SCHOLASTIC

100 SCIENCE LESSONS

NEW EDITION

TERMS AND CONDITIONS

IMPORTANT - PERMITTED USE AND WARNINGS - READ CAREFULLY BEFORE USING

Licence

Copyright in the software contained in this CD-ROM and in its accompanying material belongs to Scholastic Limited. All rights reserved. © 2007 Scholastic Ltd.

The software may not be copied, reproduced, used, sold, licensed, transferred, exchanged, hired, or exported in whole or in part or in any manner or form without the prior written consent of Scholastic Ltd. Any such unauthorised use or activities are prohibited and may give rise to civil liabilities and criminal prosecutions.

The material contained on this CD-ROM may only be used in the context for which it was intended in *100 Science Lessons*, and is for use only in the school which has purchased the book and CD-ROM, or by the teacher who has purchased the book and CD-ROM. Permission to download images is given for purchasers only and not for users from any lending service. Any further use of the material contravenes Scholastic Ltd's copyright and that of other rights' holders.

This CD-ROM has been tested for viruses at all stages of its production. However, we recommend that you run virus-checking software on your computer systems at all times. Scholastic Ltd cannot accept any responsibility for any loss, disruption or damage to your data or your computer system that may occur as a result of using either the CD-ROM or the data held on it.

SCOTTISH PRIMARY 4

YEAR 3

Minimum specification:
- PC with a CD-ROM drive and 512 Mb RAM (recommended)
- Windows 98SE or above/Mac OSX.1 or above
- Recommended minimum processor speed: 1 GHz

Malcolm Anderson

Author
Malcolm Anderson

Series Editor
Peter Riley

Editors
Nicola Morgan
Tracy Kewley
Kate Pedlar

Project Editor
Fabia Lewis

Illustrators
Kirsty Wilson, Debbie Clark , Ray and Corinne Burrows

Series Designers
Catherine Perera and Joy Monkhouse

Designer
Catherine Perera

CD-ROM developed in association with
Vivid Interactive

Published by Scholastic Ltd
Villiers House
Clarendon Avenue
Leamington Spa
Warwickshire CV32 5PR

www.scholastic.co.uk

Designed using Adobe InDesign.

Printed by Bell and Bain Ltd, Glasgow

1 2 3 4 5 6 7 8 9   7 8 9 0 1 2 3 4 5 6

Revised text © 2007 Malcolm Anderson

© 2007 Scholastic Ltd

British Library Cataloguing-in-Publication Data
A catalogue record for this book is available from the British Library.

ISBN 978-0439-94505-9

ACKNOWLEDGEMENTS

With thanks to Kendra McMahon for the use of 'Plant habitats', 'What we found out', 'Protest letter', 'Light', 'Shadow walk', 'Letting light through' and 'Shadow or not shadow?' from *100 Science Lessons – Year 4* by Kendra McMahon, © 2001, Kendra McMahon (2001, Scholastic), revised by Kendra McMahon for this edition.

With thanks to Carole Creary and Gay Wilson for the use of 'Light energy' from *100 Science Lessons – Year 2* by Carole Creary and Gay Wilson, © 2001, Carole Creary and Gay Wilson (2001, Scholastic), revised by Carole Creary and Gay Wilson for this edition.

All Flash activities developed by Vivid Interactive

Material from the National Curriculum © Crown copyright. Reproduced under the terms of the Click Use Licence.

Extracts from the QCA Scheme of Work © Qualifications and Curriculum Authority.

Extracts from the Primary School Curriculum for Ireland, www.ncca.ie, National Council for Curriculum and Assessment.

Every effort has been made to trace copyright holders for the works reproduced in this book, and the publishers apologise for any inadvertent omissions.

This new edition of *100 Science Lessons* follows the QCA Science Scheme of Work and also meets many of the demands of the curricula for England, Wales, Scotland, Northern Ireland and Eire. The book is divided into seven units – one unit to match each unit of the QCA scheme for Year 3, and one enrichment unit.

The planning grid at the start of each unit shows the objectives and outcomes of each lesson, and gives a quick overview of the lesson content (starter, main activity, group activities and plenary). The QCA objectives for Year 3 provide the basis for the lesson objectives used throughout the book.

After the planning grid is a short section on Scientific Enquiry. It is based on a QCA activity and provides a context for children to develop certain enquiry skills and for you to assess them. The section ends by showing where the activity can be embedded within one of the lessons.

Each unit is divided into a number of key lessons, which closely support the QCA scheme and all units end with an assessment lesson which is based on those key lessons. In addition to the key lessons, a unit may also contain one or more enrichment lessons to provide greater depth or a broader perspective. They may follow on from a key lesson or form a whole section, near the end of the unit, before the assessment lesson. The lesson objectives are based on the statements of the national curricula for England, Wales, Scotland, Northern Ireland and Eire, which are provided, in grid format, on the CD-ROM.

Lesson plans

There are detailed and short lesson plans for the key and enrichment lessons. About 60 per cent of the lesson plans in this book are detailed lesson plans. The short lesson plans are closely related to them and cover similar topics and concepts. They contain the essential features of the detailed lesson plans, allowing you to plan for progression and assessment. The detailed lesson plans have the following structure:

OBJECTIVES

The objectives are stated in a way that helps to focus on each lesson plan. At least one objective is related to content knowledge and there may be one or more relating to Scientific Enquiry. When you have read through the lesson you may wish to add your own objectives. You can find out how these objectives relate to those of the various national curricula by looking at the relevant grids on the CD-ROM. You can also edit the planning grids to fit with your own objectives (for more information see 'How to use the CD-ROM' on page 6).

RESOURCES AND PREPARATION

The Resources section provides a list of everything you will need to deliver the lesson, including any photocopiables presented in this book. The Preparation section describes anything that needs to be done in advance of the lesson, such as collecting environmental data.

As part of the preparation of all practical work, you should consult your school's policies on practical work and select activities for which you are confident to take responsibility. The ASE publication *Be Safe!* gives very useful guidance on health and safety issues in primary science.

BACKGROUND

This section may briefly refer to the science concepts which underpin the teaching of individual lessons. It may also highlight specific concepts which children tend to find difficult and gives some ideas on how to address these during the lesson.

Suggestions may be given for classroom displays and or obtaining resources. Safety points and sensitive issues may also be mentioned in this section, where appropriate.

VOCABULARY

There is a vocabulary list of science words associated with the lesson which children should use in discussing and presenting their work. Time should be spent defining each word at an appropriate point in the lesson.

STARTER

This introductory section contains ideas to build up interest at the beginning of the lesson and set the scene.

MAIN TEACHING ACTIVITY

This section presents a direct, whole-class (or occasionally group) teaching session that will help you deliver the content knowledge outlined in the lesson objectives before group activities begin. It may include guidance on discussion, or on performing one or more demonstrations or class investigations to help the children understand the work ahead.

The relative proportions of the lesson given to the starter, main teaching activity and group activities vary. If you are reminding the children of their previous work and getting them onto their own investigations, the group work may dominate the lesson time; if you are introducing a new topic or concept, you might wish to spend all or most of the lesson engaged in whole-class teaching.

GROUP ACTIVITIES

The group activities are very flexible. Some may be best suited to individual work, while others may be suitable for work in pairs or larger groupings. There are usually two group activities provided for each lesson. You may wish to use one after the other; use both together (to reduce demand on resources and your attention); or, where one is a practical activity, use the other for children who successfully complete their practical work early. You may even wish to use activities as follow-up homework tasks.

Some of the group activities are supported by a photocopiable sheet. These sheets can be found in the book as well as on the CD-ROM. For some activities, there are also accompanying differentiated ideas, interactive activities and diagrams – all available on the CD-ROM (for more information, see 'How to use the CD-ROM' on page 6).

The group activities may include some writing. These activities are also aimed at strengthening the children's science literacy and supporting their English literacy skills. They may involve writing labels and captions, developing scientific vocabulary, writing about or recording investigations, presenting data, explaining what they have observed, or using appropriate secondary sources. The children's mathematical skills are also developed through number and data handling work in the context of science investigations.

ICT LINKS

Many lessons have this section in which suggestions for incorporating ICT are given. ICT links might include: using the internet and CD-ROMs for research; preparing graphs and tables using a computer; using the graphing tool, interactive activities and worksheets from the CD-ROM.

DIFFERENTIATION

Where appropriate, there are suggestions for differentiated work to support less able learners or extend more able learners in your class. Some of the photocopiable sheets are also differentiated into less able support, core ability, and more able extension to support you in this work. The book contains the worksheets for the core ability while the differentiated worksheets are found on the accompanying CD-ROM.

ASSESSMENT

This section includes advice on how to assess the children's learning against the lesson objectives. This may include suggestions for questioning or observation opportunities, to help you build up a picture of the children's developing ideas and guide your future planning. A separate summative assessment lesson is provided at the end of each unit of work. One may also be provided for a group of enrichment lessons if they form a section towards the end of a unit.

PLENARY

Suggestions are given for drawing together the various strands of the lesson in this section. The lesson objectives and outcomes may be reviewed and key learning points may be highlighted. The scene may also be set for another lesson.

HOMEWORK

On occasions, tasks may be suggested for the children to do at home. These may involve using photocopiables or the setting of a research project, perhaps involving the use the books on display (as suggested in the background section) to broaden the knowledge of the topic being studied.

OUTCOMES

These are statements related to the objectives; they describe what the children should have achieved by the end of the lesson.

LINKS

These are included where appropriate. They may refer to subjects closely related to science, such as technology or maths, or to content and skills from subjects such as art, history or geography.

ASSESSMENT LESSONS

The last lesson in every unit focuses on summative assessment. This assessment samples the content of the unit, focusing on its key theme(s); its results should be used in conjunction with other assessments you have made during the teaching of the unit. The lesson usually comprises of two assessment activities, which may take the form of photocopiable sheets to complete or practical activities with suggested assessment questions for you to use while you are observing the children. These activities may include a mark scheme, but this will not be related directly to curriculum attainment targets and level descriptors. These tasks are intended to provide you with a guide to assessing the children's performance.

PHOTOCOPIABLE SHEETS

These are an integral part of many of the lessons. They may provide resources such as quizzes, instructions for practical work, worksheets to complete whilst undertaking a task, information, guidance for written assignments and so on.

Photocopiable sheets printed in the book are suitable for most children. The CD-ROM includes differentiated versions of many photocopiables to support less confident learners and stretch more confident learners.

How to use the CD-ROM

SYSTEM REQUIREMENTS
Minimum specifications:
● PC or Mac with CD-ROM drive and at least 512 MB RAM (recommended)
● Microsoft Windows 98SE or above/Mac OSX.1 or above
● Recommended minimum processor speed: 1GHz

GETTING STARTED
The accompanying CD-ROM includes a range of lesson and planning resources. The first screen requires the user to select the relevant country (England, Scotland, Wales, Northern Ireland, Eire). There are then several menus enabling the user to search the material according to various criteria, including lesson name, QCA unit, National Curriculum topic and resource type.

Searching by lesson name enables the user to see all resources associated with that particular lesson. The coloured tabs on the left-hand side of this screen indicate the differentiated worksheets; the tabs at the top of the page lead to different *types* of resource (diagram, interactive or photocopiable).

PHOTOCOPIABLES
The photocopiables that are printed in the book are also provided on the CD-ROM, as PDF files. In addition, differentiated versions of the photocopiables are provided where relevant:
● green indicates a support worksheet for less confident children;
● red indicates the core photocopiable, as printed in the book;
● blue indicates an extension worksheet for more confident children.
There are no differentiated photocopiables for assessment activities.

The PDF files can be annotated on screen using the panel tool provided (see below). The tools allow the user to add notes, highlight items and draw lines and boxes.

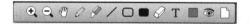

PDF files of photocopiables can be printed from the CD-ROM and there is also an option to print the full screen, including any drawings and annotations that have been added using the tools. (NB where PDF files are landscape, printer settings may need to be adjusted.)

INTERACTIVE ACTIVITIES
The CD-ROM includes twelve activities for children to complete using an interactive whiteboard or individual computers. Each activity is based on one of the photocopiables taken from across the units. Activities include: dragging and dropping shadows next to the objects that cast them; clicking on everyday items to see if they are made from rock; ordering traffic lights to create the correct sequence.

GRAPHING TOOL
The graphing tool supports lessons where the children are asked to gather and record data. The tool enables children to enter data into a table, which can then be used to create a block graph, pie chart or line graph.

When inserting data into the table, the left-hand column should be used for labels for charts; the right-hand column is for numeric data only (see example below). The pop-up keypad can be used to enter numbers into the table.

DIAGRAMS
Where appropriate, diagrams printed in the book have been included as separate files on the CD-ROM. These include examples of tables and diagrams for children to refer to when undertaking experiments or building objects, such as the marble run in 'Pushes and pulls'. These can be displayed on an interactive whiteboard.

GENERAL RESOURCES
In addition to lesson resources, the CD-ROM also includes the planning grids for each unit, as printed in the book, and the relevant curriculum grid for England, Scotland, Wales, Northern Ireland and Eire. The curriculum grids indicate how elements of each country's National Curriculum are addressed by lessons in the book. The planning grids are supplied as editable Word files; the curriculum grids are supplied as Word and PDF files. Selection of a planning grid leads to a link, which opens the document in a separate window; this then needs to be saved to the computer or network before editing.

CHAPTER 1 Teeth and eating

Lesson	Objectives	Main activity	Group activities	Plenary	Outcomes
Lesson 1 Myself	• To ascertain the children's current knowledge of themselves, how they eat and the benefits of healthy eating.	Assessment sheet focusing on knowledge and understanding of the body.	Brainstorm activity on one aspect of the body. Writing questions about themselves, food and teeth.	Discussion of issues raised, looking forward to the unit.	• Teacher can assess the level of understanding of the children in the class. • Teacher can arrange the children in appropriate class groups.
Lesson 2 Sorting foods	• To realise that food can be put into different groups. • To understand one scientific grouping of foods.	Looking at a way of classifying food into three groups.	Sorting a bag of food shopping into food groups. Designing symbols for food groups.	Reinforcement of the concept of food groups.	• Can arrange food into groups for growth and for activity.
Lesson 3 Food groups	• To know how to arrange a meal into food groups for growth and activity. • To consider first-hand experience as a source of information in order to answer a question.	Looking at the contents of packed lunches.	Completing a worksheet to record contents of a packed lunch. Keeping a food diary.	Compiling a class food list from their packed lunches.	• Can arrange the food in their meals into groups for growth and activity.
Lesson 4 Going shopping	• To know about the quantities of different food groups that should be eaten. • To know that a knowledge of food groups helps us to build healthy diets.	Assessing menus for their contents and forming a balanced diet.	Looking at shopping lists to assess them for balance and health. Letter writing about healthy foods.	Reinforcing the concept of healthy and unhealthy diets.	• Can assess how healthy their meal is. • Can show how knowledge of food groups can help build a healthy diet.
Lesson 5 Food from around the world	• To know that food from different cultures contains healthy combinations of nutrients.	Looking at pictures, menus and recipes of foods from different cultures and identifying the constituent food groups.		Discussing the nutritional balance of foods from other cultures.	• Know that food from different cultures contains a healthy balance of nutrients.
Lesson 6 Food	• To know that animals have different diets.	Comparing foods eaten by humans and other animals.	Looking at food eaten by humans and animals. Researching simple food chains.	Share findings of animal diets.	• Can identify the different sorts of food eaten by animals.
Lesson 7 Pet food survey	• To know that animals have different diets. • To use ICT to communicate data.	Survey of pet owners to determine foods eaten by pets.		Present findings and draw conclusions.	• Can identify the different sorts of food eaten by animals. • Can use ICT to communicate data.
Lesson 8 My teeth	• To know the different types of teeth and their functions.	Looking at and naming types of teeth.	Looking at our own teeth and recording on a worksheet. Using secondary sources to research information for a leaflet.	Taking part in a quiz about teeth to reinforce knowledge.	• Can recognise the different types of teeth. • Can describe the function of different types of teeth.
Lesson 9 Two sets of teeth	• To know that we have two sets of teeth.	Looking at losing teeth, at milk and permanent teeth and making models.		Discussion of the number of teeth the children have.	• Can recognise and describe the function of different sets of teeth.
Lesson 10 Tooth care	• To know that teeth and gums need care to stay healthy.	Using disclosure tablets. Looking at correct methods of brushing teeth. Designing a poster.	Survey of dental hygiene. Looking at dental health posters.	Discussion of the best advice regarding dental health.	• Can describe ways to care for teeth and gums. • Can explain why tooth and gum care is needed.
Enrichment Lesson 11 Our senses	• To know that the senses make us aware of our surroundings.	Making a class concept map of 'The senses'.	Identifying senses, sense names and sensory organs. Crisp-tasting survey.	Taking part in a quiz on matching senses, names and organs.	• Can identify the senses and the sense organs.

Lesson	Objectives	Main activity	Group activities	Plenary	Outcomes
Enrichment Lesson 12 Different tastes	• To know that the senses, including taste, make us aware of our surroundings.	Taste tests for sweet, salty and bitter.		Explaining and describing taste experiences.	• Can perform activities on the senses.

Assessment	Objectives	Activity 1	Activity 2
Lesson 13	• To assess the children's knowledge and understanding of dental health, tooth types and functions. • To assess the children's knowledge and understanding of the importance of eating a balanced diet.	Completing a 'Tooth facts' and 'Dental health' worksheet.	Completing a 'Food facts' and 'Eating a healthy diet' worksheet.

SC1 SCIENTIFIC ENQUIRY

Do the same type of pets eat the same food?

LEARNING OBJECTIVES AND OUTCOMES
- Decide how to answer the question.
- Plan a survey.
- Consider how to present evidence.
- Identify simple patterns in the data.
- Draw conclusions.

ACTIVITY
The children design and carry out a survey of pet owners to determine the foods eaten by particular pets, favourite foods and any unusual diets or food items. They use data-handling software to record, interpret and present their findings.

LESSON LINKS
This Sc1 activity forms as an integral part of Lesson 7, Pet food survey.

Lesson 1 ▪ Myself

Objective
- To ascertain the children's current knowledge of their teeth, how they eat and the benefits of healthy eating.

RESOURCES 💿
Main activity: A copy of photocopiable page 25 (also 'Myself' (red), available on the CD-ROM) for each child; pencils.
Group activities: 1 Large sheets of paper; pens; pencils. **2** Paper; pens; pencils.

BACKGROUND
In planning, developing and carrying out a unit of work with children it is important to give consideration to current understanding and previous learning. To ascertain the level of the children's understanding, use a lesson to carry out an initial assessment. This will give you a starting point from which you can move on and develop that understanding. It is important not to perceive children's ideas about a concept as 'wrong', but rather that they may need to develop their understanding of that concept to bring it nearer to the generally accepted understanding. This lesson is intended to establish what is already known by the children about their bodies, food, teeth and eating.

STARTER
Introduce the unit of work to the children by telling them they are going to begin a science topic called 'Teeth and eating'. Tell them the broad outline of the unit and that by the end of the unit they will understand more about their teeth and the importance of a healthy diet. Remind them that they will have already done some work about their bodies and healthy eating and that you would like them to be able to tell you what they already know and understand.

MAIN ACTIVITY
Distribute copies of photocopiable page 25. Ask the children to make the illustration into a picture of themselves and to label it and write as much as they can about themselves. Ask them to think particularly about the benefits of food to their bodies and the things they may know about their teeth.

Differentiation
Main activity
Some children may need reminding about what they covered in previous years.

GROUP ACTIVITIES

1 Ask the children to work together in small groups, to choose one of the ideas or concepts they have written on their drawings and to brainstorm that idea. They should write down everything they know about, for example, food groups, using words and pictures to explain their thoughts.
2 Ask the children to think of three questions about themselves, food and teeth that they would like to know the answers to.

PLENARY

Discuss the pictures the children have drawn. Highlight some of the concepts they have written about and explain the areas they will be looking at over future lessons. Avoid suggesting that the children's concepts are wrong – the work they will be doing will develop their thinking from where they are now.

OUTCOMES

- Teacher can assess the level of the children in the class.
- Teacher can arrange the children in appropriate class groups.

Lesson 2 ▪ Sorting foods

Objectives
- To realise that food can be put into different groups.
- To understand one scientific grouping of foods.

Vocabulary
body-building foods, energy-giving foods, growth, healthy, maintenance foods, activity

RESOURCES

Main activity: Stand-up labels with the words 'Meat and eggs', 'Milk products', 'Cereals, fruit and vegetables' and 'Processed foods' written on them; a carrier bag of food including examples of energy-giving foods: carbohydrates and fats; body-building foods: proteins; and maintenance foods: vitamins and minerals (see table below). If you do not get enough of each type of food, print out illustrations from your computer (copyright permitting). Most CD-ROM clip art collections have pictures of food.
Group activities: 1 Carrier bags; sets of stand-up labels with the words 'Meat and eggs', 'Milk products', 'Cereals, fruit and vegetables' and 'Processed foods' written on them; empty food packets and containers; large sheets of paper; pens. **2** Paper; drawing; painting and colouring materials.

PREPARATION

Prepare a carrier bag of shopping to use in the Starter activity containing examples from each of these groups: meat and eggs; milk products; cereals, fruit and vegetables; processed foods.

For the Group activities, prepare a carrier bag for each group of children containing a selection of the collected packets and food containers. Ensure there are examples from each of the food groups. Prepare stand-up labels for the food groups shown in the table below.

Food group	Foods	Function
Energy-giving foods:carbohydrates fats and oils	Bread, potatoes, pasta, rice, sugar, fatty and oily foods	Provide energy for activity, movement and warmth.
Body-building foods: proteins	Meat, fish, eggs, dairy produce, seeds, nuts	Help with growth and repair of the body.
Maintenance foods: vitamins and minerals	Red meats, milk, fresh fruit, vegetables	Maintain healthy bones and teeth. Prevent 'vitamin deficiency' diseases.

BACKGROUND

Food is needed to help our bodies move, grow and repair themselves after being damaged. The food and drink that we consume each day makes up our diet and while there are not any unhealthy foods, many people do eat unhealthy diets. It is important we eat a diet which contains a range of different foods, since these different foods serve different purposes. A balanced or healthy diet is one that consists of the appropriate types of food in the correct quantities. There are five main food groups.

● **Proteins:** essential for the growth and repair of the body. Muscles, skin, hair and nails are nearly 100% protein. Bone is part protein.
● **Fats and oils:** essential for the release and storage of energy and as an insulation.
● **Carbohydrates:** essential for the release of energy, for the storage of energy and as roughage for the movement of food through the gut. Fibre acts as roughage in the diet and prevents constipation.
● **Minerals:** essential for building bones and teeth, for the functioning of the nervous system and the production of haemoglobin in red blood cells.
● **Vitamins:** essential for the control of chemical reactions in the body and the control of deficiency diseases with symptoms such as poor vision, stomach ache, poor growth and weak bones.

These five food groups are often combined into three groups that can be thought of as energy-giving foods (carbohydrates and fats and oils), body-building foods (proteins) and maintenance foods (vitamins and minerals). In addition to these foods we also need water and fibre. While we could survive without food for several weeks, we could survive only for a few days without water. Most of the water we take in is through drinking, but most solid foods also contain water. Nevertheless, to maintain our bodily functions, we need to drink plenty of water every day.

STARTER

Ask the children to think about the different types of food they may see on a visit to a supermarket. How are foods grouped together in the supermarket? Use your carrier bag to show the children examples from the food groups: meat and eggs; milk products; cereals, fruit and vegetables; processed foods.

The children can help with this by coming to the front and having a 'lucky dip' into the bag. They then have to place the food by a card labelled with the appropriate category.

MAIN ACTIVITY

Ask the children if they can think of any other ways of grouping the foods. Lead them into suggesting that we could group them by their functions and uses to our body (see diagram on page 10, also available on the CD-ROM). Introduce the idea that some foods give us energy, some foods help us to grow and some foods keep us healthy. Tell the children that each food belongs in one group and that together they are going to classify the foods in the bags you have prepared. Write three column headings on the board: 'Energy-giving foods', 'Body-building foods', and 'Maintenance foods'. Talk about each food group and tell the children about the types of food in each group and their function. (See Background.) Stress that energy-giving foods are good for activity, that body-building foods are good for growth, and that maintenance foods keep us healthy.

GROUP ACTIVITIES

1 Distribute the bags of food, stand-up labels and sheets of paper. Ask the children to work in their groups to arrange their shopping into the three groups you have written on the board, using the stand-up labels as a guide. When they have sorted the food, the children should record their work on a large sheet of paper using the column headings that are written on the

Differentiation
Main activity
Some children may need adult support to sort the foods. To challenge children, ask them to write a sentence about the different food types on their chart.

board: 'Energy-giving foods', 'Body-building foods', and 'Maintenance foods'. **2** Ask the children to design symbols that could be used to accompany the food groups. You may like to compare them to computer icons. The designs should be based on the benefits to the body, for example energy-giving foods: an athlete; body-building foods: a weightlifter; maintenance foods: a toolkit.

ASSESSMENT
Monitor the children's ability to sort the foods into groups by observation.

PLENARY
Gather the class together and discuss the Group activities. Ask children to bring foods out and make a simple display of foods in each group. Write the vocabulary list on the board, and use the words to reinforce the knowledge of food groups and what each gives to our bodies by completing these sentences together on the board:
Energy-giving foods like _____ are good for _____ .
Body-building foods like _____ are good for _____ .
Maintenance foods like _____ help to keep us _____ .
Stress that energy-giving foods are good for activity, that body-building foods are good for growth, and maintenance foods help to keep us healthy, especially our teeth and bones.

OUTCOME
● Can arrange food into groups for growth and for activity.

Lesson 3 ▪ Food groups

Objectives
● To know how to arrange a meal into food groups for growth and activity.
● To consider first-hand experience as a source of information in order to answer a question.

Vocabulary
balanced diet, bones, healthy diet, teeth

RESOURCES 💿
Main activity: Prepared word cards: 'Energy-giving foods', 'Body-building foods', 'Maintenance foods', 'apples', 'bread', 'butter', 'carrots', 'cheese', 'cream', 'fish', 'ice cream', 'meat', 'oil', 'oranges', 'pasta', 'potatoes', 'rice'; Blu-Tack®, children's packed lunches.
Group activities: 1 Copies of photocopiable page 26 (also 'Food groups–1 (red), available on the CD-ROM); pens or pencils. **2** Copies of photocopiable page 27 (also 'Food groups– 2 (red), available on the CD-ROM); food group table (see Lesson 2 Background, page 11); flipchart or OHP; pens or pencils.

PREPARATION
Write to parents or guardians in advance of the lesson, explaining that the children are looking at food groups and asking them to ensure their child brings a packed lunch to school on one particular day. Try not to explain in too much detail to avoid parents putting in food types that perfectly match your groups, since this would not highlight the reality of packed lunch menus. Copy the table of food groups (see Lesson 2 Background, page 11) for whole-class use, for example on to a flipchart or OHP, for Group activity 2.

BACKGROUND
A balanced diet consists mainly of carbohydrates, fats and proteins. Vitamins and minerals are needed but in much smaller quantities. However, if they are missing altogether, it could lead to ill-health, so the adoption of a balanced diet is important. Just as eating insufficient vitamins and minerals can lead to ill-health, so too can overeating. Eating more than is needed can lead to obesity and subsequent damage to the heart, bones and joints, together with high blood pressure and sometimes a general feeling of poor self-esteem. Fatty and sugary foods are generally the main culprits in overeating, so it is important to moderate the intake of these food types.

STARTER

Reinforce the food groups and how each of these groups carries out a particular function for us by asking the children to recall that energy-giving foods are good for activity, that body-building foods are good for growth and maintenance foods help to keep us healthy, especially our teeth and bones. Stick the prepared word cards: 'Energy-giving foods', 'Body-building foods', and 'Maintenance foods' on the board as column headings, then hold up a number of the word cards with food names written on them. Ask the children to put these in the correct food groups by sticking them in the right columns.

MAIN ACTIVITY

Ask the children to think about how they could investigate the foods they eat. Ask them to open up their own packed lunch, to look at it and to try to sort the contents into the food groups. Remind the children of the importance of food hygiene. Ensure that they wash their hands prior to handling the packed lunch, and that they don't take the foods out of their wrappings if putting them out onto their desks.

GROUP ACTIVITIES

1 Ask the children to use the contents of their packed lunch to complete photocopiable page 26.
2 Ask the children to think about the meals they have eaten recently, for example breakfast or the previous day's evening meal. Ask them to complete photocopiable page 26 by writing down the foods they ate at each mealtime and then to put a tick in the appropriate column, depending on whether the food's function is growth or activity. They can refer to the food group table on the flipchart, OHP or the interactive whiteboard, if you are using the diagram from the CD-ROM. The children could then set up a database into which each child can input their findings to give a class view of the foods eaten. Alternatively, this activity could be used as homework and photocopiable page 27 filled in as a diary over the following few days.

ASSESSMENT

Discuss with the children the foods they have eaten and their ability to sort their menus into food groups. Analysis of photocopiable pages 26 and 27 will support this assessment.

PLENARY

As the children complete Group activity 1, ask them to contribute to compiling a class chart showing the number of people with items in their lunch from each food group. When the data has been compiled help the children to interpret the data by asking questions such as: *Which food is the most popular? Is it healthy? Which food is the least popular? Is it healthy? Is our class a 'healthy-eating' class?*

Be careful not to make any child feel guilty about the contents of their packed lunch as this is something over which most young children have little or no control.

Discuss the menus of a few children (from photocopiable page 26) and compile a shared class list of foods from each food group.

OUTCOME

● Can arrange the food in their meals into groups for growth and activity.

Lesson 4 ▪ Going shopping

Objectives
● To know about the quantities of different food groups that should be eaten.
● To know that a knowledge of food groups helps us to build healthy diets.

Vocabulary
carbohydrates, fats, fibre, minerals, proteins, recommended daily allowance (RDA), vitamins, water

RESOURCES 💿
Main activity: Sample menus (enlarged for class discussion) as shown below, one healthy and one unhealthy; OHP (optional).
Group activities: 1 Copy of photocopiable page 28 (also 'Going shopping' (red), available on the CD-ROM) for each child, pens or pencils **2** Paper; pens or pencils.
ICT link: 'Going shopping', interactive activity, from the CD-ROM.

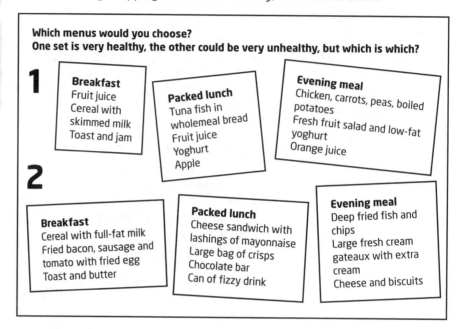

Which menus would you choose?
One set is very healthy, the other could be very unhealthy, but which is which?

1

Breakfast
Fruit juice
Cereal with skimmed milk
Toast and jam

Packed lunch
Tuna fish in wholemeal bread
Fruit juice
Yoghurt
Apple

Evening meal
Chicken, carrots, peas, boiled potatoes
Fresh fruit salad and low-fat yoghurt
Orange juice

2

Breakfast
Cereal with full-fat milk
Fried bacon, sausage and tomato with fried egg
Toast and butter

Packed lunch
Cheese sandwich with lashings of mayonnaise
Large bag of crisps
Chocolate bar
Can of fizzy drink

Evening meal
Deep fried fish and chips
Large fresh cream gateaux with extra cream
Cheese and biscuits

PREPARATION
Copy the menus above on to a flipchart or OHP for whole-class use.

BACKGROUND
A balanced diet is one that helps the body to stay healthy and gives us a supply of carbohydrates, fats, proteins, vitamins, minerals, water and fibre. In order to get all this we need to eat a variety of foods. The quantities and types of food needed by each person will vary and is dependent on things like age, sex, height, weight, health and lifestyle. For example, those people who are involved in a great deal of physical work or exercise will need to eat more than those who lead a more sedentary lifestyle. People who have a tendency to gain and retain weight may avoid fatty foods; similarly, those with medical conditions may avoid certain foods. In general, it is regarded as healthy to eat a balance of different foods from a range of groups. This is important since it is a balanced diet that provides us with all the nutrition that our bodies need.

Recommended Daily Allowances (RDA)

Age group	Energy (kcal)	Protein (g)	Iron (mg)
Under 1	776	20	6
Age 5	1764	45	8
Boy 15–17	2964	75	15
Girl 15–17	2258	58	15
Man	2964	75	10
Woman	2164	55	12

STARTER
Begin the lesson by asking the children to share with the class their 'favourite meal': share yours too! Continue by asking the children to think about what life would be like if they were to always eat their favourite meal – how long would it be before they became bored with it?

MAIN ACTIVITY
Ask the children if they can think of other, 'scientific' reasons why we do not always eat the same foods. Lead them to think about the importance of eating a variety of foods.

Explain to the children that because different foods help our bodies to perform different functions it is important to eat a balanced diet.
  Provide the sample menus and RDA figures, if appropriate, for the children to look at. Ask them to consider each menu and to decide if the menu seems to give a balanced diet. What is 'good' about them? What is 'bad'? Is the 'very unhealthy' meal necessarily 'bad'? (No, not if it is an occasional treat – no food is bad as such.)

GROUP ACTIVITIES

1 Distribute photocopiable page 28. Ask the children to consider the diets of the two people and to assess them for balance and health, then write a shopping list of their own.
2 Ask the children to write a letter to a friend that explains the foods people should eat as part of a healthy diet.

ICT LINK 💿
Children can use the 'Going shopping ' interactive, from the CD-ROM, to sort foods into two categories, 'healthy' or 'less healthy'.

ASSESSMENT
Using the photocopiable pages look for evidence of the children's understanding through their ability to explain the differences between the two lists. Look also for evidence among the more confident learners of their ability to write their own shopping list that has other healthy food ideas not already used.

PLENARY
Look again at the menus from the start of the lesson and ask the children to think about the unhealthy diet and to make suggestions for how it could be improved to make it healthy.

OUTCOMES
● Can assess how healthy their meal is.
● Can show how knowledge of food groups can help build a healthy diet.

LINKS
PSHE: developing a healthy, safer lifestyle.

Lesson 5 ▭ Food from around the world

RESOURCES
Pictures of foods from different places, for example chilli from Mexico, risotto from Spain, fish and rice from Thailand, vegetable curry from India; recipes for meals from different countries (optional); menus from Indian, Chinese and Italian restaurants (optional).

MAIN ACTIVITY
Show the children the pictures of foods from around the world and ask them to identify the food items and say whether they are energy-giving foods, body-building foods or maintenance foods. They could record their ideas in a table. They could also look at recipes for meals from different countries and assign the ingredients to food groups or more simply they could look at menus from Indian, Chinese and Italian restaurants.

ICT LINK 💿
The children could use the graphing tool, from the CD-ROM, to make graphs from the results recorded in their table.

Differentiation
Children who need support could work with the pictures and menus. More confident learners could work with the recipes.

ASSESSMENT
Assess the children on the construction of their table and the accuracy of their answers.

PLENARY
Review the children's work and point out that meals from around the world are balanced to provide healthy amounts of the different food groups.

OUTCOME
● Know that food from different cultures contains a healthy balance of nutrients.

Lesson 6 ▸ Food

Objective
● To know that animals have different diets.

Vocabulary
carnivore, food chain, food web, food, herbivore, omnivore, processed

RESOURCES ◉
Main activity: Board or flipchart and a felt-tipped pen.
Group activities: 1 and **2** Photocopiable page 29 (also 'Food' (red), available on the CD-ROM); long strips of paper (for food chains); reference sources about animals such as books; videos; CD-ROMs; internet access.

PREPARATION
Ensure suitable secondary source material is available.

BACKGROUND
In years past, people got their food by gathering seeds and fruit and by hunting. Today, most of our food is produced for us by farmers and food processing companies and, instead of gathering the food ourselves, we visit shops and supermarkets to buy our food. In the wild, things are very different. Wild animals eat very different foods and spend much of their time finding and eating food. Animals that eat plants do not usually need to move very far to feed since plants tend to be rooted in one place. On the other hand, carnivores (meat-eaters) usually have to catch their food.

The 'diet' of an animal is its complete food intake. Some animals have very varied diets, others tend to eat only a limited range of foods. The plants and animals living in a community are closely linked through their feeding habits as they may feed on other members of the same community. For example, a rabbit eats plants, and in turn is eaten by a fox. So we get a food chain: plants are food for rabbits which are food for foxes.

Since some animals eat a varied diet, food chains can quickly build to form a food web, with great interdependence between the plants and animals in the web. For example, a lack of food for smaller creatures at the lower end of a food chain has a 'knock-on' effect as you travel higher up the chain. Hence, if for some reason there was a problem with the growth of suitable plant life, the number of rabbits may be reduced, which in turn could affect the number of foxes.

STARTER
Begin by talking to the children about the foods that their pets may eat. Ask them a few silly questions such as: *Does your pet rabbit eat jam sandwiches? Did your goldfish have a boiled egg for breakfast?*

MAIN ACTIVITY
Ask the children to think about the different foods that they eat. Compile a list on a board or flipchart. Now ask them to think about the food that is eaten by animals and list these separately. Compare the lists: in general the foods eaten by animals will be different. Encourage the children to think about the ways in which an animal's food may differ – human food is often cooked or processed, whereas food for wild animals is raw and unprocessed

Differentiation
Group activity 1
For children who need support, use 'Food' (green), from the CD-ROM. This sheet asks the children to draw the foods rather than writing their names.
Group activity 2
Some children will draw simple food chains showing just one or two relationships. Other children may be able to draw a simple food web by linking sets of food chains together as shown in the example below. compare the information in a table.

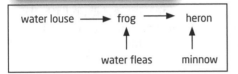

for example. Talk about food chains and the way in which animals and plants are food for other animals. Give an example of a food chain.

GROUP ACTIVITIES

1 Give out copies of page 29 for the children to complete. Encourage the children to think about how our food is eaten raw, cooked or processed. The children should use a range of secondary sources to find out about the range of foods eaten by one particular animal. Encourage them to relate what is eaten to where the animal lives. They can use the 'Animal diet factfile' at the bottom of the sheet to record their findings.
2 Working in small groups, the children should then use their research skills and findings to build up a food chain based on the diet factfile. These can be drawn on strips of paper for illustration and display.

ICT LINK

Children could use presentational software to present the diet factfiles.

ASSESSMENT

Look at the children's work for evidence of an understanding of the different diets eaten by humans and animals and also between different animals.

PLENARY

Share the findings of the children's research into animal diets

OUTCOME

● Can identify the different sorts of food eaten by animals.

Lesson 7 ▪ Pet food survey

Objective
● To know that animals have different diets.
● To use ICT to communicate data.

RESOURCES

Computer and data-handling software.

MAIN ACTIVITY

Design and carry out a survey of the pet owners amongst the children to determine the foods eaten by particular pets, favourite foods and any unusual diets or food items. Use data-handling software to record, interpret and present findings.

ICT LINKS

Children could use data handling software to record and present the findings and to enable others to interrogate the data or use the graphing tool, from the CD-ROM, to present data in the form of a bar graph or pie chart.

ASSESSMENT

Assess ability to explain findings and to carry out the data research.

Differentiation
Some children may need support with data collection. Other children may be able to ask and answer questions about the data they have collected such as 'What is the most popular food eaten by rabbits?'

PLENARY

Present findings, discuss and try to draw some conclusions about foods eaten by different pets.

OUTCOMES

● Can identify the different sorts of food eaten by animals.
● Can use ICT to communicate data.

Lesson 8 ▶ My teeth

Objective
● To know the different types of teeth and their functions.

Vocabulary
biting, canines, cutting, grinding, incisors, molars, premolars, tearing

RESOURCES 💿
Main activity: Illustrations or models of teeth, hard fruits such as apples and pears.
Group activities: 1 Mirrors; copies of photocopiable page 30 (also 'My teeth' (red), available on the CD-ROM). **2** Secondary sources of information about ourselves, food and teeth – books; videos; CD-ROMs; the internet; paper, pens and pencils.
ICT link: 'My teeth' interactive activity from the CD-ROM.

PREPARATION
Cut up fruit into small portions.

BACKGROUND
The hardest part of the human body is the surface of the teeth. Made from enamel, this surface protects the teeth from being worn away and attacked by chemicals. Teeth play a vital role in the initial stages of food digestion in that, before it is swallowed, food is chewed. Most mammals have specialised teeth that are shaped in particular ways to carry out different tasks. Teeth are used to bite food, break it up and grind it into small pieces. Humans are omnivores (we eat both plants and animals as food), and our teeth are capable of eating both, unlike some other animals. Carnivores (or meat-eaters) have teeth suited to killing other animals and tearing their flesh, whereas herbivores (plant-eaters) have teeth more suited to eating vegetation. As humans we have different types of teeth, each of which has a different function.

Human babies are generally born without teeth and by the age of one their milk teeth have appeared. Between the ages of six and twelve these milk teeth are replaced by permanent teeth. The table below shows how many of each teeth we usually have.

We lose our milk teeth as we grow, but we can also lose our permanent teeth for a variety of reasons – through injury, gum disease or tooth decay. It is important, though, that we maintain healthy teeth for as long as possible, so that we can chew properly and also be spared the pain of a

Tooth type	Shape	Function
Incisors	Sharp, chisel shape	Biting off food, cutting food
Canines	Sharp pointed shape	Biting off food, tearing food
Molars	Cube shape	Grinding, chewing and crushing food

decaying tooth. Most adults have 32 teeth in their second, or permanent, set. These consist of: eight incisors, four canines, eight premolars and twelve molars.

The part of the tooth that you can see is the crown, which is about half of the full tooth. The crown is covered with enamel, below which is a layer of dentine. The centre of the tooth is filled with a soft pulp which contains the blood supply and nerve endings. Long roots anchor the tooth to the jaw.

Age	Tooth set	Tooth type	Number	Total
Birth	None			
1 year	Milk teeth	Incisors Canines Premolars	8 4 8	20
6-12 Adults	Permanent	Incisors Canines Premolars Molars	8 4 8 12	32

STARTER
Ask the children to think about what they use when they are eating. Bring the discussion around to how they use their teeth.

Enamel on outside of crown

Crown

Gum

Dentine

Pulp

Root

Jaw bone

MAIN ACTIVITY

Look at your illustrations or models of teeth. Talk about how we use our teeth when eating, how we have different types of teeth, the names we give them and their functions. Think about the different types of teeth we have and the jobs they do. Hand out pieces of fruit so the children can watch each other eat and observe the functions of the teeth – incisors to bite; canines to hold and tear; molars and premolars to grind the food up. (The children will not have permanent molars yet.)

GROUP ACTIVITIES

1 Give each child a copy of photocopiable page 30. Tell the children to use mirrors to help them to see their own teeth. Tell them to complete the worksheet by drawing each tooth type and then writing about its function.

2 Ask the children to use secondary sources to find out how many teeth children and adults should have. Use this research to make an information leaflet about teeth.

ASSESSMENT

By observation and discussion with the children, assess their ability to recognise different types of teeth. The photocopiable page will provide documentary evidence.

ICT LINKS

Children could visit appropriate dental health websites for Group activity 2 or use the 'My teeth' interactive, from the CD-ROM, to label names of teeth.

PLENARY

Discuss the activity and have a quiz-style 'question and answer' session to reinforce knowledge of different types of teeth. Use the illustrations or the model of the teeth as prompts.

OUTCOMES
● Can recognise the different types of teeth.
● Can describe the function of different types of teeth.

Differentiation
Group activity 1
For children who need support, use 'My teeth' (green), which allows them to choose the function of each tooth from a list of options. To extend children, use 'My teeth' (blue), which challenges children to label the different types of teeth and asks them to provide examples to support their explanations of how the teeth work.

Lesson 9 ▸ Two sets of teeth

Objective
● To know that we have two sets of teeth.

RESOURCES

Illustrations or models of teeth; mirrors; red paper; white paper; glue; scissors.

MAIN ACTIVITY

Talk about losing teeth and the reasons why we lose teeth: replacement, disease and decay or damage. Develop the idea of the first teeth (milk teeth) being replaced by permanent teeth. Discuss how, as our teeth sets change and develop, so do the range and type of foods we eat.
Use mirrors to enable the children to look at their teeth to assess permanent and milk teeth. Make models of gums and teeth using red paper for the gums and white paper for the teeth. The children can stick teeth on to the gums to create a replica of their mouth.

ICT LINK

Children could use digital cameras to look at their own teeth.

Differentiation
Differentiate by outcome.
Most children should be able
to produce a model in this
activity.

ASSESSMENT
Assess the ability to observe their teeth and draw a plan of their
arrangement in the mouth.

PLENARY
Gather the children together and discuss their findings. Talk about how
many milk and permanent teeth the children have.

OUTCOME
● Can recognise and describe the function of different sets of teeth.

Lesson 10 ▫ Tooth care

Objective
● To know that teeth and
gums need care to stay
healthy.

Vocabulary
acid, bacteria, gum disease,
milk teeth, permanent teeth,
plaque, tooth decay

RESOURCES ◉
Main activity: Disclosure tablets; children's own toothbrushes; toothpaste
(these are often available in dental health packs that are frequently supplied
to schools by toothpaste companies); cola fizzy drink; a small milk tooth
(supplied by a child).
Group activities: 1 Paper; pens; computer and data-handling software.
2 A collection of dental health leaflets available from dental surgeries; paper
and art materials.
ICT link: Use data handling software to collate data on frequency of tooth-
brushing or use the graphing tool from the CD-ROM, to present data using
graphs and charts.

BACKGROUND
As children lose their milk teeth they are replaced by permanent teeth. For
various reasons these may not be so permanent. If we do not take care of
both our teeth and gums, we can lose our permanent teeth. It is important,
therefore, for the children to have some awareness of tooth decay and gum
disease and how they can be prevented.
   Tooth decay occurs when holes develop in what is the hardest substance
in the body – tooth enamel. The holes are formed when acid is released from
bacterial plaque that forms on the teeth. The presence of sugar in the
mouth encourages the growth of bacteria. The best way to prevent the
build-up of plaque and tooth decay is to avoid eating sweet and sugary
foods and drinks. Regular brushing of teeth and drinking of fluoridated
water also help to prevent the build-up of plaque and can strengthen
enamel.
   Gum disease occurs when bacteria enter the gaps between the gums and
the surface of the teeth. This can lead to the fibres that hold the teeth in
place becoming damaged, meaning the teeth can work loose and may be in
danger of then falling out. Again, regular and correct brushing of the teeth
can prevent this happening.
   Prevention of tooth decay is helped by saliva, which is produced in the
mouth while we are eating. Saliva is alkaline and this means it is able to help
neutralise the acids produced by the bacteria in the mouth and can help to
prevent tooth decay. However, the best ways of stopping tooth decay are to
eat sensibly, without too much sugar, to clean teeth after each meal and
visit a dentist for a check-up every six months.

STARTER
Ask the children to recall why we sometimes lose teeth. Referring to the
food the children eat, introduce the idea that sugary foods cause tooth
decay. Explain how and why this happens (see Background). Demonstrate
the effect of sugary foods on teeth by leaving a small milk tooth in cola (the
tooth enamel will break down and the tooth will decay).

Differentiation
Group activity 2
To support children, encourage them to design a simple poster that contains just one clear message. Other children may be able to design more complex posters that deliver a more coherent message.

MAIN ACTIVITY

Ask the children to think of ways in which we could reduce the risk of tooth loss. If there is not a familiar toothpaste advert that you can refer to running on TV at the time you may need to introduce the idea of fluoridation and fluoride toothpaste. Discuss the importance of good dental health practice. Ask at least one child to use disclosure tablets to show where plaque builds up on the teeth. Then ask them to brush their teeth correctly: only correct brushing will remove all the disclosure colouring.

GROUP ACTIVITIES

1 Carry out a simple survey to find out how often the children brush their teeth. Use a simple database program to record the findings anonymously – there is no need to collect names, just the number of times per day that each child brushes their teeth. You may like to extend the survey to other classes in school. One group can visit each class to collect their data.
2 Ask the groups to work collaboratively to design posters that highlight and inform other children about the good and bad practices of dental hygiene. The children could use the dental health leaflets as a source of further information.

ICT LINKS ⊙

Children could use data handling software in the Group activity 1 or use the graphing tool, from the CD-ROM, to present data.

ASSESSMENT

Assess the posters to determine understanding and ability to describe ways to care for teeth. Ask the children to explain their posters.

PLENARY

Summarise the learning by asking the children what advice they would give you if you were concerned about your dental health.

OUTCOMES
- Can describe ways to care for teeth and gums.
- Can explain why tooth and gum care is needed.

ENRICHMENT
Lesson 11 ◗ Our senses

Objective
- To know that the senses make us aware of our surroundings.

Vocabulary
eyes, ears, tongue, nose, skin, sight, sound, taste, hearing, smell, touch

RESOURCES ⊙

Main activity: Large sheets of paper; pens; A4-sized pictures to illustrate the sense organs (suitable images are available on many clip art packages); large print labels of the organ names, the senses and functions of the sense organs (also used in Plenary).
Group activities: 1 A copy of photocopiable page 31 (also 'Our senses' (red), available on the CD-ROM) for each child. **2** Bags of flavoured crisps; pens and paper.

BACKGROUND

In order to survive, all living things need a system that allows them to respond to changes and events occurring around them. Humans have a sensory system which keeps us in touch with our surroundings by processing information received from our surroundings and sent to our brain. In common with other mammals, we have a number of sensory organs that help us to monitor and make sense of our environment. Although our sensory system can respond to many things, we tend to regard ourselves as having just five senses with associated sensory organs (see overleaf).
      The information received by the senses is sent around the nervous

system of the body as a series of nerve impulses. The central nervous system (the brain and the spinal cord) responds in an appropriate way. For example, if you touch an object the receptors in your skin detect a great deal of information about that object, including whether it is hot or cold. If it is hot your central nervous system will instantly send a message back saying 'that object is too hot to hold, let go!' There are many other examples that you could use to illustrate the role of our senses in making us aware of our surroundings. These changes in our surroundings that our bodies detect are called stimuli; our reactions to them are called responses.

● **Sight:** our eyes help us to detect light and to form images. The iris controls the amount of light entering the eye; the lens and cornea focus that light onto the retina at the back of the eye. Here, light-sensitive cells send a message to the brain which interprets the image.

● **Hearing:** our ears detect sound because of the movement of the air (vibration). When, for example, someone bangs a drum, the drum skin vibrates. This causes the air in contact with it to also vibrate and these vibrations, like ripples on a pond, spread out. As that vibrating air enters your ear then a series of vibrations occur in the ear drum and the ear bones. This causes the fluid-filled 'cochlea' to vibrate. Nerve cells detect this movement and send a message to the brain.

● **Smell:** we detect smells using groups of sensory cells, called receptors, in the nasal passages.

● **Taste:** we detect tastes using groups of sensory cells, called receptors, located on the tongue.

● **Touch:** we are able to detect the many sensations associated with touch because of the receptors in the skin which are sensitive to touch, pain and temperature.

STARTER

Begin by asking the children to think about their favourite foods. Invite some children to share with everyone a description of the foods they really enjoy. Ask the children to say why they enjoy the food, and they should begin to talk about liking the taste.

MAIN ACTIVITY

Continue by asking the children to tell you more about their favourite foods, asking them to talk about other ways of identifying and enjoying foods apart from taste. Move the discussion on to learning about their surroundings: the classroom, the weather, various atmospheric smells or sounds, and so on. Ask the children to think about how we know about all these things. Encourage the children to think about the senses as a means of making us aware of our surroundings. Use A4-sized pictures of the sense organs to illustrate the discussion.

As a class, draw a concept map of the senses in which you include all the senses, the sensory organs and any other relevant information. Use this to help support the Group activities. Start by writing 'The senses' in the centre and note all the children's ideas and contributions around this. Then ask the children to try to link up words which are connected in some way and to say what that link is. For example, for eyes – sight, the link would be 'We use our eyes to see things'. This could be used as the basis for a 'senses' display.

GROUP ACTIVITIES

1 Distribute copies of photocopiable page 31. Tell the children to fold the page in half on the central line (the 'valley' fold) and back on the line to the left of centre (the 'mountain' fold). The sheet can then be completed with information on the senses, sensory organs and functions of the senses according to the children's knowledge or by research.

2 Carry out a 'Tasty crisp survey', but ask: Can you identify flavours of crisps blindfolded? Ask the children to hold their noses to see if it makes a difference to their ability to choose. Encourage the children to decide on a suitable way of recording and presenting the findings.

ASSESSMENT
Does the children's work on the photocopiable page indicate that they can identify the senses and show that they understand how senses tell us about our surroundings?

PLENARY
Have a quiz where the children have to match your A4 pictures of the sense organs with their names, senses and functions. Highlight how much our senses work together, such as the relationship of smell to taste.

OUTCOME
● Can identify the senses and the sense organs.

ENRICHMENT
Lesson 12 ▪ Different tastes

Objective
● To know that the senses, including taste, make us aware of our surroundings.

RESOURCES
A variety of foods (sweet, salty and bitter); paper and pens.

MAIN ACTIVITY
Use a variety of foods to get the children to distinguish and classify foods into one of these tastes: sweet (sugar cakes), salty (salted crisps), bitter (lemons). Get the children to record their results in a table, like the one shown below.

ICT LINK
Children could create a simple database using the data collected to help them see which foods are sweet, salty or bitter.

ASSESSMENT
Through discussion with the children, identify if they demonstrate understanding of what the senses tell us.

Differentiation
Most children should be able to work on this task since the different tastes are quite distinctive.

PLENARY
Ask the children to explain their findings and to describe what effect the different tastes had on them.

OUTCOME
● Can perform activities on the senses.

Sweet	Salty	Bitter

Lesson 13 ▪ Assessment

Objective
● To assess the children's knowledge and understanding of dental health, tooth types and functions.
● To assess the children's knowledge and understanding of the importance of eating a balanced diet.

RESOURCES 💿
Assessment activities: 1 Copies of photocopiable page 32 (also 'Assessment- 1' (red), available on the CD-ROM); pens or pencils. **2** Copies of photocopiable page 33 (also 'Assessment -2' (red), available on the CD-ROM); pens or pencils.

STARTER
Begin the Assessment activities by giving the children a vocabulary test. This could be oral or written. Remember the activity is an assessment of scientific knowledge and understanding. Either give a word and ask for a definition or give a definition and ask for a word.

ASSESSMENT ACTIVITY 1

Distribute copies of photocopiable page 32 to the children and allow them time to complete it individually. You may wish to tell the children that you wish to find out what they have understood and that it is important to complete the sheet individually. You will need to collect these in to mark them effectively.

ANSWERS

For Assessment activity 1 the children should answer that it is important to look after our teeth because they help us to tear, break, cut up and eat our food. To keep our teeth healthy we should eat sensible food without too much sugar, clean our teeth regularly (at least twice a day), and visit the dentist every six months.

LOOKING FOR LEVELS

For Assessment activity 1, all the children should be able to describe orally and in words a number of relevant tooth facts. Most children will be able to answer the questions correctly. Some children will be able to give a more reasoned answer with greater use of appropriate vocabulary.

ASSESSMENT ACTIVITY 2

Distribute copies of photocopiable page 33 to the children and allow them time to complete it individually. You may wish to tell the children that you wish to find out what they have understood and that it is important to complete the sheet individually. You will need to collect these in to mark them effectively.

ANSWERS

For Assessment activity 2 the children should answer that it is important to eat a healthy balanced diet because our bodies need different types of nutrients that different foods can give us. Too much of one food type would therefore be unhealthy. They should know that their diet is unhealthy if it consists of all the same types of food, for example too much fat or sugar.

LOOKING FOR LEVELS

For Assessment activity 2, all the children should be able to plan a healthy meal. Most children will be able to answer the questions correctly. Some children should be able to give a more reasoned answer with greater use of appropriate vocabulary.

PLENARY

You may wish to give some feedback to the children, celebrate their achievements and correct any areas of recurrent misunderstanding.

Myself

■ Make this picture into a picture of you.

■ Write labels around the picture for all the things that you know about your body and how it works. One label has already been put on for you. Think particularly about how you eat and how food benefits you.

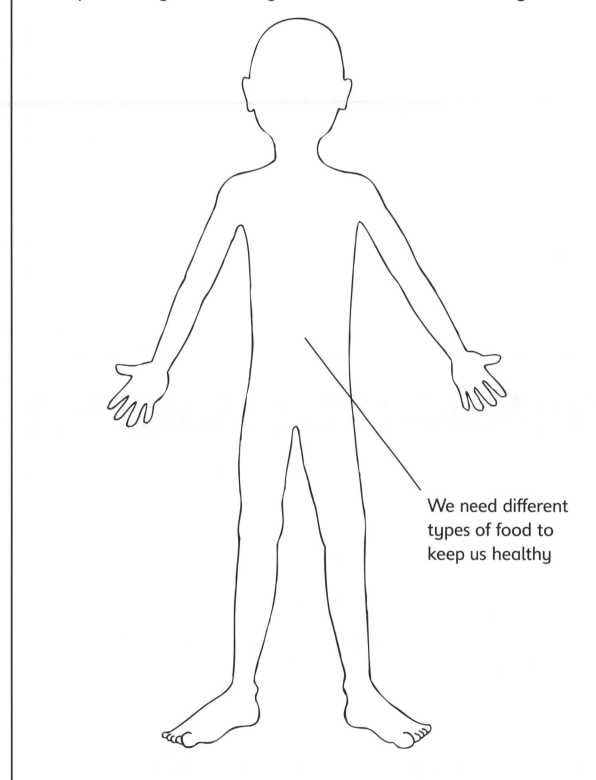

We need different types of food to keep us healthy

Food groups –1

■ Draw pictures of all the food in your packed lunch.

■ Now write down the name of each item in your packed lunch under these headings.

Energy-giving foods	Body-building foods	Maintenance foods

Which foods in your packed lunch are you looking forward to eating the most and why?

_____

_____

■SCHOLASTIC

Food groups – 2

■ Write in the table the foods you have eaten in the past 24 hours for breakfast, lunch, evening meal and any other snacks.

✓ Tick the correct food group.

Foods eaten at mealtimes	Food groups	
	Body-building (for growth)	Energy-giving (for activity)
Breakfast		
Lunch		
Evening meal		
Snacks		

PHOTOCOPIABLE

Going shopping

◗ Different people eat different kinds of foods.

◗ Here are the food shopping lists for two people. Look at them carefully and think about the balance of the foods on each list.

LIST A

bananas
carrots
apples
chicken
yoghurt
skimmed milk
low fat spread
rice
pasta
wholemeal bread
fish

LIST B

chips
cream
sausage
full fat milk
chocolate biscuits
butter
fizzy drinks
cheese
chocolate bars

1. Write your thoughts about the balance of food on each list.

List A _____

_____

List B _____

_____

2.a) Which diet is healthy and balanced? _____

   b) Which diet is unhealthy and unbalanced? _____

◗ Now write your own shopping list. Include a range of items to give you a healthy, balanced and tasty diet. A few 'treats' are allowed!

My shopping list

Food

◼ Write down the foods you and your family like to eat in the 'Foods eaten by humans' column.

◼ Then think about the foods that animals eat. Write these down in the 'Foods eaten by animals' column.

Foods eaten by humans	Foods eaten by animals

◼ Now choose one animal and find out as much as you can about where it lives and what it likes to eat.

Animal diet factfile
Name of animal:
Habitat (where it lives):
Main foods eaten:

PHOTOCOPIABLE

My teeth

◼ Look at the diagram of teeth below. Colour the teeth to show the position of each type.

incisors – red   canines – blue   molars – green

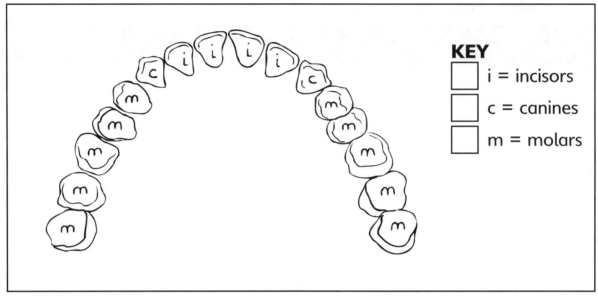

KEY

☐ i = incisors

☐ c = canines

☐ m = molars

◼ Use a mirror to look at your teeth.
◼ Draw each different type of tooth and write about the job it does.

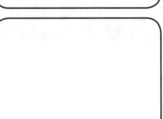

molar _____

_____

_____

canine _____

_____

_____

incisor _____

_____

_____

Illustration © Kirsty Wilson

■ SCHOLASTIC

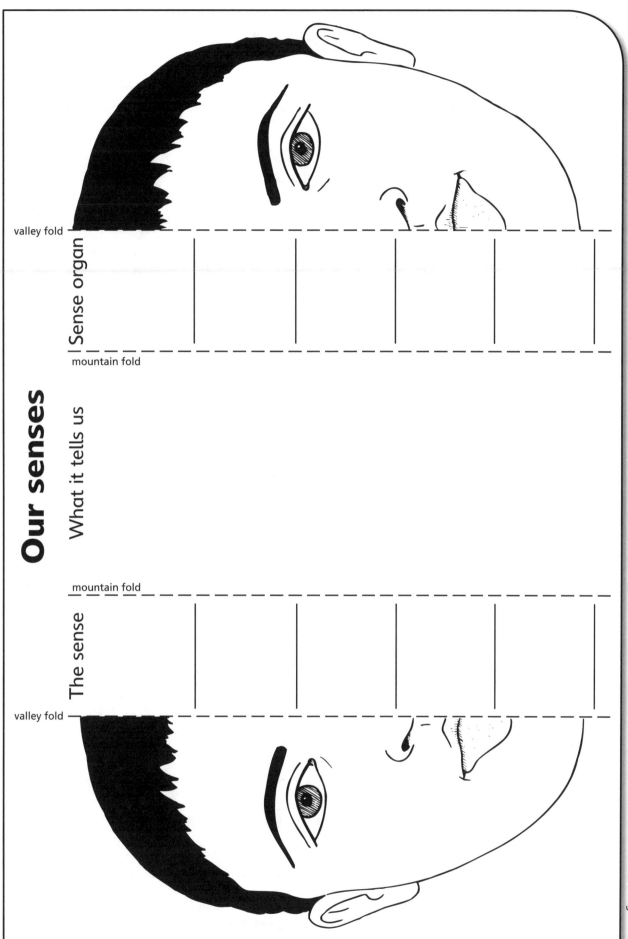

Our senses

valley fold

Sense organ

mountain fold

What it tells us

mountain fold

The sense

valley fold

PHOTOCOPIABLE

Assessment – 1

◀ What have you learned about teeth? Write in the tooth all you know about teeth. Write about their growth, why they are important and how to look after them.

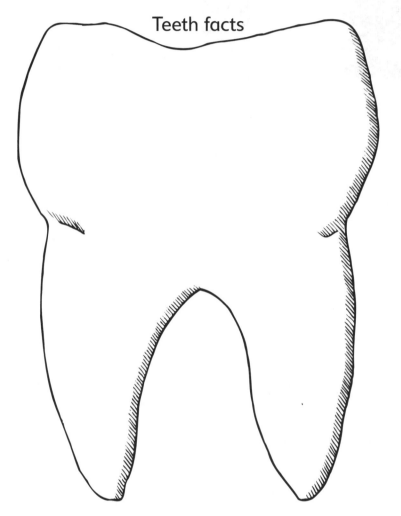

Teeth facts

Why is it important to look after your teeth?

_____

_____

What should you do to make sure your teeth are healthy?

_____

_____

▬ SCHOLASTIC

Illustration © Kirsty Wilson

Assessment – 2

◼ Think about all the things you have learned about food. Draw and write what you would include in a healthy balanced meal on these plates.

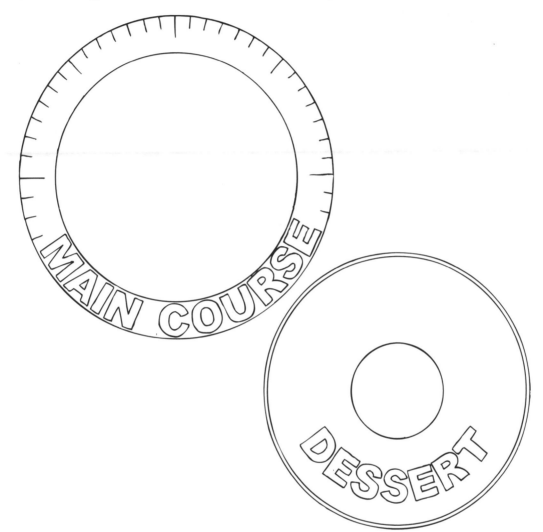

Why is it important to eat a healthy balanced diet?

_____

_____

How would you know if your diet was healthy or not?

_____

_____

Illustration © Kirsty Wilson

CHAPTER 2 Helping plants grow well

Lesson	Objectives	Main activity	Group activities	Plenary	Outcomes
Lesson 1 Food sources	• To know that most of our diet comes from plants.	Identifying foods that come from plants and animals. Supermarket visit.	Looking at food chains. Tracing foods back to plants.	Discussion from visit to supermarket.	• Can recognise that most of our diet comes directly from plants.
Lesson 2 Plant care	• To know that plants are carefully tended so that they produce large crops.	Preparation of a 'Guide to caring for plants' booklet.		'Question and answer' session with guest gardener.	• Can recognise that plants need care in order for them to supply us with food.
Lesson 3 Leaves and plant growth	• To know that plants need leaves in order to grow well. • To know that previous experimental results can help make predictions in new experiments.	Investigations involving plants with and without leaves to determine importance of leaves.		Groups to report back and together draw conclusions.	• Can recognise that leaves are needed for healthy plant growth. • Can describe an investigation on the relationship of plant leaves and plant growth. • Can make observations and comparisons.
Lesson 4 Plant parts	• To know that the roots take up water and anchor the plant to the ground. • To use systematic observation and measurement.	Looking at plant specimens.	Drawing a labelled diagram of a plant. Investigating the function of roots as water carriers.	Review the investigation and draw conclusions.	• Can describe two functions of roots. • Can use systematic observation and measurement.
Lesson 5 How plants carry water	• To know that water travels in tiny 'pipes' through plants. • To know that information from previous experiments can be used in planning new experiments.	Observing the effects of a stick of celery standing in coloured water as a way to show the 'pipes' in the stem of a plant.		Reinforce the concept through discussion of the effects on the celery.	• Can recognise the importance of previous information in planning experiments. • Can recognise where water moves up inside a plant. • Can recognise the importance of leaves in drawing water up the plant.
Lesson 6 Water and growth	• To know that plants need water, but not an unlimited amount, for healthy growth.	Investigations with water as a variable factor in plant growth.		Groups to report back and together draw conclusions.	• Can recognise that too little or too much water prevents healthy plant growth.
Enrichment Lesson 7 Wild plant survey	• To know that different plants prefer different places in which to grow.	Plan a wild plant survey.	Carry out the survey. Present results of observations.	'Wild plant' quiz.	• Know that different plants prefer different places in which to grow.
Lesson 8 Light and growth	• To know that plants need light for healthy growth.	Investigations with light as a variable factor in plant growth.		Groups to report back and together draw conclusions.	• Can recognise that light is needed for healthy plant growth.
Lesson 9 Temperature and growth	• To know that temperature affects plant growth.	Investigations with heat as a variable factor in plant growth.		Groups to report back and together draw conclusions.	• Can recognise that temperature affects plant growth.
Lesson 10 Growing seeds	• To know that experimental work can be related to the growing of food plants. • To make predictions about what will happen. • To consider what makes a fair test. • To make observations. • To present results in drawings and tables. • To draw conclusions and make generalisations.	Planning an investigation into plant growth using different variables to determine ideal conditions.	Carry out the investigation. Record findings as a diary.	Groups to report back and together draw conclusions.	• Can describe the conditions plants need for healthy growth. • Can explain why plants need roots and leaves. • Can make predictions about what will happen. • Can consider what makes a fair test. • Can make observations. • Can present results in drawings and tables. • Can draw conclusions and make generalisations.

Lesson	Objectives	Main activity	Group activities	Plenary	Outcomes
Enrichment Lesson 11 Plant habitats	• To investigate plants found in certain habitats. • To compare the numbers of different plants found. • To suggest reasons for differences in plants. • To devise a record sheet.	Predicting how plants might vary in different habitats.	Carrying out a survey of plants growing in two different habitats.	Comparing plants found in two habitats and suggesting reasons for any differences.	• Can investigate the plants found in a certain habitat. • Can compare the numbers of different types of plants in the two habitats. • Can suggest reasons for differences in the plants that grow in different habitats. • Can devise their own record sheet.
Enrichment Lesson 12 What we found out	• To communicate findings about the habitats investigated. • To begin to explore the relationships between the physical aspects and the plants living in a habitat.	Making a book to communicate their findings about two different habitats.		Sharing books that have been made.	• Can communicate findings. • Can make suggestions about the relationships between the physical aspects and the plants living in a habitat.

Assessment	Objectives	Activity 1	Activity 2
Lesson 13	• To assess the children's level of understanding of the needs of plants, their functions and uses.	Completing a worksheet to assess level of understanding of plants.	Re-ordering data showing the growth of a plant and creating a table and bar chart.

SC1 SCIENTIFIC ENQUIRY

Do plants need unlimited amounts of water to grow?

LEARNING OBJECTIVES AND OUTCOMES
- Decide how to answer the question.
- Devise a fair test, consider what evidence to collect and what equipment to use.
- Make predictions of the outcomes.
- Make systematic observations and measurements.
- Use ICT to record data.
- Consider the collected data and draw conclusions.

ACTIVITY
Prior to the lesson the children need to grow a packet of seeds. When they have germinated and grown into small seedlings, the children should set up an investigation in which they have a number of samples, each receiving varying amounts of water: some are under-watered, some over-watered, some not watered at all. The children observe and measure the growth and general health of the plants over a period of time and then draw conclusions.

LESSON LINKS
This Sc1 activity forms an integral part of Lesson 6, Water and growth.

Lesson 1 ◗ Food sources

Objective
- To know that most of our diet comes from plants.

Vocabulary
animals, food chains, plants

RESOURCES
Main activity: 1 Flipchart; paper; pens; pencils. **2** Computer and online shopping disk (optional); extra adult supervision (if visiting a shop or supermarket).
Group activities: 1 and **2** Paper; pens; pencils.

PREPARATION
If arranging to visit a local shop or supermarket, contact the manager first to arrange permission, and arrange extra adult supervision for each group. If this is not a practical option, you could access supermarket websites and use the online shopping service.

BACKGROUND
A characteristic of all living things is the necessity to feed. Almost all plants and animals depend directly or indirectly on the sun for their food. Unlike animals, plants are able to make their own food. They do this through the process of photosynthesis, where plants use carbon dioxide, water and the energy from the sun to make a type of sugar that is the plant's source of energy. The plant then becomes food for animals, which in turn may be food for other animals, including humans. Thus most of the food we eat in our diet can be traced back along a food chain to plants and ultimately the sun. These links in the food chain are often difficult to trace when faced with some of the processed foods we eat today and the many additives and preservatives they contain. None the less, the bulk of foods that children will come across will be just one link in a food chain, where we as humans are at the very end.

STARTER

Ask the children to tell you some of the foods they have eaten recently. Write them down on the board. Ask the children to consider where the food came from originally, before it arrived in the shops. Ask them to see if they can put the food into groups, not according to the type of food or its benefits to us, but in some other way. Guide their thinking towards the idea of food from plants and food from animals.

MAIN ACTIVITY - PART 1

As a whole-class activity, the children should now rewrite their earlier food suggestions, this time in two lists on the flipchart, one headed 'Plants', the other headed 'Animals'. Before recording their ideas, encourage the children to predict which they think will give the longest list, then discuss the table. After filling in the table, ask the children to think about the food that is eaten by those who are in the 'Animals' list, and what those animals that provided the food were fed on themselves.

GROUP ACTIVITIES

1 Ask the children to trace back some of the food they have eaten to its source in a food chain, then to draw these as a series of linked illustrations. Challenge the children to see if they can find a food that does not start with a green plant.
2 Ask the children to work in groups to share and explain to each other their food chain drawings. At this stage the children should then be able to come to an understanding that, either directly or through a food chain, most of our diet comes from plants.

MAIN ACTIVITY - PART 2

Arrange a visit to a local shop or supermarket or, if that is not possible, look at an online shopping service on a supermarket website on an interactive whiteboard. These are often organised into aisles, just like the real thing. Either using the computer or in the real supermarket, allocate an aisle to each group. The children's task is to record and consider the foods in that aisle and determine if they come directly from plants or animals. The results will reinforce the principle that most of our diet comes from plants.

ASSESSMENT

Marking the children's work will give an indication of whether or not they have understood the concept. All the children should have been able to sort the foods into groups, so will have understood that foods come from one of these two sources. Most should have been able to understand that most of our food can be traced directly or indirectly back to plants.

PLENARY

Discuss the findings from the supermarket visit, reinforcing the concept of plants being the major source of food and highlighting one or two foods that make food chains where plants are at the bottom of the chain, such as milk and some meats.

OUTCOME

● Can recognise that most of our diet comes directly from plants.

LINKS

Unit 3a, Lessons 3-5, human feeding.

Lesson 2 ▪ Plant care

Objective
● To know that plants are carefully tended so that they produce large crops.

RESOURCES
Find a parent or grandparent who is a keen gardener to visit the school to talk about looking after plants.

MAIN ACTIVITY
Ask your gardening expert to talk to the children about growing plants and looking after them so that they produce a good crop. The children can then prepare a 'Guide to Caring for Plants' booklet.

ASSESSMENT
Through observation and discussion, identify those children who understand how to care for plants.

PLENARY
Have a 'question and answer' session, with the children as the 'experts' answering questions from your guest.

OUTCOME
● Can recognise that plants need care in order for them to supply us with food.

Lesson 3 ▪ Leaves and plant growth

Objective
● To know that plants need leaves in order to grow well.
● To know that previous experimental results can help make predictions in new experiments.

RESOURCES
Potted plants of the same species: one with leaves and one with leaves removed.

MAIN ACTIVITY
Talk to the children about the work they have done previously about the parts of plants. Recall the parts they know about and talk briefly and in simple terms about the functions of those parts: roots take up water and nutrients and anchor the plant; stems carry water to the leaves and keep the plant upright; flowers produce seeds; leaves take in sunlight and make food.

Talk about what might happen if the plant was deprived of one of these parts, for example if all the leaves were removed.

Plan and carry out an investigation into the need plants have for leaves. Observe two plants (of the same species) - one that has leaves and one that has had its leaves removed. Keep them in the same conditions, observe what happens and measure growth over a period of time.

ASSESSMENT
Discussion with the children during their investigation and scrutiny of written work will indicate understanding. Look for evidence that the children know that without leaves the plant would not be able to grow. Some children may be able to explain that without leaves the plant cannot produce food and therefore will not grow healthily.

PLENARY
Discuss observations and draw conclusions about what happened to those plants without leaves that were not growing well. Reinforce the knowledge that leaves are important in order for plants to grow well.

OUTCOMES

● Can recognise that leaves are needed for healthy plant growth.
● Can describe an investigation of the relationship of plant leaves and plant growth.
● Can make observations and comparisons.

Lesson 4 ▪ Plant parts

Objectives
● To know that the roots take up water and anchor the plant to the ground.
● To use systematic observation and measurement.

Vocabulary
anchor, roots, water

RESOURCES ●

Main activity: Washed weeds with roots in shallow trays; a copy of photocopiable page 50 (also 'Plant parts -1' (red), available on the CD-ROM) for each child.
Group activities: 1 Copies of photocopiable page 50 (also 'Plants parts–1 (red), available on the CD-ROM). **2** Copies of photocopiable page 51 (also 'Plant parts– 2' (red), available on the CD-ROM); beakers; washed weeds (complete with roots); water; cling film.
ICT link: 'Plant parts' interactive activity, from the CD-ROM.

PREPARATION

Dig up and clean sufficient weeds to provide one for each group.

BACKGROUND

Roots are vital to the well-being of a plant. Gardeners go to great lengths to develop a healthy and substantial root system on their plants. It is this system that performs two very important functions in the plant and without such a system the plant would become unhealthy and die.

The first function is that of supplying water to the plant. If a plant becomes short of water it will eventually wilt and die: the plant needs water in order to survive. The roots of the plant draw up water and trace minerals from the ground. These are transported from the roots to the leaves where photosynthesis takes place. The plant also loses some of this water as it evaporates into the air from the leaves and flowers. This water loss is called transpiration. The water in the roots and stems moves due to a combination of pushing and pulling. The roots often push the water a little way up the stem while the evaporation from the leaves draws up more water to replace that lost.

As well as taking up water for the plant, the roots also perform another very important function: the root system acts as an anchor to hold the plant firmly in place. Without a well-established root system to keep the plant in place it would rock about and become loose; very soon it would fall over, become unhealthy and die. The root system of a plant is very often quite extensive and can spread out as far and wide as the branches above ground. The roots of some larger plants and trees are also very strong and can cause serious structural damage if allowed to develop near buildings.

STARTER

Ask the children to think about what they feel like on a lovely, hot and sunny day, particularly when they are inside or if they have just been for a long walk or finished playing games. Encourage them to think about being hot and in need of some refreshment. Ask them to think about what being thirsty does to you.

Show them a wilting plant and ask them to think about what this plant may need and why it is wilting. They should suggest that the plant needs a 'drink' of water. Draw again on the analogy of themselves needing water and the plant needing water. Ask the children to think about how we drink to take in water and how the plant might take in water through its roots.

Differentiation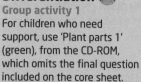

Group activity 1
For children who need support, use 'Plant parts 1' (green), from the CD-ROM, which omits the final question included on the core sheet.
To extend children, use 'Plant parts 1' (blue), which uses open-ended questioning.

Group activity 2
Some children will need support during the setting up of the investigation and may benefit from using a simplified scale on the beaker (or writing on the beaker with a waterproof pen to mark the falling water level). Give them 'Plant parts 2' (green), which includes multiple choice answers for question 1, to record their investigation.
Other children will be able to give reasoned answers to questions and may have a beaker marked in smaller units, such as millilitres, that can be read off and recorded.

MAIN ACTIVITY

Distribute the weeds that you have prepared and copies of photocopiable page 50. Ask the children to take great care as they will be using the plants later in an investigation. Ask them to look carefully at the plant, its roots, stem and leaves. Talk about how water moves up the roots and stem to the leaves and about the functions of the roots, stem and leaves.

GROUP ACTIVITIES

1 Ask the children to draw a labelled diagram of their plant on a copy of photocopiable page 50. They should then pair up the names of the parts with the description of their function.

2 Suggest to the children that, while we think water is taken up through the roots of the plant, we need to be sure and so they are going to carry out an investigation to show that water does travel through the roots of the plant. The children will need copies of page 51, the weeds, plastic beakers, water and cling film. During the investigation, which could last a week, the children will need to observe the water levels every day and record their observations on page 51. At the end of the investigation there are two questions to answer that will help the children to draw some conclusions.

ICT LINKS

Children could use digital cameras to record what happens to the plants during the investigation. They could also use the 'Plant parts' interactive, from the CD-ROM, to match plant parts to their functions.

ASSESSMENT

Mark the children's work to show understanding of the functions of the roots. Have they been able to identify the two functions? During the investigation, assess the children's ability to take simple measurements.

PLENARY

Bring the children together, with their plants, and ask each group to describe what has happened to theirs. (The water levels will have dropped.) You may need to reinforce the idea that because the beaker was sealed the water could not have 'escaped' directly into the air, so it must have been taken up by the plant's roots and travelled through and out of the plant.

OUTCOMES

- Can describe two functions of roots.
- Can use systematic observation and measurement.

Lesson 5 ▪ How plants carry water

Objective
- To know that water travels in tiny 'pipes' through plants.
- To know that information from previous experiments can be used in planning new experiments.

RESOURCES
Celery; containers; food colouring.

MAIN ACTIVITY
As an introduction to the lesson, take a bunch of cut flowers and put them in a vase of water. Ask the children why we put cut flowers into water. Talk about the tiny pipes through which a plant carries the water. Look at the ends of the cut flowers. The children will find it difficult to see any pipes clearly. Continue by suggesting that if they place a stick of celery in a container of coloured water the children will be able to see the pipes. Do this and leave it for a few days. Cut the stalk and examine the end of the celery. The children can write and draw about their observations of how water travels in tiny pipes through plants.

Children could take a series of digital images or video at intervals to create a 'time lapse' record of the celery over a few days. This will show the leaves of the celery changing colour as the coloured water travels up the stalk.

ASSESSMENT
Examine the children's explanations and drawings to assess whether they understand the concept of water travelling through pipes.

PLENARY
Discuss the investigation and the colour of the celery. Reinforce the concept of water travelling up the stem of the celery.

OUTCOMES
● Can recognise the importance of previous information in planning experiments.
● Can recognise where water moves up inside a plant.
● Can recognise the importance of leaves in drawing water up the plant.

Lesson 6 ▪ Water and growth

RESOURCES
Seeds; compost; water.

MAIN ACTIVITY
In the context of previous work related to plants, grow a packet of seeds. When they have germinated and grown into small seedlings set up an investigation in which you have a number of samples, each receiving varying amounts of water: some are under-watered, some over-watered, and some not watered at all. Observe and measure the growth and general health of the plants over a period of time.

ASSESSMENT
Discussion with the children during the investigation and scrutiny of written work will indicate understanding. Ask the children to explain their investigation and what the results mean. Ask questions such as: *Why did this plant die? Do you think plants like to stand in water? What happens if you over-water a plant?*

PLENARY
Discuss the results of the investigation, draw conclusions related to the amount of water plants need. The children should find that too little or too much water is not going to benefit a plant. Too little and the plant will dry out and die, too much and the roots may rot, also causing the plant to die.

OUTCOME
● Can recognise that too little or too much water prevents healthy plant growth.

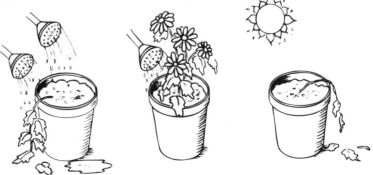

ENRICHMENT
Lesson 7 ▪ Wild plant survey

Objective
● To know that different plants prefer different places in which to grow.

Vocabulary
wild plant, survey, hedges, waste ground, field

RESOURCES
Main activity: Secondary sources of information; a map of your locality, paper; pens; pencils.
Group activities: 1 Paper; pens; pencils; clipboards. **2** Secondary sources of information; paper; pens; pencils; art materials.

PREPARATION
Ensure that a variety of common wild plants grow in your chosen locations.

BACKGROUND
As most gardeners will tell you, certain plants like to grow in particular types of soil and in certain conditions. Many garden centres will set out their stocks of plants according to whether those plants prefer, for example, clay soil or sandy soil; whether they should be planted in a shady site or a sunny site and so on. As we look around our environment, we are able to see a real variety of wild plants that also prefer certain conditions. Some, such as the dandelion, grow well in dry open sunny sites whilst others, such as mosses, prefer the shady dampness offered by a sheltered north-facing position.

STARTER
Begin the lesson by telling the children that they are going to be explorers and that they are going to explore local plant life. Ask the children if they can name any wild plants that they know of and that they think they may be able to see and possibly identify locally. Most of the children should be able to identify some common wild plants such as the dandelion, daisy and buttercup. It may be worth discussing here the difference between a wild plant and a weed. (Weeds are plants that are not wanted in the location where they are growing.)

MAIN ACTIVITY
Together, plan a wild plant survey. Ask the children to suggest areas in the locality in which they could look to survey the wild plants growing there. Try to get a range of different places, such as the school field, under a hedge, in a wild area or on waste ground. (These will depend on the location of your school.) Have available a range of secondary sources of information that the children can use to familiarise themselves with some of the possible wild plants they may see. Discuss with the children exactly what it is they are going to be observing, for example, the characteristics of the location (damp, dry, dark, light and so on) or the plants growing there.

GROUP ACTIVITIES
1 Let the children carry out their survey. They should record their observations in an appropriate way. They could devise a record sheet that includes detail such as: place, date and season, the conditions and plants growing there. A sketch of the location and its plants could also be made.
2 The children should then try to identify the wild plants they have seen using secondary sources as an aid. The children could present their findings in the form of a location sketch, painting or collage, which may also give extra detail on the plants seen.

ASSESSMENT
All of the children should be able to identify a few of the more common wild plants. Most should be able to identify more common wild plants and understand that they grow in different places. Some may be able to explain more about each of the common wild plants they have seen and begin to explain where they generally grow.

Differentiation
Some children may prefer to present their observations in a simple picture form. Other children could present their observations with additional research and background information.

PLENARY
Bring the children together and discuss their observations from their surveys. Have a simple quiz where the children have to try to identify a wild plant from the description you give of the plant and the location where it typically grows.

OUTCOME
● Know that different plants prefer different places in which to grow.

LINKS
Enrichment unit, Lessons 2–4.

Lesson 8 ▫ Light and growth

Objective
● To know that plants need light for healthy growth.

RESOURCES
Seeds; compost; pots.

MAIN ACTIVITY
Set up a number of investigations with plants where light is a variable factor. These could include: growing seeds with and without light; leaving some seedlings in the dark and bringing others out; keeping existing plants in light and dark conditions; studying covered and uncovered patches of grass.

ASSESSMENT
Discussion with the children during their investigation and scrutiny of their written work will indicate understanding. Ask the children to explain what they have done in their investigation and what they have found out. Do the children understand that for healthy growth plants need light?

PLENARY
Ask each group to report back their findings. Bring results together and encourage the children to draw conclusions. Highlight that the plants deprived of light have not grown as well or as healthily as those with the benefit of light.

Differentiation
Differentiate by outcome.

OUTCOME
● Can recognise that light is needed for healthy plant growth.

Lesson 9 ▫ Temperature and growth

Objective
● To know that temperature affects plant growth.

RESOURCES
Seedlings; warm and cold places.

MAIN ACTIVITY
Grow a number of seedlings where the only variable is temperature. Heated and unheated propagators would give the ideal variables. Try to ensure that light and other conditions remain the same for all the samples.

ASSESSMENT
Discussion with the children, during the investigation, and scrutiny of their written work will indicate understanding. Ask them to explain to you the conditions in which their plants are kept and what will happen. They should be able to explain that plants with insufficient heat will not grow as well as those with sufficient heat and that some plants may not like too much heat.

Differentiation
Differentiate by outcome.

PLENARY

Discuss the results of the investigation, draw conclusions related to the effect variables in temperature have on plants. The children should discover that too much or too little heat are not ideal conditions for healthy growth.

OUTCOME

- Can recognise that temperature affects plant growth.

Lesson 10 ◗ Growing seeds

Objectives
- To know that experimental work can be related to the growing of food plants.
- To make predictions about what will happen.
- To consider what makes a fair test.
- To make observations.
- To present results in drawings and tables.
- To draw conclusions and make generalisations.

Vocabulary
conclusion, fair test, observation, prediction, results

RESOURCES ◉

Main activity: Paper; pens; pencils.
Group activities: 1 Cress (or other fast-germinating seeds); compost; eight small containers per group, sticky labels; photocopiable page 52 (also 'Growing seeds' (red), available on the CD-ROM); pens; pencils. **2** Paper; pens; pencils.

BACKGROUND

There are about 380,000 known species of plant in the world, the most abundant and successful being those which reproduce by making seeds. There are two main groups of seed-bearing plants:
- flowering plants, which produce seeds that are enclosed in a fruit
- non-flowering plants, which produce seeds that are not enclosed in a fruit (such as ferns).

The abundance and success of plants is of benefit to humankind since we harvest and eat a large range of fruits, vegetables, cereals and grain as food. Many food crops are grown throughout the world and are a major part of the diets of large parts of the world population. It is humankind's general success in growing crops that has helped to sustain life throughout the world, despite problems in some countries.

A plant's unique ability to make its own food has been particularly important for humans. Without plants, animals (including humans) would die. Plants need water, light, moderate temperatures and carbon dioxide in order to survive. Plants will suffer and die if they do not get the correct amount and balance of these things. Too much or not enough water, insufficient light, too high or low a temperature will all affect the growth of plants. This lesson brings together the work from previous lessons into one investigation. It is designed to encourage the children to consider factors that affect the growth of plants in combination with each other.

STARTER

Remind the children of the recent lessons they have had and the investigations they have carried out looking at plants, particularly plants and light, plants and water, plants and temperature. Reinforce the previous learning, asking questions such as: *What things do plants need to grow? Can anybody tell me what effect light has on plants? If I kept a plant in very cold temperatures what would happen to it? Tell me why water is important to plants.* Address any misunderstandings that may become apparent as a result of such questions and ask other children to share and discuss solutions.

MAIN ACTIVITY

Tell the children that they are going to carry out an investigation to try to find out the ideal conditions for growing plants, particularly those that we can use for food. Together discuss how this could be done. Ask the children to plan a fair test that would investigate the growth of plants with combinations of these variables: light, heat and water. Ask the children to

Differentiation

Group activities

For children who need support, use 'Growing seeds' (green), from the CD-ROM, which includes fewer questions than the standard sheet.

work out how many different combinations there are and therefore how many samples they will need to grow. They will also need to consider: how much water they will give the plants and how often (perhaps daily, every three days, weekly); where to keep the plants needing light and those needing dark (perhaps in a store room, on a window sill); where to keep those that need heat or not (perhaps in a cold store room, outside, in a fridge).

GROUP ACTIVITIES

1 Make the resources the children need available, and distribute and talk through photocopiable page 52. The children can then work in groups of three or four to set up their part of the investigation. Remind them to put sticky labels on the pots that include the group's names, the plant number, the conditions (whether given water, light or warmth).

2 Ask the children to write the first part of the record of their investigation. This can be in diary format, but needs to include details of: what they are investigating, how they are carrying out the investigation, what they think will happen, and what they have done so far.

ASSESSMENT

During the investigation, try to find time to talk to each child about the investigation. Try to elicit their level of understanding of what they are doing and why. Marking of the children's completed work should also be indicative of understanding. The children should have been able to keep accurate records of their work, presenting their results and drawing some conclusions that would indicate they understand that seeds that have water, light and heat grow better, and maybe suggest why.

PLENARY

At the end of the first investigation lesson, ask some children to talk about how they have set up the investigation. Remind the children of the aims and also to continue to observe their seeds on a daily basis. At some point each day, set aside a few minutes for groups to report on any progress. Remind the groups to record everything they observe during the experiment.

OUTCOMES

- Can describe the conditions plants need for healthy growth.
- Can explain why plants need roots and leaves.
- Can make predictions about what will happen.
- Can consider what makes a fair test.
- Can make observations.
- Can present results in drawings and tables.
- Can draw conclusions and make generalisations.

ENRICHMENT

Lesson 11 ▪ Plant habitats

Objectives
- To investigate plants found in certain habitats.
- To compare the numbers of different plants found.
- To suggest reasons for differences in plants.
- To devise a record sheet.

RESOURCES

Main activity: Two hoops of different sizes; a flipchart or whiteboard and marker pens.

Group activities: 1 Writing materials. **2** One hoop per group; writing materials; clipboards; adhesive tape; digital cameras (optional); reference books and keys on plants.

PREPARATION

Copy the sample record chart below on to the flipchart. Have the resources for the Main teaching activity to hand. Have the resources for the Group activities ready to be taken outside.

Vocabulary
compare, fair test, hoop

BACKGROUND

In this lesson, children will begin to gain an appreciation of the diversity of plant life, even in places that at first glance seem to be just grass. They can draw on prior knowledge to help them make predictions about the types of plants that grow in different places.

It is good to extend children's knowledge of the names of different plants, but this should not become too threatening for you, and different strategies are recommended below for dealing with unknown plants. It is not expected that they will gain a detailed knowledge of which plants are suited to different conditions, but more that they begin to develop awareness that the nature of the habitat will affect what can live there.

STARTER

Explain that this lesson will focus on plant habitats in locations near the school and the plants that live in these habitats.

	Under tree	In playing field
daisies	1	6
clover	0	2
moss	Lots	2 patches
dandelion	0	1

MAIN ACTIVITY

Write the descriptions of two habitats on the board, for example 'Under a large tree', 'In the middle of the playing field'. Ask: *What plants might we expect to find under the tree or in the field? What differences might there be in the plants that grow in each place? Why do you think that?* (Fewer plants might grow under the tree because it is dark; fewer might grow in the field because it is mown and trampled on; daisies might grow in the field but not under the tree because they like the sun.)

Write a prediction on the board to model this process. Ask: *How could we find out if our predictions are right?* (We can look.) Explain that to help them concentrate on one patch in their habitat, the children could put a hoop down and look at the plants that are growing inside the hoop. Hold up the large hoop and say: *Imagine I have put this on the field and I have counted six daisy plants.* Now take the smaller hoop and say: *Imagine that I put this hoop under the tree and I counted one daisy plant.* (If children find this difficult to visualise, then draw it on the board.) Ask: *Is this a fair test?* (No, it is not a fair test.) Ask: *Why not?* (Because you would be looking at different-sized areas.) *What must we do to make it a fair test?* (Use same-sized hoops.)

Show the children the example of recording on the flipchart (see above), explaining how the chart is organised into rows and columns. Ask questions such as: *How many daisies did we find under the tree? How many clover plants were found in the field? Did we find any moss growing under the tree?* Explain that they might want to use this way of recording, or they might want to find their own way.

GROUP ACTIVITIES

1 Before going outside, ask the children to write down what they predict they will find and if they expect to find any differences in the plants in the two different habitats they are going to study.

2 When outside, the children can begin investigating the plants in each habitat and recording their findings. If children do not know the name of a particular plant, they could either draw it or take a digital photograph. It may be possible to identify them either by asking an adult or using reference books. If not, they could name the plant themselves.

Discuss questions that arise as the children are working such as: *Do you count the number of flowers, or try to work out if they all belong to one plant? How do you record the number of grass plants?* (You estimate.) Ask: *Did you choose where you put your hoop, or did you just drop it down? Which would be fairer?* (Dropping, so that there is no pre-selection of 'interesting bits'.)

Differentiation
Challenge children by asking them to link the physical aspects they recorded with the plants that grow there.

ASSESSMENT

Can the children record the different plants that they find? Can they devise a table to record quantitatively? Can they make comparisons between the two habitats and suggest reasons for the differences?

PLENARY

Return to the classroom and ask the children to write at least a sentence comparing what they found in the two different habitats. You may want to provide a structure for this, for example: 'We found _____ in both habitats, but we only found _____ in the _____. We think this is because _____'. Ask: *Did you find any plants you didn't recognise? What did you do?* Ask the children to compare the different habitats by asking: *Did you find different plants in each habitat? Can you suggest why that might be?*

OUTCOMES

- Can investigate the plants found in a certain habitat.
- Can compare the numbers of different types of plant in the two habitats.
- Can suggest reasons for differences in the plants that grow in different habitats.
- Can devise their own record sheet.

ENRICHMENT
Lesson 12 ▷ What we found out

Objectives
- To communicate findings about the habitats investigated.
- To begin to explore the relationships between the physical aspects and the plants living in a habitat.

RESOURCES

Writing materials, ready-made books into which items can be glued, coloured paper and card, glue, scissors, example pages on presentation, such as photographs mounted with a caption and questions in speech bubbles.

MAIN ACTIVITY

Ask the children to have their notes and records about the habitats from the previous lesson with them. Recap the previous lesson, noting the two aspects they gathered information on: physical aspects of the habitats and plants. Ask: *Do you think there are any connections between these two things?* Listen to the children's ideas, intervening with further questions when necessary (for example, 'I think daisies like it better in the playing field'. *Why do you think they prefer the playing field? Is there more sunlight?*)

Ask each group to work collaboratively to make a book about the two habitats they studied. Provide some examples of how they might set out their work.

As the children work, help them to make connections by asking questions such as: *Why do you think the clover lives there, but not there? What kinds of places do you think dandelions grow best in?*

ASSESSMENT

Have the children communicated their findings clearly and presented them well? Are they making connections between the physical conditions and plants in a habitat?

PLENARY

The books can be shared with each other, each group showing one of their pages. The books could be taken to another class and the children could share their books and new expertise with younger children.

OUTCOMES
- Can communicate findings.

• Can make suggestions about the relationships between the physical aspects and the plants living in a habitat.

Lesson 13 ◘ Assessment

Objectives
• To assess the children's level of understanding of the needs of plants, their functions and uses.

RESOURCES 💿
Assessment activities: 1 Copies of photocopiable page 53 (also Assessment' (red), available on the CD-ROM); pens or pencils. **2** Pens or pencils.

STARTER
Begin the assessment by having a vocabulary quiz. Either give a word and ask for the definition or give a definition and ask for the word. Here are some words to use: leaf, root, stem, flower, seed, growth, habitat, food chain.

ASSESSMENT ACTIVITY 1
Distribute copies of photocopiable page 50 to test the children's understanding and let them complete it individually. It would be best if you could mark the test but you may wish the children to mark each other's. You may need to scribe for some of the children.

ANSWERS
1. Roots collect water from the ground and anchor the plant into the ground; stems hold the plant upright and carry water from the roots to the leaves; leaves produce food for the plant; flowers produce seeds. 2. The drawing should show a wilting plant and the words should suggest that the plant may be wilting due to a lack of water. 3. There should be appropriate examples of plant- and animal-originated foods. 4. Most of our food comes from plants.

LOOKING FOR LEVELS
All the children should be able to answer questions 1 and 2 correctly. Most should be able to answer question 4 and some will be able to answer question 3.

ASSESSMENT ACTIVITY 2 💿
Write the information outlined below on the board in the order shown. Tell the children that the table shows the results of a plant-growth experiment performed by a group of children, but that the data has been recorded in the wrong order. Ask the children to set out the data correctly in the table and then produce a bar chart of the results. You could use the graphing tool on the CD-ROM to create your bar chart.

You could also ask the following questions: *Between which days did the plant grow the most? Between which days did the plant grow the least?*

Day 7   24mm
Day 3   14mm
Day 1   10mm
Day 5   21mm
Day 2   12mm
Day 6   22mm
Day 4   17mm

ANSWERS
The correct order in the table is:
Day 1   10mm
Day 2   12mm

Day 3   14mm
Day 4   17mm
Day 5   21mm
Day 6   22mm
Day 7   24 mm
Question 1: Between days 4 and 5;
Question 2: Between days 5 and 6.

LOOKING FOR LEVELS
All of the children should be able to rearrange the data and fill in the table correctly. (Note that they do not need to put mm after each number in the second column as it is included in the column heading). The children may have varying degrees of success in constructing the bar graph. More confident learners may show the greatest success at answering the two questions.

ICT LINKS
Display 'Assessment' (red) from the CD-ROM on an interactive whiteboard. Complete the exercises as a whole-class activity, or as part of the plenary as a means of check the children's answers and assessing their understanding of the unit.

As part of Assessment activity 2, use the interactive graphing tool on the CD-ROM to convert the information from the table into a bar chart and use this to analyse the data as a class.

PLENARY
You may wish to review the unit with the children and work through any misconceptions that the children still have.

PHOTOCOPIABLE

Plant parts – 1

◢ Look carefully at the plant in front of you.

◢ Draw it in the box on the right.

◢ Label these parts of the plant:

roots

stem

leaves

◢ Each part of the plant has a special job to do.

◢ Match the part of the plant with its job.

leaves

roots

stem

These take water into the plant from the soil.

These are where the plant makes its food.

This keeps the plant upright.

◢ One of these plant parts has another job.

Which one is it and what does it do? _____

_____

_____

📖 SCHOLASTIC

Plant parts – 2

◼ You are going to carry out an investigation to show that water is carried up the roots of a plant. Use your weed, beaker, cling film and water to set up your investigation as shown in this diagram.

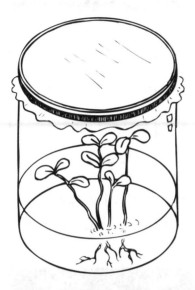

Why is it important to put a seal around the top of your beaker?

_____

_____

_____

Now put your plant in a safe place and record the water level every day, starting with today.

Date	Days after start	Water level
Difference between first and last water levels		

What has happened to the water level?

_____

Why do you think this has happened?

_____

Growing seeds

◗ Use this table to record the conditions that your plant will be kept in

Plant number	Water		Light?		Heat?	
	Yes	No	Yes	No	Yes	No
1						
2						
3						
4						

◗ Use the table below to keep a record of how well your plant is growing.
◗ You may want to draw or write your observations down. You may be able to measure the growth of your plant.

	Day 1	Day 2	Day 3	Day 4	Day 5
1					
2					
3					
4					

	Day 6	Day 7	Day 8	Day 9	Day 10
1					
2					
3					
4					

◗ As you observe your plant what do you begin to notice?
◗ Remember to write down everything that is happening in your diary.
◗ At the end of two weeks what has happened?
◗ Write down which of your plants has grown the best. What do you think this tells us about the conditions that your plant was kept in?

Assessment

1. What job does each of these plant parts do?

roots _____

stem _____

leaves _____

flower _____

2. Draw an unhealthy plant. Write down why you think it may be like this.

_____

_____

_____

_____

3. What have you eaten in the past two days? Fill in the table to show whether it was food from an animal or from a plant.

Food from animals	Food from plants

4. Complete this sentence:

Most of our food comes from _____

CHAPTER 3 | The environment

Lesson	Objectives	Main activity	Group activities	Plenary	Outcomes
Enrichment Lesson 1 In the garden	• To ascertain the children's level of knowledge and understanding about the environment from their work in Key Stage 1/ Primary 1–3.	Completing a worksheet to assess understanding of animal habitats, seasonal changes and the environment.	Writing a list of seasonal characteristics. Using secondary sources to research human effects on the environment.	Discussion of outcomes and looking forward to the unit.	• Teacher can assess the level of the children in the class. • Teacher can arrange children in appropriate class groups.
Enrichment Lesson 2 World climates	• To understand how the climates of world environments differ.	Researching people who live in different climates.		Sharing research findings.	• Can understand how the climates of world environments differ.
Enrichment Lesson 3 What's this place like?	• To develop an understanding of the characteristics of different climates.	Describing individual climates.		Role-play a TV holiday programme.	• Has developed an understanding of the characteristics of different climates.
Enrichment Lesson 4 My weather chart	• To know that the world environment can be divided into parts. • To think about how to collect sufficient evidence. • To use simple measuring equipment safely. • To present results in tables.	Completing a class weather study.	Week-long individual weather study. Looking at different environments and writing a postcard.	Children share postcards with the class.	• Can recognise the major environments on the planet. • Can describe how the atmosphere brings changes in the weather.
Enrichment Lesson 5 Looking at climates	• To know that the climate affects where plants and animals live.	Identifying different climates by criteria: heat, moisture, temperature.	Using secondary sources to research details of animals living in a chosen environment. Making 'estate agent' descriptions of environments.	Creating an environmental 'estate agency'.	• Can recognise places with different climates. • Can describe some of the living things that live in rainforests, deserts and at the poles.
Enrichment Lesson 6 Polar habitats	• To know how the wildlife of the polar regions is suited to the environment.	Identifying how animals keep warm in extreme low temperatures.		Children share their annotated drawings.	• Can identify common factors in the suitability to live in polar regions.
Enrichment Lesson 7 Tundra regions	• To know how the wildlife of the tundra regions survive in its environment.	Preparing a tundra factsheet.		Share ideas and discuss why the tundra is so inhospitable.	• Can identify some of the characteristics, locations and wildlife of the tundra regions.
Enrichment Lesson 8 Temperate forests	• To use keys to identify a range of trees that are typically found in temperate forests.	Investigating the range of trees to be found in the locality.		Children quiz each other about the identity of different trees.	• Can identify a range of trees found in temperate forests, with or without the use of a key.
Enrichment Lesson 9 Desert conditions	• To understand the range of environmental conditions to be found in a desert.	Comparing the desert during the day and the desert during the night.		Share findings using creative media of their choice.	• Can explain the reasons for, and range of, environmental conditions in a desert.
Enrichment Lesson 10 Life in the rainforest	• To begin to understand about the range of plants and animals found in a rainforest.	Researching the range of plants and animals to be found in each 'layer' of a rainforest.		Consider the characteristics of animals within each 'layer' of the rainforest.	• Can appreciate the range of plants and animals in a rainforest and the way in which there is interdependence.
Enrichment Lesson 11 Protest letter	• To know that human activities can affect habitats. • To communicate ideas effectively.	Discussing the impact of new paving on a grassy area on the food chain in that habitat.	Writing letters of protest about damage to habitats.	Discussing how humans can act to protect habitats.	• Can give examples of how human activities can affect habitats. • Can communicate ideas effectively in the form of a letter.

Lesson	Objectives	Main activity	Group activities	Plenary	Outcomes
Enrichment Lesson 12 Habitats	• To know that living things in a habitat are affected by light and shade, dryness and moisture, heat and cold. • To make predictions.	Walking around the school grounds to look at two contrasting environments.	Looking at characteristics of contrasting environments. Using secondary sources to research living things seen on the walk.	Discussion of findings in the environment.	• Can recognise how environmental factors vary in a habitat. • Can recognise a relationship between environmental factors and the distribution of plants and animals. • Can make predictions.
Enrichment Lesson 13 Litter survey	• To know that litter is an environmental problem.	Looking at litter. Carrying out a litter survey and planning an anti-litter campaign.		Children share plans for an anti-litter campaign.	• Can explain why litter in the environment is harmful to living things including humans.
Enrichment Lesson 14 Decaying materials	• To know that some materials decay and some do not and how we can use this in waste disposal.	Studying different materials as they decay.		Discussion of investigation and materials that did or did not decay.	• Can recognise that some materials decay and some do not.
Enrichment Lesson 15 What a waste!	• To know that there are many waste products that can affect the environment.	Studying waste produced in the locality.	Mapping the locations of waste products seen. Creating posters to show the effects of waste on the environment.	Displaying maps and posters.	• Can recognise a range of wastes that can affect the environment.

Assessment	Objectives	Activity 1	Activity 2
Lesson 16	• To assess the children's level of understanding of animal habitats and environments of the world. • To assess the children's level of understanding of the environmental effects of waste products.	Completing a worksheet to identify different habitats and creatures living there.	Designing an environmental awareness poster.

SC1 SCIENTIFIC ENQUIRY

Hiding from the Sun

LEARNING OBJECTIVES AND OUTCOMES
- Decide how to answer the question.
- Devise a fair test, consider what evidence to collect and what equipment to use.
- Make predictions of the outcomes.
- Make systematic observations and measurements.
- Use ICT to record data.
- Consider the collected data and draw conclusions.

ACTIVITY
Many animals have skins, which prevent water from leaving their bodies but some, like frogs and woodlice, do not. When searching for these animals in the environment you have to look under stones or wood. Children can investigate whether hiding in this way helps the animals to conserve water, by testing the idea with model animals made from sponge. Children should decide to use two identical pieces of sponge, placed on plastic trays then soaked in water and weighed. One sponge, in its tray, should then be placed on a sunny windowsill while the other is placed in a box in the shade. After a number of hours the trays are weighed again. This process can be repeated with the two sponges at the end of the experiment.

LESSON LINKS
This Sc1 activity forms an integral part of Lesson 1, In the garden, to explain the distribution of woodlice and frogs in a garden.

ENRICHMENT
Lesson 1 ▪ In the garden

Objective
- To ascertain the children's level of knowledge and understanding about the environment from their work in Key Stage 1/Primary 1–3

RESOURCES 💿
Main activity: A copy of photocopiable page 72 (also 'In the garden' (red), available on the CD-ROM) for each child.
Group activities: 1 Paper; pens; pencils. **2** Books; CD-ROMs; internet access.

BACKGROUND
This unit builds on the children's previous understanding of the environment through the work they have carried out on habitats, the animal and plant life within a habitat and the seasonal changes in plants and animals. It takes the children on to learn about world environments, the effects of climate on plants and animals, environmental factors in differing habitats and waste in the environment.

STARTER
Begin by asking the children a number of questions like: *Do moles live in trees? Do fish live on dry land? Do polar bears live in the desert? Do camels walk across the ice?* While these questions may be silly, they will capture the imagination of the children and you will begin to gain an understanding of what knowledge the children have. Ask the children if they can think of any similar questions.

MAIN ACTIVITY
Continue by asking the children if they know what the word 'habitat' means. Say that you would like them to show you what they already know and

Differentiation 🖸
Main activity
For children who need
support, use 'In the garden'
(green), from the CD which
does not require children to
provide reasons for their
answers.
Group activity 1
Some children may benefit
from using a wordbank.

understand about habitats and how the seasons can affect habitats. It is important, therefore, that they carry out this first task. Distribute copies of photocopiable page 72 and ask the children to work on their own.

GROUP ACTIVITIES

1 Ask the children to write a list of the characteristics of each season, for example, in the UK summer usually has longer daylight hours, warm weather, flowers in bloom and in winter many trees have lost their leaves and the weather is cold. The children should record their work in an imaginative way that reflects the season, for example, written inside the outline of a snowman for winter.

2 Let the children use secondary sources such as books, CD-ROMs or websites to find out about the effects we are having on our environment. Encourage them to think about what has changed recently in the local environment and about places in the world where humans have not had a dramatic effect. You could visit the websites for organisations such as the Royal Society for the Protection of Birds (www.rspb.org) or the World Society for the Protection of Animals (www.wspa.org.uk). These and many other environmental organisations have sections for young people.

PLENARY

Discuss the task the children have completed, highlighting some of the concepts the children have covered and explaining the areas they will be looking at in future lessons. Avoid suggesting that the children's concepts are wrong – the work they will be doing will develop their thinking from where they are now.

OUTCOMES

- Teacher can assess the level of the children in the class.
- Teacher can arrange children in appropriate class groups.

ENRICHMENT
Lesson 2 ▪ World climates

Objective
- To understand how the climates of world environments differ.

RESOURCES

Pictures of people from different climatic regions of the world; secondary sources of information; paper; pens; pencils.

MAIN ACTIVITY

Use pictures of people dressed appropriately for the different climates of the world as a basis for discussion about how these climates differ. For example, you could use pictures of people dressed in warm clothing suited to very cold conditions (polar climate), people dressed in minimal clothing who live in very warm conditions (tropical climate) and those dressed for a temperate climate. Ask the children to draw their own pictures of people who live in these three different climates and describe the characteristics of the climates using secondary sources of information.

ASSESSMENT

Through scrutiny of their work, questioning and observation, assess the children's understanding of how climates of the world differ. Can they identify three distinct climates?

Differentiation
Some children may need to concentrate on just one climatic region. Others may be able to research and compare all three.

PLENARY

Bring the children together to share their findings. Reinforce the idea of different climates in the world and use the work of the children to begin to find simple differences and similarities between the regions.

OUTCOME

● Can understand how the climates of world environments differ.

ENRICHMENT

Lesson 3 ◗ What's this place like?

Objective
● To develop an understanding of the characteristics of different climates.

RESOURCES
Secondary sources of information; atlases; paper; pens; pencils.

MAIN ACTIVITY
Ask the children to imagine they are one of the people they drew in Lesson 2 and to write about the sort of place in which they live. The children could use secondary sources of information to identify a particular country that has, for example, a tropical climate to write and draw about in a holiday brochure style, with an emphasis on the climate. These could then be compiled into a large class holiday booklet.

ASSESSMENT
Through scrutiny of their work, questioning and observation, assess the children's understanding of and ability to describe one particular climate.

PLENARY
Bring the children together and role-play a television holiday programme. The children should pretend they are presenters reporting on a particular country, again with an emphasis on climate.

Differentiation
Some children may prefer to write about a country with which they are familiar. Others could research an unfamiliar country and write a clear detailed description.

OUTCOME
● Has developed an understanding of the characteristics of different climates.

ENRICHMENT

Lesson 4 ◗ My weather chart

Objectives
● To know that the world environment can be divided into parts.
● To think about how to collect sufficient evidence.
● To use simple measuring equipment safely.
● To present results in tables.

RESOURCES 💿
Main activity: Class weather chart; weather measuring and observation equipment such as thermometers; an anemometer; flipchart or board; OHP (optional).
Group activities: 1 Copies of photocopiable page 73 (also 'My weather chart' (red); available on the CD-ROM). **2** Pens; pencils; colouring materials; postcard-sized cards for each child.

PREPARATION
Prepare a class weather chart based on photocopiable page 73. You will need to mark on a temperature range depending on the season. Prepare a piece of card the size of a postcard for each child.

Vocabulary
cities, deserts, forests, freshwater, grasslands, lakes, land, mountains, oceans, polar, rivers, seashore, sea water, towns, tundra, wetlands, woodland

BACKGROUND
Living things are found everywhere in the world: on land, in the air, in water and underground. Different living things live in different places, these are called habitats. While children will be familiar with habitats in their local environment, there are millions of other habitats in the world offering a variety of conditions, some hot, some cold, some dry, some wet. It is the surroundings, not the actual location, which make an environment. The place where something lives is generally called a 'habitat', whereas 'environment' is the term used to describe the surroundings of a habitat. These surroundings affect the things that exist there. The factors that contribute to creating a particular environment may include such physical things as

temperature and rainfall, or biological things such as the creatures living there. For example, when ecologists study the environment of an animal such as a rabbit, they study everything - living and non-living - that is connected with it. This includes animals that hunt it, its food, other rabbits, the weather, air and soil. So we can see that there is a very diverse range of environments into which our world can be divided. The environments give character to a number of 'ecosystems'. An ecosystem is a community of living things, for example, a lake or a forest. These ecosystems can be broadly grouped into land, sea (salt water) and freshwater.

One of the main factors that characterises an environment is climate. There are different climates ranging from extremely cold and dry at the poles to hot and wet at the equator. Living things like plants and animals have often changed so that they can be more suited to the local conditions in which they live.

STARTER

Tell the children that for this science topic they are going to be thinking about the environment and how we can affect it. Tell them the outline of the unit and that by the end of the unit they will understand more about how important the environment is and why it is important to them.

Begin by asking the children to think about where they live: the town, city, village or rural location. *What is it that makes that place what it is?* Ask questions about the characteristics of their local environment, such as: *Is it built up? Are there any parks or fields? Is it near the coast? Are there rivers or lakes nearby?*

Now compare the local environment to somewhere further afield - even abroad if you have Internet links with a school a long way away. Introduce the idea that there are a number of different types of 'environments' in the world. Ask the children if anyone can guess what we mean by an environment. Explain that it is everything that is around us - our surroundings - that makes a place what it is.

Land	Sea (salt water)	Freshwater
Seashore Polar and tundra Towns and cities Mountains Grasslands Forests and woodlands Wetlands Deserts	Seashore Beaches Seas and oceans	Rivers and lakes Wetlands

MAIN ACTIVITY

Ask the children to think about different types of environments there are in the world. Copy the headings 'Land', 'Sea (salt water)' and 'Freshwater' from the table above on to the board or OHP and ask the children to help you fill in the table. Explain any potentially unfamiliar words such as 'polar' or 'tundra'.

Introduce the idea that one of the factors that influences the environment is the weather. Talk about the types of weather we generally have, how our weather changes from day to day, and seasonal variations. Explain that each day they are going to study and record the weather. Children can take it in turns to complete a class weather chart for each day. They will need to record: temperature, measured using a simple thermometer; wind speed, measured using an anemometer; cloud cover in terms of 'no cloud', 'some clouds', 'very cloudy'; general comments like 'It is wet and windy today'.

Ask the children to draw illustrations to show typical weather in each of the four seasons.

GROUP ACTIVITIES

1 Give each child a copy of photocopiable page 73 to help them make individual weather records which they can keep for themselves each day for a week.

2 Give each child a postcard-sized piece of card and ask them to think about the range of environments in the world. Tell them to imagine that they are

Differentiation 💿
Children who need support can use 'My weather chart' (green), from the CD-ROM, to record some of their observations in pictorial form.

on holiday in an environment very different from home. Ask them to write a postcard from that place describing its characteristics and climate.

ICT LINKS
Children could use data logging hardware and software to log the temperature during the week. They could use the internet to look at satellite images of weather systems for your region and record the weather using a digital camera. An interactive whiteboard could be used to keep a class weather record or you could record a daily TV or radio weather report.

ASSESSMENT
Are the children able to identify environments and their characteristics? Most children will be able to identify some environments, but some may identify less familiar ones such as polar, tundra and wetlands.

PLENARY
Discuss the environments the children have identified. Ask some children to read out their postcards. Reinforce the concept of the world being made up of a number of different environments. Remind the children about their weather study and the observations they are going to carry out.

OUTCOMES
● Can recognise the major environments on the planet.
● Can describe how the atmosphere brings changes in the weather.

ENRICHMENT
Lesson 5 ▫ Looking at climates

Objective
● To know that the climate affects where plants and animals live.

Vocabulary
climate, cold, environment, hot, temperature, temperate

RESOURCES 💿
Main activity: A copy of photocopiable page 74 (also 'Looking at climates' (red), available on the CD-ROM) for each child.
Group activities: 1 Secondary sources of information related to climate; pens; white and coloured paper; art materials. **2** Paper; pens; pencils;
ICT link: 'Looking at climates' interactive activity from the CD-ROM.

PREPARATION
Copy photocopiable page 74. Ensure secondary resources, various types of paper, pens and art materials are available.

BACKGROUND
The climate of an area or region depends on its position on the Earth's surface. For example, land near the equator has a hot climate because it gets sunshine from almost directly overhead. As you travel further away from the equator, the climate gets cooler until you reach the North and South Poles where the Sun is always low on the horizon and the temperatures are constantly low. There are, however, other factors that affect climate: the oceans carry warmth around the world and affect the land climate, as do winds and the height of land above sea level. Climates are classified into eight main groups, within which there are also variations.

The climate of a region affects the plants and animals that live there. Different plants and animals are able to thrive in different climates. For example, bears are well suited to living in polar regions because of their diet of fish and their thick fur. On the other hand, an elephant would not survive in such conditions due to its diet of vegetation, the slow speed at which it moves and its unprotected skin. A number of climatic factors affect living things and their environment. These include temperature, light intensity, rainfall and wind speed. The most profound of these climatic factors is without doubt temperature. Generally, living things prefer to live in an

Differentiation

Main activity
For children who need support, use 'Looking at climates' (green) from the CD-ROM, which does not ask for written explanations to support the drawings of different climates.
Group activity 2
Some children may need to use secondary sources to help with ideas. Other children will make greater use of estate agent jargon in descriptive writing.

```
                    WET
         ┌──────────────┬──────────────┐
         │              │              │
         │ Rainforests  │   Oceans     │
   HOT   │              │              │   COLD
         ├──────────────┼──────────────┤
         │              │              │
         │  Deserts     │   Poles      │
         │              │              │
         └──────────────┴──────────────┘
                    DRY
```

environment with warm temperatures and a supply of water and food. This is why as you travel from temperate climates to ones that are more extreme, like the poles or deserts, there is a marked reduction in the number of species of living things to be found.

STARTER
Remind the children of their work from the last lesson and how they were identifying different environments. Ask them to recall some of those. Also remind them that they have been studying the weather. Discuss the weather findings briefly and ask the children to sum up the weather over the past week. *Has it been warm and dry, sunny, wet and windy, cold and frosty?* Ask the children to think about how our weather changes and what happens to plants and animals when it does. Some children will be able to tell you about hibernation or migration, although they may not recall the correct terms.

MAIN ACTIVITY
Talk about why some animals, particularly birds, tend to move around to different environments. Introduce the idea that the climates within environments are not always suitable for plants and animals at all times of the year and that some plants and animals prefer different climatic conditions. Give examples of climatic conditions with different combinations of heat and moisture: hot and dry; hot and wet; cold and dry; cold and wet. Photocopiable page 74 provides a simple Carroll diagram on which the children can see the different combinations of temperature and moisture to help them identify four examples of environments with these climates.

GROUP ACTIVITIES
1 In pairs, the children can use secondary sources of information to find out about some of the living things that live in a chosen climate. Research could be presented in a novel way, for example information about rainforests on paper the shape of a large tree, the poles on paper the shape of an iceberg and deserts on paper the shape of a sand dune.
2 Ask the children to write an estate-agent-style description of three or four habitats of living things, for example, 'Accommodation under deceptively spacious damp and dark stone. Would ideally suit someone who does not like the Sun...'

ICT LINK
The children can use the interactive 'Looking at Climates', from the CD-ROM, to match environments to their descriptions.

ASSESSMENT
Most children should be able to complete photocopiable page 74. Discuss with the children their ideas to gain an idea of their level of understanding.

PLENARY
Create an 'Environmental estate-agents' window to display the children's descriptions and ask the children to read them to the class.

OUTCOMES
● Can recognise places with different climates.
● Can describe some of the living things that live in rainforests, deserts and at the poles.

LINKS
Unit 3f, Lesson 10, The Sun in the sky.
Geography: weather and climate.
Literacy: using jargon.

ENRICHMENT
Lesson 6 ▪ Polar habitats

Objective
● To know how the wildlife of the polar regions is suited to the environment.

RESOURCES
Secondary sources of information such as text books, CD-ROMs, websites, posters which make specific reference to the polar regions, paper, pencils.

MAIN ACTIVITY
Using secondary sources for research, the children should make an annotated drawing to show the ways in which particular examples of polar wildlife are suited to their environment in ways that allow them to survive the extremes of low temperatures. For example, the children could look at the polar bear, the walrus and penguin and consider how they keep warm and what common characteristic they share, such as thick outer layers (fur or skin) and thick layers of fat.

ICT LINK
Children could use CD-ROMS and the internet as secondary sources of information.

ASSESSMENT
Through scrutiny of the annotated drawings, assess the children's ability to identify characteristics that indicate an understanding of environmental suitability.

Differentiation
Some children might consider how just one creature is suited to their environment while others could begin to make comparisons between wildlife at the poles and other environmental regions of the world such as rainforests.

PLENARY
Encourage the children to share their annotated drawings and begin to draw some conclusions. Consider how humans survive in similar conditions.

OUTCOME
● Can identify common factors in the suitability to live in polar regions.

ENRICHMENT
Lesson 7 ▪ Tundra regions

Objective
● To know how the wildlife of the tundra regions survives in its environment.

RESOURCES
Secondary sources of information; paper; access to ICT resources.

MAIN ACTIVITY
Using secondary sources of information ask the children to prepare a Tundra Factfile that addresses issues such as:
● What is tundra?
● Where is tundra to be found?
● What is permafrost?
● What plants live in the tundra regions?
● What animals live in the tundra regions?
● A tundra food web
This could be developed further using ICT and displayed using presentational software such as Powerpoint®.

ICT LINKS
Children could use CD-ROMs and the internet as secondary sources of information. They could present their findings using presentational software bringing together words, pictures and sounds.

ASSESSMENT

Through scrutiny of work, assess the children's depth of understanding of the tundra regions. Are they able to describe the key characteristics of tundra and identify some of the wildlife living there?

PLENARY

Ask the children to share their ideas with each other and discuss with the children why tundra is an inhospitable area for us to live in.

OUTCOME

● Can identify some of the characteristics, locations and wildlife of the tundra regions.

Differentiation
This activity can be differentiated by the range and depth of detail covered. Some children will need to focus on a few significant areas while others children can begin to build food webs and consider how pollution is affecting the tundra regions of the world.

ENRICHMENT
Lesson 8 ◘ Temperate forests

Objective
● To use keys to identify a range of trees that are typically found in temperate forests.

RESOURCES

Tree identification keys; a branching database; access to leaves or winter buds.

MAIN ACTIVITY

Investigate the range of trees to be found in your locality or in an area that you choose to visit. Use a simple branching database or identification key as a means of identifying and recording. This could be done using leaves or winter buds.

ICT LINK

Children could use a branching database such as 'FlexiTREE' to present their findings.

ASSESSMENT

Through discussion and questioning, assess the children's ability to use an identification key or database to identify a range of trees typical of their locality. Most children should be able to identify the most commonly found trees, some will be able to do so without using a key.

Differentiation
Some children could record their findings by taking leaf rubbings or prints. Others may be able to write their own dichotomous key or identification chart using yes/no answers to simple observational questions.

PLENARY

Let the children quiz each other about the identity of different trees, talk about temperate forests and some the threats that human activity is imposing on these forests.

OUTCOME

● Can identify a range of trees found in temperate forests, with or without the use of a key.

ENRICHMENT
Lesson 9 ◘ Desert conditions

Objective
● To understand the range of environmental conditions to be found in a desert.

RESOURCES

Craft materials; selection of coloured paper; ICT resources; secondary sources of information.

MAIN ACTIVITY

Working collaboratively in small groups, ask the children to think creatively and to present a comparison between the desert during the day and the desert at night. This could be presented as a table or more visually using pictures and 3D effects such as stand-up sand dunes. Others could use ICT to present their findings, dramatise the desert environs or write creatively and descriptively about a journey across the desert.

ICT LINKS
Children could use CD-ROMs and the internet as secondary sources of information. They could display their findings using presentational software bringing together words, pictures and sounds.

ASSESSMENT
Through discussion and questioning, assess the children's understanding of the environmental conditions that exist during the day and night in the desert. Assess their ability to identify the significant differences in temperature and behaviour of animals.

PLENARY
Let children share their findings using their chosen creative media.

OUTCOME
● Can explain the reasons for, and range of, environmental conditions in a desert.

ENRICHMENT
Lesson 10 ▪ Life in the rainforest

Objective
● To begin to understand about the range of plants and animals found in a rainforest.

RESOURCES
Draw and photocopy (either A3 or A4) a picture of a tree with the rainforest layers labelled from the top down: emergent layer, canopy, understorey and forest floor; secondary sources of information; pencils and colouring pencils.

MAIN ACTIVITY
Using secondary sources of information, ask the children to research the range of plants and animals to be found in each 'layer' within a rainforest. They could then present these pictorially to use as part of a display.

ASSESSMENT
Ask the children to take on the role of one animal in their picture and to describe orally the plants and other animals that they see around them.

ICT LINKS
Children could use CD-ROMs and the internet as secondary sources of information. They could display their findings using presentational software bringing together words, pictures and sounds. Using the interactive graphing tool, on the CD-ROM, the children could create a bar graph or pie chart showing the different types of plants and animals found in a rainforest.

PLENARY
Talk about the layers within the rainforest and encourage the children to consider the characteristics of the animals in each layer and why they live where they do. Begin to introduce the notion of interdependence.

OUTCOME
● Can appreciate the range of plants and animals in a rainforest.

ENRICHMENT
Lesson 11 ▪ Protest letter

Objectives
● To know that human activities can affect habitats.
● To communicate ideas effectively.

Vocabulary
affect, effect, habitat, protect

RESOURCES 💿
Main activity: An enlarged copy of photocopiable page 75 (also 'Protest letter' (red), available on the CD-ROM); a flipchart or board; marker pens.
Group activities: 1 The habitat books made in Unit 3b, Lesson 12; sugar paper and felt-tipped pens; writing materials. **2** Writing materials.

PREPARATION
Enlarge photocopiable page 75 so that the whole class can read it.

BACKGROUND
This lesson asks children to consider the effects that humans may have on the environment. It brings together the work on individual habitats and ideas about food chains as children imagine the impact of changes on the different living things in a habitat. Children sometimes find it hard to grasp why animals cannot just 'move somewhere else' or 'eat something different' when their habitats are destroyed or damaged. This can be addressed by helping them think about where the animals would move to - and the impact on the living things already there.

STARTER
Ask the children to think about the habitats studied in Unit 3b, Lessons 11 and 12. Each group could spend five minutes reviewing the book they have made.

MAIN ACTIVITY
Ask: *What things might humans do that could change a habitat?* (They might trample on it; cut long grass short; cut down a tree; dig up bushes; spray it with weedkiller; put down slug pellets.) Make a list of the ideas the children have on the board or flipchart and introduce some more suggestions if necessary.

Explain that the children are going to think about one example together, then each group will think about their own habitats. Give the example of putting paving slabs down on an area of the school field that has long grass. Ask: *What living things might that affect?* Help the children to apply their understanding of food chains, for example: So you are saying that there won't be anywhere for the snails to live. *What animals eat snails?* (Thrushes and other birds eat snails.) *So what effect will the paving have on the thrushes?* (They will have less food, so will have to go elsewhere and some may not survive.) Together, read the copy of photocopiable page 75.

Differentiation
Some support for the initial ideas about damage to the habitat will come from working as a group, but you may need to spend more time discussing the possibilities with some groups than others. Some children may need support with the writing - a writing frame for the letter could be provided for them, or they could work with another child or adult assistant.

GROUP ACTIVITIES
1 Ask each group to decide on a change that humans could make to a habitat and to collaboratively brainstorm the effects it might have on that habitat. These ideas can be recorded on sugar paper. Then, individually, each child can write a letter of protest to the relevant people, explaining the impact the change might have on their habitat.
2 The children could imagine the headteacher's response to the letter on photocopiable page 75 and write back to Kate Lucas 'in role'. This may help the children's understanding of conflicting points of view.

ASSESSMENT
Can the children make suggestions about the impact of the imagined damage to the habitat? Can they give examples of living things that would suffer? Are they able to communicate these ideas in the form of a letter?

PLENARY

Ask some of the children from each group to read their letters to the rest of the class. Ask: *What things can humans do to help protect habitats?* (Leave corners of lawn unmown to grow wild; protect areas of the countryside; set up areas in towns for wildlife.)

OUTCOMES

● Can give examples of how human activities can affect habitats.
● Can communicate ideas effectively in the form of a letter.

LINKS

Literacy: letter-writing, persuasive writing.

ENRICHMENT
Lesson 12 ▪ Habitats

Objectives
● To know that living things in a habitat are affected by light and shade, dryness and moisture, heat and cold.
● To make predictions.

Vocabulary
cool, dark, dry, habitat, light, warm, wet

RESOURCES ◉

Main activity: A copy of photocopiable page 76 (also 'Habitats' (red), available on the CD-ROM) for each child; a simple plan of the area to be visited; a clipboard and pencil for each child.
Group activities: 1 Paper; pens and pencils. **2** Secondary sources of information; paper and art materials.

PREPARATION

Plan to visit an area where the children can study two contrasting environmental conditions, such as two areas of your school field or local park. Ensure that you have adequate adult supervision. Ask some parents to help you and, if they are going to lead a group, ensure your adult helpers are well briefed and know what they are looking for. Organise your visit to allow plenty of time for both fieldwork and follow-up. Draw and copy a simple plan of the area you are going to visit for each child.

BACKGROUND

Plants and animals interact with their environments in order to create habitats. A habitat is simply the place where a plant or animal lives. Habitats vary greatly in size, from large forests to small puddles, but all have to satisfy the needs of the animals and plants that live there. Not only do they vary in size: habitats also vary greatly in character. Some are hot, some cold, some light, some dark, some dry, some wet. Whatever their differences they all have the same function – the support of living things. It is these differences in habitats that mean different habitats are capable of supporting varying types of plants and animals.

STARTER

Children always enjoy going outside and hunting around. In this lesson, the children will get the opportunity to do just that. Ask the children to think about where they would choose to live if they had unlimited money: in what sort of house, in which location and why. After a short discussion ask them to imagine they are a tiny woodlouse and to think about where they would choose to live and why. Encourage the children to think about the conditions that would be most suitable. Some creatures like hot and dry conditions, others prefer dark and damp conditions. Explain that they are going to look in some different habitats to find out what type of creatures are living there and why they think that may be so.

MAIN ACTIVITY

Distribute the plans and copies of photocopiable page 76. Encourage the children to choose two contrasting areas around the school grounds, for

Differentiation

Main activity

For children who need support, use 'Habitats' (green), from the CD-ROM, which includes a simplified version of the habitat record chart.

To extend children, use 'Habitats' (blue), which encourages children to think about why the animals found live where they do. Some children may also be able to record observations and locations on the plan. They could indicate minibeasts found at each location using a colour code to show the distribution.

example, the playground and a wildlife area, a playing field and a garden, under a hedge and a pond. Before visiting the sites, ask children to predict the animals they expect to find in each area.

Take a walk around the school grounds, visit a local park or wild area with a variety of habitats. Ask the children to use photocopiable page 76 to help them record the living things they see in the two contrasting habitats. They should complete the photocopiable page with details of each habitat and what they saw. Some children will also be able to mark these locations on their plan. Observe birds feeding in the playground (after break is a good time, especially if the children have been eating snacks). As you walk around, talk with the children about what animals they have found and where they were found.

GROUP ACTIVITIES

1 Back in the classroom, ask the children to use drawings and writing to describe the differences between the two areas they studied. Ask them to think about why the two areas are different and whether they found the animals they expected.

2 Ask the children to use secondary sources to find out more about any of the living things they saw. They should present their findings in an imaginative way, perhaps in the shape of the creature they are writing about.

ASSESSMENT

Assess the ability of the children to carry out the observations and record their findings.

PLENARY

Discuss with the children the creatures they have found in a number of locations. Draw conclusions about the creature's habitat preferences.

OUTCOMES

● Can recognise how environmental factors vary in a habitat
● Can recognise a relationship between environmental factors and the distribution of plants and animals.
● Can make predictions.

ENRICHMENT
Lesson 13 ▫ Litter survey

Objective
● To know that litter is an environmental problem.

RESOURCES
Paper and art materials.

MAIN ACTIVITY

Identify a local area to visit to look at the litter there. Carry out a litter survey. Be very conscious of health and safety issues: the spread of diseases, the dangers of cuts from glass and of discarded syringes. The children must not touch any of the litter, particularly outside school. Also be vigilant for risks from dog faeces, for example, in public parks. Consider: *Where is most of the litter? Why is it there? Are there any litter bins and are they in the best places?* (Mark positions on a map and relate to paths, dog-walking routes and so on.)

Discuss why litter is a problem. (Because it's a danger to animals, it spreads diseases, it smells and so on.)

Design and run an anti-litter campaign in school with posters, leaflets and an assembly presentation. If you contact a local shopping centre, they may be willing to provide a more public forum for the children's work.

Differentiation
Differentiate by outcome.

ICT LINKS
Children could use desktop publishing software to create the posters. They could also use a digital video to make a short anti-litter advertisement.

ASSESSMENT
Discuss the children's campaign proposals, looking for an understanding that litter is a problem.

PLENARY
Discuss the children's findings and plans for an anti-litter campaign.

OUTCOME
● Can explain why litter in the environment is harmful to living things including humans.

ENRICHMENT
Lesson 14 ▫ Decaying materials

Objective
● To know that some materials decay and some do not and how we can use this in waste disposal.

RESOURCES
Trays; soil; leaves; cardboard; aluminium foil; orange peel; an apple core; a crisp bag.

MAIN ACTIVITY
Bury the same six items deep in several pots full of soil, or in the school garden. Vary the conditions, try: warm and dry, warm and wet, cold and dry, cold and wet.
Check at weekly intervals to monitor and note the rates of decay. Take photographs, perhaps, with a camera as evidence.
   At the end of three or four weeks, draw some conclusions by asking: *Which has decayed the most? Which has not decayed at all? Which materials would be suitable for disposal in a landfill site?*

ICT LINK
Children could record their observations using a digital camera.

ASSESSMENT
Through observation and questioning, identify the children's level of understanding of decaying materials.

PLENARY
Gather together to discuss observations at regular intervals.

Differentiation
Differentiate by outcome.

OUTCOME
● Can recognise that some materials decay and some do not.

ENRICHMENT
Lesson 15 ▫ What a waste!

Objective
● To know that there are many waste products that can affect the environment.

RESOURCES 💿
Introduction: A bag of classroom waste; gloves; a bag for waste.
Main activity: Photocopiable page 77 (also 'What a waste' (red), available on the CD-ROM); paper; pens.
Group activities: 1 Paper and pencils. **2** Pictures and samples of waste packets; large sheets of paper; glue; art materials.

PREPARATION
Arrange to make a visit around your locality to identify the types of waste

Vocabulary
exhaust, fumes, landfill, litter, recycling, refuse, waste

being produced and to carry out a study of waste products from the home, transport and industry. Visit the location for your walk and ensure there are appropriate examples for the children to see and that the route you will take is safe. Ensure you have adequate adult supervision for the visit. Ask some parents to help and brief them as to the purpose of the visit.

BACKGROUND

By its very nature, the industrial society of which we are a part produces, whether we like it or not, a huge amount of waste. Some of these effects are local to us all (for example litter). The effects of nuclear waste, and damage caused to the ozone layer are global issues. This lesson will concentrate not on the global issues, but on the effects that waste like rubbish and fumes have on the environment. Recent legislation has been introduced in an attempt to regulate the production of waste and its disposal, since it is not always the waste itself that causes environmental concern, rather the way its disposal is managed. The children will be familiar with many waste products, and many will be aware of the environmental concerns they raise. On the right are examples of some waste products, where they are found and their environmental effects.

As part of this work it may be possible to arrange for a local industrialist and/or a local authority waste officer to come and talk about the problems of waste and how they are dealing with it.

Location	Waste products	Type of waste	Environmental effects
Home	Litter, packaging, food waste	Rubbish	Danger to wildlife, danger of disease
In the street	Vehicle exhausts	Fumes	Air pollution
	Litter	Rubbish	Danger to animals and humans, attraction of vermin
Factories	Fires	Fumes	Air pollution
	Production waste and scrap	Rubbish	Disposal of potentially dangerous waste
	Smoke and smells	Fumes	Air pollution

STARTER

Ask the children to guess what is in your bag. Wearing gloves, transfer items from the rubbish bag into the second bag. (Later dispose of both carefully.) The children will quickly work out it is rubbish. Show them the quantity of waste they have produced in just one day, in the classroom. Ask them if they know what will happen to this waste and all the waste from school. They may be able to explain that it will be taken away by the refuse collectors (for dumping or incineration). In many areas, there are recycling schemes that require the waste to be sorted before collection. Pose a few questions and seek responses: *But where is the rubbish taken to? What happens to it? What about all the other waste we produce? What effect does waste have on our environment? What types of waste are there?* Tell the class that they will be finding out answers to some of these questions.

MAIN ACTIVITY

Prior to your walk around the locality, discuss with the children what types of waste they think they will observe and where it will be. Try to move them beyond litter, to think about fumes from cars, for example.

As they walk around, they should use photocopiable page 77 to record their observations.

On return to the classroom, discuss what the children saw and recorded, and consider the effects that the waste may be having and what could be done about the problem.

GROUP ACTIVITIES

1 Following the visit, the children should draw a map of the area they have surveyed and use a key to record where certain waste products were found. This will give some indication of particular problem areas. For example, at a bus stop there may be litter and traffic fumes.

Differentiation 💿
Main activity
For children who need support, use 'What a waste!' (green) from the CD-ROM, which includes a simplified version of the waste recording sheet.

2 Collect pictures or samples of waste products (be sure they are clean and safe) to produce posters explaining the effects that waste has on the environment. For example, display plastic bags and bottles to highlight them as a danger to wildlife; use pictures of cars to highlight car exhaust fumes and their effect on people's health.

ASSESSMENT
Assess the children's ability to understand and appreciate the range of waste produced. Their work should reflect their understanding, having identified a range of waste products during the visit.

PLENARY
Bring the class together to look at the maps of waste and the posters. Ask the children to explain their findings, and involve the children in a discussion reinforcing the types of waste and their effects on the environment.

OUTCOME
● Can recognise a range of wastes that can affect the environment.

LINKS
PSHE: caring for the environment; personal responsibility; health and safety issues.
Geography: investigating the local area.

Lesson 16 ▸ Assessment

Objectives
● To assess the children's level of understanding of animal habitats and environments of the world.
● To assess the children's level of understanding of the environmental effects of waste products.

RESOURCES 💿
Assessment activities: 1 A copy of photocopiable page 78 (also 'Assessment' (red), available on the CD-ROM) for each child; pens; pencils; colouring materials. **2** Large sheets of paper; art materials.
ICT link: 'Looking at habitats' interactive activity, from the CD-ROM.

STARTER
Begin the Assessment activities by giving the children a vocabulary test, which could be oral or written. Remember the activity is an assessment of scientific knowledge and understanding. Either give either a word and ask for a definition or give a definition and ask for a word. For example, ask, *Who can tell me what a habitat is? Can you give me some examples of different habitats? What is the word we use to describe the weather and temperature in a particular place?*

ASSESSMENT ACTIVITY 1
Distribute copies of photocopiable page 78 to the children and allow them time to complete it individually. You may wish to tell the children that you wish to find out what they have understood and that it is important to complete the sheets individually. You will need to collect these in order to mark them effectively.

ANSWERS
I am a hot place with lots of tall trees - rainforest.
It is very cold here all year long - polar region.
I am hot during the day but cold at night - desert.
I am a very wet place and I can be calm or rough - ocean.
I begin my journey in the hills and travel towards the sea - river.

ICT LINK

Children can use the 'Looking at climates' interactive from the CD-ROM to match habitats with their correct descriptions.

LOOKING FOR LEVELS

Assess the children's work for evidence of understanding. Most children should be able to match the habitat descriptions with their names. While most should be able to name creatures living in each habitat, the list will vary in complexity. Some children may be able to name only one or two creatures, whereas others should name a varied selection.

ASSESSMENT ACTIVITY 2

Ask the children to design an environmental awareness poster that explains the dangers to the environment of litter and encourages people to be litter conscious. It should make people aware of the quantities and types of waste that we all produce and how we can prevent damage to the environment.

LOOKING FOR LEVELS

Most children will be able to create a poster for Assessment activity 2. Some will be able to create a poster with a single simple message, while others will produce one that is more complex and puts forward clear points and arguments.

PLENARY

Discuss the Assessment activities and address any misconceptions still held by the children. For example, young children may commonly believe that animals grow thick fur so they can live where it is cold. (Animals don't decide to equip their bodies to live in a particular environment.) Young children may also believe that all of the effects we have on the environment are negative. (We do many things to create and improve environments.)

In the garden

- These animals live in this garden, but they have different habitats.
- Draw an arrow to where in the garden you think each animal might live.
- Say why you think it lives there.

A fox lives here because	A squirrel lives here because	A blackbird lives here because
_____ _____	_____ _____	_____ _____

A slug lives here because	A snail lives here because	A hedgehog lives here because
_____ _____	_____ _____	_____ _____

- Add to the picture to show that it is autumn in the garden.
- Do you know anything that might harm the plants and animals?
- Tell your teacher or write about it on the back of this sheet.

Illustration © Kirsty Wilson

■SCHOLASTIC

My weather chart

■ Use this sheet to record your weather observations over one week.

	Monday	Tuesday	Wednesday	Thursday	Friday
Morning temperature in degrees Celsius					
Afternoon temperature in degrees Celsius					
Wind					
Cloud					
General comments					

Looking at climates

■ Draw a picture in each box to show the different climates in the world.
■ For example in the box where the climate is both wet and hot you could draw a place such as a rainforest. Write a brief description to explain why you chose that place.

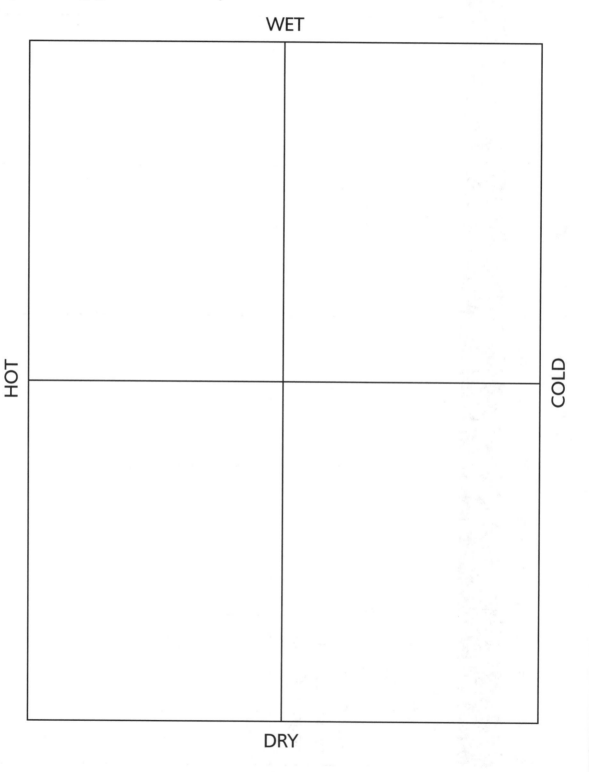

📖 SCHOLASTIC

Protest letter

The Headteacher

Kate Lucas
Class 4M
Fairways Primary School
18th September

Dear Mrs Hayward

I am writing to you about the new pavement that is going to be built along the edge of the school field.

I am very worried because I think it will destroy the habitat of the snails, because they need long grass for food and protection. If there is nowhere for the snails to live then we might not have so many different sorts of birds, like thrushes, that eat snails.

Please will you think about this and if the pavement has to be built, could we have a different part of the field that does not get mown so that long grass can grow there instead?

Yours sincerely

Kate Lucas

Kate Lucas

PHOTOCOPIABLE

Habitats

■ Look carefully at two different habitats in which an animal lives. Use this sheet to record what you observe.

Habitat (Name or description)	Light or dark?	Hot or cold?	Creatures found (Name or drawing)	How many? (Estimate)

◣SCHOLASTIC

What a waste!

◼ Go on a walk around your locality. As you walk, look out for examples of waste products. Make a note of where you are, what you saw and from where the waste was being produced.

Location	Waste seen	Producer		
		Home	Transport	Industry

◼ Look at the results of your survey. Which types of waste did you see most examples of?

_____

_____

What effects do you think each type of waste has on the environment?

Type of waste	Effects on the environment

Assessment

■ Draw a line to match the description with the name of the habitat.

Description	Habitat
I am a hot place with lots of tall trees.	ocean
It is very cold here all year long.	desert
I am hot during the day but cold at night.	river
I am a very wet place and I can be calm or rough.	rainforest
I begin my journey in the hills and travel towards the sea.	polar region

■ Different creatures like to live in different conditions. Write the names of as many creatures as you can think of that live in each of these places. On the back of this page draw an example from each habitat.

Under a hedge	
Around houses	
Under a stone	
In a wood	
In a garden	

CHAPTER 4 Characteristics of materials

Lesson	Objectives	Main activity	Group activities	Plenary	Outcomes
Lesson 1 Changing materials	• To ascertain the levels of the children in their understanding of materials from their work in Key Stage 1/Primary 1–3, particularly in relation to simple properties and how they can be changed by heating or cooling.	Concept mapping.	Sorting materials. Changing materials worksheet.	Review concept maps, reinforce learning about changing materials by heating and cooling.	• Teacher can assess the level of the children in the class. • Teacher can arrange children in appropriate class groups.
Lesson 2 Materials	• To know a range of common materials and that a material may have different uses.	Using senses to identify materials.	Materials survey worksheet. Identifying materials used.	Feedback from Group activities.	• Can recognise common materials. • Can describe how some materials have several uses.
Lesson 3 Properties of materials	• To know that different materials have different properties. • To know that any material may have more than one property.	Describing the properties of materials.	Identifying the properties of given materials. Tabulating properties by criteria.	'Guess the material' quiz.	• Can state one or two characteristics of a range of common materials. • Can compare the properties of different materials.
Lesson 4 Uses of materials	• To know that materials are selected for making objects according to their properties. • To understand that the use and wear an object will need to withstand governs the materials from which it can be made.	Identifying why objects are made from particular materials.		Agreeing why certain materials are used.	• Can recognise how materials are selected according to their properties when an object is being made.
Lesson 5 Investigation	• To know that the properties of materials can be compared by investigation. • To plan and carry out a fair test, make predictions and observations and draw conclusions.	Identifying which properties can be investigated and how. Ensuring fair tests.	Planning an investigation. Carrying out and recording the investigation. Making and testing carrier bags.	Sharing group investigations and findings.	• Know that the properties of materials can be compared by investigation. • Can plan and carry out a fair test, make predictions and observations and draw conclusions.
Lesson 6 Fit for purpose	• To use materials for a specific purpose and to test their suitability for that purpose. • To identify what scientific questions need to be asked.	Using appropriate materials to suit a function.		Drawing conclusions about the best materials.	• Can use materials for a specific purpose • Can test their questions about the material's suitability for that purpose.
Enrichment Lesson 7 Natural and man-made materials	• To know that some materials occur naturally and others do not.	Sorting materials into 'natural' and 'man-made'.	Looking for materials that derive from plants, animals and under the ground. Survey of objects made from man-made and natural materials.	Quiz, identifying the mystery material.	• Can recognise that some materials occur naturally and others do not.
Enrichment Lesson 8 From raw material to finished product	• To be able to compare finished objects with raw materials.	Sorting raw materials, processed materials and finished objects into groups.		Sharing ideas and reinforcement of lesson objectives.	• Can compare finished objects with raw materials.

Assessment	Objectives	Activity 1	Activity 2
Lesson 9	• To assess the children's knowledge and understanding of materials and their uses.	Completing a worksheet, identifying materials used in houses and why they are used.	Completing a worksheet about planning an investigation and matching the properties of materials with their meanings.

SC1 SCIENTIFIC ENQUIRY

Comparing materials

LEARNING OBJECTIVES AND OUTCOMES

● Ask questions about the properties of materials that can be investigated, such as strength, elasticity, hardness, reflectivity, magnetism, absorbency.
● Plan and carry out a fair test making predictions and observations and drawing conclusions.

ACTIVITY

The children should be supported in planning this investigation into one of the properties above. They measure the effects that their test has on the property of a range of different materials. These individual tests are repeated three times to ensure validity. The children should construct a table to record their results before presenting and interpreting their findings. They can then draw conclusions from their investigation.

LESSON LINKS

This Sc1 activity forms an integral part of Lesson 5, Investigating materials.

Lesson 1 ▪ Changing materials

Objective

● To ascertain the children's level of understanding of materials from their work in Key Stage 1/Primary 1-3, particularly in relation to simple properties and how they can be changed by heating or cooling.

Vocabulary

cooling, heating, ice, materials, steam, water

RESOURCES ◉

Main teaching activity: Flipchart or board; large sheets of paper; pens; a small number of common objects from the classroom.
Group activities: 1 A selection of everyday materials such as paper; plastic; metal; wood; water; wool; cotton and so on; A2 sheets of art paper; marker pens or thick crayons for recording. **2** Copies of photocopiable page 92 (also 'Changing materials' (red), available on the CD-ROM); pens; pencils; drawing materials.
ICT link: 'Changing materials' interactive activity, from the CD-ROM.

BACKGROUND

This first lesson reintroduces the children to materials. They should already have done some work about the properties of materials and how materials can be changed. They should have some understanding of a range of everyday materials and know that some materials are natural while others are manufactured (man-made). They should also have some understanding that materials can be changed physically or by heating and cooling, for example, through experience of baking or clay modelling.

STARTER

Begin the lesson by showing the children the objects that you have collected. Try not to talk about the identity of the objects so much as the materials from which they are made. Encourage the children to look carefully and to say what each object is largely made from. Remind the children that they have already done some work on materials and that in this lesson you are going to see what they can remember from that work.

MAIN ACTIVITY

Review the children's work on materials by working with them to draw a concept map. Use a flipchart or board to record key words and facts from the children as they brainstorm the ideas they have learned in Key Stage 1/

Primary 1-3. When you have these words and phrases scattered around the board, attempt to link the phrases and also justify those links. For example, the children should be able to name a range of everyday materials and might identify that some are natural while others are manufactured.

GROUP ACTIVITIES

1 Give the children a collection of materials or pictures of materials and ask them to sort them according to their own criteria, and to explain what the criteria are. These could be hard/soft, heavy/light, magnetic/non-magnetic, shiny/dull and so on. This could be a collaborative task recorded on large sheets of art paper.
2 Distribute photocopiable page 92 and ask the children to recall their work on how materials change when subjected to temperature changes.

ICT LINK

Children can use the 'Changing materials' interactive to match pictures of changing materials to the process that is taking place.

ASSESSMENT

Note the children's individual contributions to the concept-mapping exercise as an indication of their general understanding. Most children should be able to name some materials and say a little about how they are used. Most should be able to describe what happens to water when it is heated and cooled but some may not have reached this level of conceptual understanding.

PLENARY

Review the children's work. Return to the concept map and ask the children if they would like to add or change anything. Reinforce the key points raised in the concept mapping. Ask each group to explain their sorting work in Group activity 1. Check each child's work on photocopiable page 92. With the class, revise how these materials change when they are heated or cooled.

OUTCOMES

- Teacher can assess the level of the children in the class.
- Teacher can arrange children in appropriate class groups.

Differentiation
Group activity 1
Some children may be able to present their findings in a table.
Group activity 2
For children who need support, use 'Changing materials' (green), from the CD-ROM which allows them to present their ideas pictorially.
   To extend children, use 'Changing materials' (blue), which asks for children's ideas in writing using the correct scientific words where possible.

Lesson 2 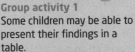 Materials

Objective
- To know a range of common materials and that a material may have different uses.

Vocabulary
brick, glass, metal, paper, plastic, sight, stone, touch, wood

RESOURCES

Main teaching activity: A selection of everyday materials such as paper, plastic, metal, wood, water, wool, cotton and so on.
Group activities: 1 Copies of photocopiable page 93 (also 'Materials' (red), available on the CD-ROM); clipboards; pens; pencils. **2** Paper; pens; pencils.
ICT link: 'Materials' interactive activity, from the CD-ROM.

PREPARATION

Decide and agree where around school your class will be surveying materials.

BACKGROUND

No matter how we choose to classify different materials, it is important to remember that all materials ultimately come from the natural resources of the Earth; either in a form that makes them useful immediately, like wood, or as a raw material in the production of other materials, such as oil for plastics.
   Our ability to manipulate the materials around us has played a major part

Differentiation

Group activity 1

For children who need support, give them 'Materials' (green), from the CD-ROM, which asks them to draw rather than write the names of the objects that they find.

To extend children, use 'Materials' (blue), which asks for three examples of uses for each material and, in the second part of the sheet, challenges them to find sources of the materials used.

Object	Old material	New material
Kettle	Steel	Plastic
Window frames	Wood	uPVC
Carrier bag	Paper	Polythene
Bottles	Glass	Plastic

Object and material	How we identified it
Wooden chair	By the look (and smell?) of the wood
Plastic spoon	By the feel of the plastic

in our development from the ages of stone and iron for tools and weapons, to the modern age of synthetic and 'man-made' materials. This unit considers in more depth the sources of our materials and how their uses and properties must be matched up.

The designs of many everyday items today may have changed little since their invention, but the materials they are made from have often been replaced by newer alternatives.

Many materials can serve the same purpose, and some materials can serve many different purposes, as shown in the table below.

Clearly this range can be expanded very significantly. However, what is key is that to make good use of the range of available materials it is necessary to know about and understand their properties in order to choose the best material for the job. Children often have the idea that when we talk about 'materials' we mean 'fabrics'. However, the word 'material' is used to describe the full range of substances that things are made from such as wood, metal, plastic, paper, ceramics, glass and so on. In the scientific world, the word 'material' is used to describe an even wider spectrum of substances. When scientists refer to 'materials' they think and talk about the whole physical substance of the Universe.

STARTER

Bring into the classroom an unusual or old object that the children are unlikely to recognise, or something that has changed over recent years: perhaps a 78rpm record, a flat iron or a chamber pot! Ask the children to look at the object and then tell you what they think the item may be used for. Discuss how they identified the object – which senses did they use? Relate the activity to their earlier work on the senses and how they use their senses to inform them about the world around them.

MAIN ACTIVITY

Present the children with a selection of samples of materials. Ask them to tell you how they would identify each material. Talk about how they find out about anything to do with the world around them. Encourage the children to recall the senses they would use in identifying an unknown material – sight and touch mainly.

GROUP ACTIVITIES

1 Distribute copies of photocopiable page 93 and tell the children that they are going to use their senses to identify a range of materials around the school that have been used to make particular objects. Go out and survey the chosen area to complete the photocopiable sheet.

2 When they have completed their investigation, ask the children to think about how they knew, or what helped them to decide, what an object was made from. They should find a way to record their thoughts.

ICT LINK

Children can use the 'Materials' interactive, from the CD-ROM, in order to match everyday objects to the materials from which they are made.

ASSESSMENT

All the children should know that they use their senses to help them identify materials, and which senses are most often used. Most should be able to complete Group activity 1 and be able to identify the uses of these materials.

PLENARY
Ask the children to feed back their findings, giving examples of objects made from particular materials and the materials used in various objects.

OUTCOMES
● Can recognise common materials.
● Can describe how some materials have several uses.

Lesson 3 ▪ Properties of materials

Objectives
● To know that different materials have different properties.
● To know that any material may have more than one property.

Vocabulary
clay, glass, hard, opaque, paper, plastic, properties, rough, smooth, soft, steel, translucent, transparent, wood

RESOURCES ◉
Main teaching activity: A selection of materials; flipchart or board; pens.
Group activities: 1 Copies of photocopiable page 94 (also 'Properties of materials' (red), available on the CD-ROM); materials, including glass (in a window); paper; steel; plastic; wood; clay. **2** Paper; pens; pencils.
ICT link: 'Properties of materials' interactive activity from the CD-ROM.

BACKGROUND
To make the best use of materials it is important to know the properties they possess, so we can select the correct material for the job we are doing. For example, we construct buildings using concrete, bricks, steel and so on because we know that they are strong, durable and available relatively cheaply. Similarly, we use plastic for bottles because it is cheap, lightweight, can be coloured, moulded and recycled. Of course, whole objects can be made from a number of different materials, as well as their individual components. Likewise, one material can be made into very many different objects. In deciding which material to use for a particular purpose, the manufacturer needs to consider the range of different properties that the material possesses and may sometimes have to compromise on some aspects of the properties of some materials.

   The material may be: hard or soft; heavy or light; opaque, transparent or translucent; smooth or rough; reflective or non-reflective; rigid or flexible; easily cut, moulded or otherwise changed; cheap or expensive; smelly; easily available; magnetic or non-magnetic; able to conduct electricity or be an insulator; a good insulator of heat; recyclable. Some of these properties are explored in this unit, and others are touched on in other units (such as magnetism in Unit 3e).

STARTER
Recap on how the children identified the various materials in the previous lesson. Then ask: *How would you tell the difference between two different people?* Begin to introduce the children to the idea that just as humans have certain things about them that make them who they are, so too can materials have certain 'properties'.

MAIN ACTIVITY
How would you tell the difference between two different materials? We use our senses to help us identify materials, but how do we sort one material from another? How do we know that what we are touching is glass?

   Let the children observe and handle some materials. Talk about the properties of those materials, asking the children to describe them as: hard or soft; opaque, transparent or translucent; smooth or rough. You may like to keep the number of properties limited at this stage (depending on the ability of your class), as too many could lead to some confusion. Compile a list of properties that the children could use in describing materials (see Background). This should be revision, so try to extend the properties identified to take in the children's more recent experiences.

GROUP ACTIVITIES

1 Distribute copies of photocopiable page 94. Ask the children to compile lists of properties of these common materials. For example: glass - rigid, transparent, smooth, reflective and so on. (You may prefer to amend the sheet to match the materials you have available.)
2 Ask the children to use the information from Group activity 1 to draw up a table similar to that above to show which materials have particular properties such as hard, soft, smooth, rough.

ASSESSMENT

All the children should be able to identify a number of properties such as hard, soft, smooth, rough and so on. Most should be able to look at examples of materials and list some properties that each has. Some will be able to use that information to group materials by these properties in increasingly sophisticated ways.

PLENARY

Ask the children to think of a material and to begin to describe it by referring only to its properties; the other children must try to guess the identity of the material.

OUTCOMES

● Can state one or two characteristics of a range of common materials.
● Can compare the properties of different materials.

LINKS

Unit 3e, Lessons 3-5: exploring the functions and uses of magnets.
Unit 3e, Lessons 10-12: exploring elasticity.
Unit 3f, Lessons 6, 7 and 18: the occurrence and uses of lights, reflective materials and colour in the environment.
Unit 3f, Lessons 5 and 8: exploring which materials make the best shadows, reinforcing transparent, translucent and opaque.
Maths: organising data in tables and charts, for example into a Carroll diagram.

Lesson 4 ▪ Uses of materials

Objective
● To know that materials are selected for making objects according to their properties.
● To understand that the use and wear an object will need to withstand governs the materials from which it can be made.

RESOURCES

A variety of classroom objects; a video of glassmaking or similar material changing.

MAIN ACTIVITY

Look at a variety of objects and suggest reasons why a particular material was used in its making. Ask the children to give sensible reasons why each object is made from the material it is. Ask them to suggest alternative materials that could be used and to say why. Suggest materials that would be unsuitable, again ask the children to say why they are unsuitable. Refer back to the survey of materials around the school in Lesson 2 - does the place where the object is used affect the choice of materials it is made from: *Why are our chairs made from metal or plastic and not finely carved wood?*

ASSESSMENT

Through scrutiny of the children's work and discussion with them, assess their understanding of the suitability of materials for particular uses.

PLENARY

Discuss the children's findings and come to some agreement about the use of certain materials due to their properties, for example, wood is used for furniture because of its looks and strength. Show the children a video where materials are being used to make things, for example, wooden furniture or glass bottles. Focus on the appropriateness of these materials.

This lesson is followed up practically in Lesson 5, Group activity 3, but you may like to discuss and plan for that activity as part of this lesson.

OUTCOME
● Can recognise how materials are selected according to their properties when an object is being made.

Lesson 5 ▸ Investigating materials

RESOURCES 💿
Main teaching activity: Copies of photocopiable page 95 (also 'Investigation – 1' (red); available on the CD-ROM) for each child or pair (or an enlarged copy displayed for whole-class use); appropriate pens or pencils.
Group activities: 1 Paper; pens; pencils. **2** A selection of man-made and natural materials such as stone, brick, paper, cloth, clay, plastic, steel, wood; carrier bags made of paper, fabric, rafia, leather and different types of plastic; copies of photocopiable pages 96 and 97 (also 'Investigation – 2' (red) and 'Investigation – 3' (red), available on the CD-ROM). **3** Different materials, including paper, fabric, rafia, leather and different types of plastic; copies of photocopiable page 98 (also 'Investigation – 4' (red), available on the CD-ROM); adhesive and or sticky tape; needles and a variety of threads (optional); scissors; weights (for example, large potatoes); thin card (see Preparation).

PREPARATION
The template on photocopiable page 98 is for half a bag and needs enlarging to A3 size, copying on to thin card and perhaps assembling before the children can use it to draw and cut out bag shapes. You may prefer to make the bag template from card for the children first (see instructions on photocopiable page 98).

BACKGROUND
In order to make the best use of materials, it is essential to know and understand their properties and to know how they will perform under certain conditions. Often this knowledge can be gained from simple observation, at other times we need to carry out an investigation into the properties of a range of possible materials and compare the results of those investigations to make the best choice. Investigations into materials involve doing things to the material such as exerting a force and trying to break it and measuring the effects. This lesson offers a 'pure' science investigation through which to explore this, but also offers a design and technology task, relating the appropriateness of a material to its purpose when made into an object. You may prefer to use only one of these tasks, use both in a circus, or use them sequentially.

In carrying out the activities in this lesson you will need to support the children as they continue to develop their investigative skills. While many of them may have done similar tests before (for example, in Key Stage 1/ Primary 1–3 it is common to explore suitable waterproof materials for a teddy's umbrella), they may not have carried out an investigation so systematically or with consideration of controlling any of the variables.

STARTER
Begin by talking about why we need to know about the properties that

---

Property	Description of material	What could you test?	How could you test it?
Strength	strong/weak	How much force is needed to break it?	Hang weights on it.
Elasticity	elastic/inelastic	Does it spring back after being stretched or compressed?	Apply push and pull forces.
Hardness	hard/soft	How easily can you change its shape by squeezing it?	Try to squash it into a different shape.
Reflective	reflective/non-reflective	Can you see a reflection in it?	Observation of the object.
Magnetic	magnetic/non-magnetic	Is it attracted by a magnet?	Use a magnet to try to attract the material.
Absorbency- probably a new word!	absorbent/ waterproof	Does it absorb or repel water?	Drip water on to the material - does it run off or need to be squeezed out?

certain materials possess. Discuss the outcomes of the previous lesson in the context of establishing a suitable material from which to make a carrier bag.

MAIN ACTIVITY – PART 1

Talk to the children about ways of finding out the properties of materials. Ask the children to think of properties that could be investigated and how. Work together as a class to complete photocopiable page 89, with information such as that shown in the table on the left.

GROUP ACTIVITIES

1 Tell the children that they are going to plan an investigation into just one of the properties they have looked at on photocopiable page 95. The question they will answer is 'Which material is the... (hardest, strongest, most absorbent)?' You will need to work very closely with each group as they do this. They will need to decide four things: which property to investigate (such as strength or absorbency); what exactly they will test for (perhaps how much force is needed to break something or whether a material absorbs water); how the test will be carried out (perhaps by adding weights or dripping water on to a material); and which materials to test.

MAIN ACTIVITY – PART 2

When the children have carried out their planning, bring them back together to discuss how they are going to ensure that the tests they carry out are fair. Discuss the idea of fairness when playing games and apply this to their investigations. (A game is fair if everyone has the same opportunities, for example, a team game is fair if the sides are equal and both are playing to the same rules.) Emphasise that for their tests to be fair the children need to treat all the materials the same: if they drip water on materials to test for absorbency they need to drip the same quantity of water on each.

GROUP ACTIVITIES

2 Some groups can carry out their investigation. You may like to use photocopiable pages 96–97 for the children to record their results, or for the children to devise their own method of recording their work. At this stage, to ease resource pressures, others can carry out Group activity 3.

3 Ask the children to make carrier bags using the template and instructions on photocopiable page 98. First they should try to decide what makes a good carrier bag. Have some bags available for the children to look at and examine their construction. The children should think about: strength - whether it can carry a heavy load; weight - whether the bag itself is heavy or light; colour - whether it can be coloured (for decoration or advertising); waterproofing - whether it can still be used when it gets wet.

Each group should use just one main material to make the body of the carrier bag, with each group using a different material. They will also need to consider how to fasten the sides of the bag together, perhaps using sticky tape, by gluing, or even sewing. Let them test their bags to see which material is the most suitable. Watch out for unprotected toes if the bag breaks and the load (perhaps a big potato) falls out. Encourage the children to try to write a set of instructions telling other people how to make a strong carrier bag.

Differentiation

Some children will need more support in planning and carrying out the Group activities. Support them with adult supervision wherever possible. Some children should be able to work on these tasks with less support and begin to draw some conclusions from their investigations.

Encourage these children to justify their choice of material for their carrier bag or why their material was unsuitable (depending on how much choice they had in the material).

ICT LINKS

Encourage the children to use ICT as a means of recording and communicating their findings.

ASSESSMENT

Through scrutiny of the children's work, observation and discussion during the lesson, assess the children's ability to plan and carry out the investigation. Most should be able to carry out the investigation although some support may be needed at the planning stage. What consideration did the children make towards fairness?

PLENARY

Bring the class together before tidying away the groups' investigations so that each group can report to the rest of the class on how they carried out the investigation, their observations and their conclusions.

Conclude the lesson by reinforcing the idea that in choosing appropriate materials to use we need to investigate the properties of possible materials to establish the most appropriate material. The children may describe the 'best' material, but highlight how 'best' is also dependent on purpose.

OUTCOMES

- Know that the properties of materials can be compared by investigation.
- Can plan and carry out a fair test, make predictions and observations and draw conclusions.

Lesson 6 ▪ Fit for purpose

Objective

- To use materials for a specific purpose and to test their suitability for that purpose.
- To identify what scientific questions need to be asked.

RESOURCES

A wide variety of flexible materials such as paper; tissue paper; card; cloth; plastic; scissors; glue; adhesive tape; carrier bags.

MAIN ACTIVITY

Ask the children to make a specific item using a particular material, for example, an envelope or a small box to keep an item safe. The children should be able to think of a question they need to answer or test to see if their chosen material might be suitable, for example, 'What happens to tissue paper when it gets wet?' and thus, 'What would happen to an envelope made from tissue paper?', or 'What happens to a paper box when we put a heavy weight on it?' and thus, 'Would a paper box protect an egg?' You may like to use photocopiable pages 96 and 97 (see Lesson 5) to help the children record their results, or for the children to devise their own ways of recording.

ASSESSMENT

Through observation and discussion, assess whether or not the children are able to test the appropriateness of the materials used.

PLENARY

Bring the children together and share experiences. Draw some conclusions about suitable and unsuitable materials.

Differentiation

Differentiate by outcome.

OUTCOMES

- Can use materials for a specific purpose.
- Can test their questions about the material's suitability for that purpose.

ENRICHMENT

Lesson 7 ▸ Natural and man-made materials

Objective
● To know that some materials occur naturally and others do not.

Vocabulary
man-made, manufactured, natural, source

RESOURCES

Main teaching activity: A collection of different natural and manufactured materials; flipchart or board; pens.
Group activities: 1 A copy of photocopiable page 99 (also 'Natural and man-made materials' (red); available on the CD-ROM) for each child; pens; pencils. **2** Clipboards; paper; pens; pencils.

BACKGROUND

There are many ways to group materials. Some groupings are based on the properties of the materials and others are to do with their origins. Materials are often grouped as being 'natural' or 'manufactured' (man-made).

Many years ago, people had access to a limited range of natural materials such as stone and wood. Natural raw materials can be traced to several sources: animals, plants, or the ground ('animal, vegetable or mineral').

Today, while we still use a number of natural materials, we also use a large number of 'man-made' or manufactured materials. These materials are designed and produced to have quite specific properties. For example, plastic is a strong, light and very versatile material that has replaced many natural products. Many materials are manufactured from natural raw materials or derivatives of natural materials. Glass, for example, is manufactured from pure sand.

In the production of objects, materials often go through intermediate stages and are processed as they are turned from a raw material into a finished product. This processing can confuse what is natural and what is manufactured. A wooden chair, for example, is made from the timber of a tree which is sawn into planks; a pullover can be made from a ball of wool which previously was the fleece of a sheep.

In summary: 'natural' materials, such as raw wool, wood and cotton, are produced by natural processes. What we might call 'processed' materials are usually grouped as natural materials as they are changed physically by humans, although the change does not alter the nature of the material, examples include spun wool and cotton, planks of wood, or cut and finished slabs of stone. 'Manufactured' materials are made by processes that change raw materials into different materials, for example, crude oil is used to manufacture plastics and artificial fibres.

STARTER

Have ready in the classroom a collection of objects made from materials that have been discussed in previous lessons. Talk about the materials, recapping on their properties and uses. Ask: *Could these materials be sorted in a different way to the ways they have been sorted before – not by their properties?*

Differentiation
Some children may need extra support in determining whether or not a material is man-made or natural, and may benefit from you providing extra examples. Help will also be needed with drawing and completing the Carroll diagram. Some children will be able to work with the Carroll diagram to add more examples.

MAIN ACTIVITY

Look at the collection of materials. Encourage the children to consider the origins of the materials: which ones occur naturally and which have been manufactured. Make a list of natural and manufactured materials.

GROUP ACTIVITIES

1 Distribute copies of photocopiable page 93. Ask the children to make a list of materials and where they come from, under the headings on the sheet. Ensure that they only record materials and not objects.

	CHANGED/SHAPED BY HUMANS	NOT CHANGED/ SHAPED BY HUMANS
NATURAL MATERIAL USED	woollen jumper paper book wooden pencil chair	plant
NOT NATURAL MATERIAL USED (manufactured)	plastic ruler pen	

2 Ask the groups to carry out a survey around the classroom to find objects that are made from natural materials or manufactured materials. Use the information and that gained from Group activity 1 to create a Carroll diagram similar to the one, here.

ASSESSMENT
Can the children recognise manufactured materials and naturally occurring materials? Assess their understanding from their ability to sort materials into groups using photocopiable page 93.

PLENARY
Have a quiz in which the children have to find the identity of a mystery material by asking five questions. The respondent can say only 'Yes' or 'No'. The children can use the Carroll diagrams to help them, together with other visual information such as samples of the materials.

OUTCOME
● Can recognise that some materials occur naturally and others do not.

LINKS
Maths: organising data into tables and charts, for example Carroll diagrams.

ENRICHMENT

Lesson 8 ▷ From raw material to finished product

Objective
● To be able to compare finished objects with raw materials.

RESOURCES
A selection of raw materials, their corresponding processed materials and finished objects, or pictures of these. For example, raw materials could be a sheep's fleece, a tree trunk and cotton; corresponding processed materials could be a ball of wool, a plank of wood or a sheet of paper and a reel of cotton; finished objects could be a knitted jumper, a wooden table or a book and a cotton shirt. Also provide secondary sources of information relating to how materials are processed and manufactured.

MAIN ACTIVITY
Compare raw materials, processed materials and finished products. Ask the children to sort the materials into related groups, for example, a sheep's fleece, a ball of wool and a knitted jumper in one group. They can then present their ideas in pictorial form to show the links and groupings.

ASSESSMENT
Use the children's work to check that they have an understanding and ability to sort the various items into groups that show raw materials, processed materials and finished products.

PLENARY
Share ideas and reinforce the understanding that manufactured items and materials come from natural raw materials.

OUTCOME
● Can compare finished objects with raw materials.

Differentiation
For children who need support, provide sets of cards of the three phases of manufacturing to sort into order.
Other children can go on to carry out their own research looking at how some raw materials are processed and how man-made materials are manufactured, for example, how paper or bricks are made.

Lesson 9 ▪ Assessment

Objective
● To assess the children's knowledge and understanding of materials and their uses.

RESOURCES 💿
Starter: Objects brought in from home (less familiar than the usual classroom items).
Assessment activities: 1 Copies of photocopiable page 100 (also 'Assessment – 1' (red), available on the CD-ROM); pens; pencils. **2** Copies of photocopiable page 101 (also 'Assessment – 2' (red), available on the CD-ROM); pens; pencils.
ICT link: 'Investigating Materials' interactive activity, from the CD-ROM.

STARTER
Ask the children to bring in one simple object from home (a letter home may ensure they do not bring valuables to school). Ask them to help you to sort the objects according to the materials they are made from. Discuss alternative groupings. Encourage the children to begin to identify the natural raw materials that are used in some of the objects.

ASSESSMENT ACTIVITY 1
Distribute copies of photocopiable page 100 and ask the children to complete the sheet unaided. The tasks are designed to give the children the opportunity to identify the uses of materials used to build houses.

ANSWERS
1. There may be several alternative answers:

Part of house	Made from	Why?
Window	Frames: wood, metal, plastic Window: glass	Accept reasons that make sense in light of the materials chosen.
Roof	Slate, tile, reeds, felt	
Door	Wood, plastic, glass	
Guttering	Plastic, metal	
Walls	Brick, concrete, stone	
Door handles	metal	

2. An umbrella made from paper would disintegrate when it rained or tear when it was windy. The material is not strong enough and is not waterproof.
3. A hammer made from glass would shatter when used because glass is too brittle and is not as strong as iron.

LOOKING FOR LEVELS
All the children should be able to suggest materials for some of the components listed, and most should be able to give one good reason why each material could be used. Most should also be able to give explanations of what would happen if we used the wrong materials for making objects, and a few should be able to give reasons why.

ASSESSMENT ACTIVITY 2
Distribute copies of photocopiable page 101 and ask the children to complete the sheet unaided.

ICT LINK 💿
Some children could use the interactive, 'Investigating materials', from the CD-ROM to match properties to their definitions.

Differentiation
For children who need support, provide sets of cards of the three phases of manufacturing to sort into order.
Other children can go on to carry out their own research looking at how some raw materials are processed and how man-made materials are manufactured, for example, how paper or bricks are made.

ANSWERS

1. Look for evidence that the children have some understanding of how to carry out a fair test investigation. This may include treating all paper samples the same, using the same amount of paper and liquid together with the same equipment.

2.

Property	Meaning
Strength	How much force is needed to break it
Elasticity	How easily it springs back after being stretched
Hardness	How easily it can be shaped
Reflective	How easily you can see yourself in it
Magnetic	How easily it is attracted by a magnet
Absorbency	How easily it will absorb a liquid

Words such as these and others may be suggested:
Wood: hard, strong, non magnetic.
Paper: soft, flexible, non magnetic, absorbent.
Plastic: soft (could also be hard), elastic (although could also be quite brittle), non magnetic.
Glass: hard, reflective, non magnetic, non elastic.

LOOKING FOR LEVELS

All the children should be able to begin to identify ways of carrying out an investigation; some will be able to use more accurate vocabulary. Most should be able to match the properties of materials and identify the properties of the specified materials. Some may be able to use scientific vocabulary when describing these materials although you may want to accept other words of similar meaning.

PLENARY

Discuss the Assessment activities and address any further misunderstandings. Reinforce the link between rock and how soil is made.

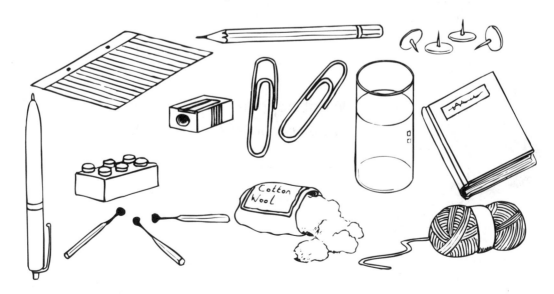

Changing materials

◖ What happens to materials when you change their temperature?
◖ Draw these things in the boxes.

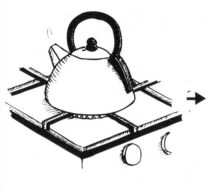

What happens when water is heated?

_____

_____

_____

➡

What happens when ice is heated?

_____

_____

_____

➡

What happens when dough is heated?

_____

_____

_____

➡

What happens when water is cooled?

_____

_____

_____

➡

Illustration © Kirsty Wilson

Materials

■ Find examples around school of things that are made from each of the materials below.

Remember: a material is the substance something is made from.

Material	Example of its use
Metal	
Wood	
Plastic	
Glass	
Paper	
Stone	
Brick	

■ Now try to find out what materials these objects in your school are made from. There may be several materials used in making each object.

Object	Materials used
Table	
Chair	
Book	
Pen	
Computer and monitor	
Your classroom	

Properties of materials

◼ Look at the examples of these materials on your table.
◼ Write a list of properties that belong to each one.

Glass	Paper
Steel	Plastic
Wood	Clay

◖SCHOLASTIC

Investigation – 1

■ How would you investigate these properties of materials? Complete the table. One has been done for you.

■ Can you add two more properties to test?

Property	Description of material	What could you test?	How could you test it?
Strength	strong/weak	How much force is needed to break it?	Hang weights on it.
Elasticity			
Hardness			
Reflective			
Magnetic			
Absorbency			

PHOTOCOPIABLE

Investigation – 2

Name _____ Date _____

Our question:

What we will do to find the answer:

What we will need:

What we think will happen:

■ SCHOLASTIC

Investigation – 3

Name _____ Date _____

This is what we did:

This is what we found out:

This is what we now know:

Investigation – 4

■ Copy this template twice onto thin card.

1. Cut out two template shapes.

CUT OUT FOR HANDLE

2. Stick them together like this.

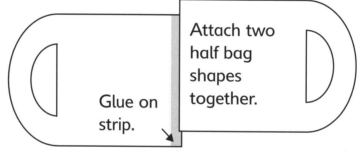

Glue on strip.

Attach two half bag shapes together.

GLUE

GLUE

Your teacher may do steps 1 and 2 for you.

3. Draw around the bag template on your chosen material and cut it out.

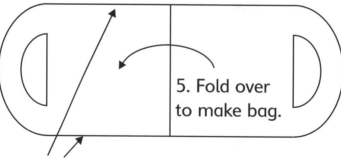

5. Fold over to make bag.

4. Glue on both edges.

GLUE

Natural and man-made materials

Where do natural materials come from? See if you can complete this table with examples of materials from each of these sources.

Materials that come from plants

Materials that come from animals

Materials that come from the ground

What sorts of materials are made by people – 'manufactured'?

Materials that are made by people

PHOTOCOPIABLE

Assessment – 1

1. Look at this picture of a house.

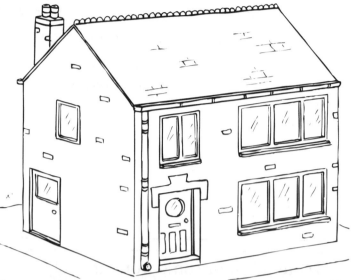

■ Think about the materials that each part listed below is made from. Say why that material is used for that part.

Part of house	Made from	Why?
Window		
Roof		
Door		
Guttering		
Walls		
Door handles		

■ Try these questions about what would happen if we used the wrong materials:

2. What would happen if we made an umbrella out of paper?

_____

_____

3. What would happen if we made a hammer out of glass?

_____

_____

■SCHOLASTIC

Illustration © Kirsty Wilson

Assessment – 2

1. Draw a labelled diagram to show how you would carry out an investigation to find out which was the best kitchen paper for mopping up spillages. This should be a fair test.

2. Match these properties with their meanings.

Strength	How easily it can be shaped
Elasticity	How easily you can see yourself in it
Hardness	How easily it is attracted by a magnet
Reflective	How much force is needed to break it
Magnetic	How easily it will absorb
Absorbency	How easily it springs back after being stretched

3. Which words would you use to describe the properties these materials usually have?

Wood _____

Paper _____

Plastic _____

Glass _____

CHAPTER 5 Rocks and soils

Lesson	Objectives	Main activity	Group activities	Plenary	Outcomes
Lesson 1 Uses of rocks	• To ascertain the level of understanding of rocks and soils. • To recognise the ways in which rocks are used.	Identifying ways in which rocks are used, for example as a construction material on buildings, walls and roads.	Concept mapping. Drawing uses of rocks.	Reviewing concept maps, sharing ideas and asking questions.	• Can identify the ways in which humans use rocks.
Lesson 2 Types of rock	• To be able to recognise and describe a range of different rocks.	Observing, examining and naming rock samples.	Grouping rocks by characteristics. Using secondary sources.	Using descriptions of rocks to help others identify rock samples.	• Can recognise and describe a range of different rocks. • Can put rocks into groups.
Lesson 3 Rock rubbing test	• To know that rocks can be tested for their wear.	Compare rock samples for wear by rubbing.		Ranking rocks for wear.	• Can compare and rank rocks according to their ease of wearing.
Lesson 4 Rock permeability	• To know that rocks can be tested for their permeability.	Compare rock samples for permeability by dripping water.		Concluding which rock samples are least permeable.	• Can compare and rank rocks according to their permeability.
Lesson 5 Rock trail	• To know that rocks are chosen for particular purposes because of their characteristics.	Go on a 'rock trail' around the school or the neighbourhood to identify the ways in which rocks have been used because of their characteristics.	Prepare a group presentation on the uses of rocks.	Share observations on the uses of rocks.	• Know that rocks are used for particular purposes because of their characteristics.
Lesson 6 Under our feet	• To understand that rock is below all surfaces.	Create model rocky landscape.		Identifying why soil may have been eroded from rock surfaces.	• Can explain some rock is exposed due to erosion and the structure of the Earth's crust.
Lesson 7 Types of soil	• To know there are different kinds of soil. • To know that there is rock beneath soil.	Learning how soil is formed.	Describing soil samples. Using secondary sources.	Looking at coloured layers in soil.	• Can describe how soil lies on top of rock. • Can recognise that there are different kinds of soil.
Lesson 8 Soil observation	• To know that different soils have different-sized particles and different colours.	Mixing soil with water and observing settlement.		Discussion of the different layers from different soil samples.	• Can compare soils in terms of particles and colour.
Lesson 9 Separating soil particles	• To understand that particles of differing sizes can be separated by the use of sieves.	Sieving wholemeal, seeded flour using sieves with different sized holes.	Sieving sand and gravel mixture using different sieves. Designing a poster.	Discuss process of sieving.	• Can understand that particles of differing sizes can be separated by the use of sieves.
Lesson 10 Growing seeds in different soils	• To use simple apparatus to measure volumes of liquids and to measure time. • To recognise when a test is unfair.	Watching an unfair test into soil permeability and discussing how to make the test fair.	Growing cress to investigate different soils.	Reviewing work and sharing ideas about how to improve soil permeability.	• Can use simple apparatus to measure volumes of liquids and to measure time. • Can recognise when a test is unfair.
Lesson 11 Testing soil permeability	• To plan a fair test. • To make and record measurements of time and volume of water. • To use results to make comparisons and draw and explain a conclusion.	Demonstration of testing soil permeability.	Devising and carrying out a fair test into different soil samples. Growing cress in different soils.	Reinforcing the concept of permeability and why some land does not drain well.	• Can plan a fair test. • Can make and record measurements of time and volume of water. • Can use results to make comparisons and explain conclusions.

Assessment	Objectives	Activity 1	Activity 2
Lesson 12	• To assess the children's knowledge and understanding of rocks and soils.	Completing a worksheet about the different types of rock.	Completing a worksheet on uses of rock and how soil is formed.

SC1 SCIENTIFIC ENQUIRY

Which soil drains the best?

LEARNING OBJECTIVES AND OUTCOMES
- Decide how to find the answer to the question.
- Decide what equipment and materials to use.
- Make a fair test.
- Take action to control risk.
- Review their work.

ACTIVITY
The children should devise together, with support, a fair test to investigate permeability of soil types. Ensure the children consider what factors will make the investigation a fair test. The children should pour equal amounts of water over equal quantities of soil and time how long it takes for the water to drain through, or how much water drains through in a given time.

The children could record their findings in a table format. Throughout they should be aware of the health and safety risks involved in handling soil. At the end encourage the children to reflect on the way they carried out the investigation.

LESSON LINKS
This Sc1 activity forms an integral part of Lesson 11, Growing seeds in different soils.

Lesson 1 ▸ Uses of rocks

Objectives
- To ascertain the level of understanding of rocks and soils.
- To recognise the ways in which rocks are used.

RESOURCES
A3 paper and pencils for concept maps; paper; samples of rocks; secondary sources of information; concept-mapping software if available.

BACKGROUND
In Key Stage 1/Primary 1-3 and in the unit 'Characteristics of materials' the children will have been given the opportunity to find out about classifying and sorting materials and about the characteristics they present. This unit considers rocks and soils and draws on some of the skills and knowledge that the children will have used when looking at the properties of materials.

Rock is a solid, natural material that is quite literally a piece of a planet, in this case the Earth. Most rocks are made up of one or more minerals, that is, a material that has a specific chemical composition. There are usually no more than six types of mineral in each type of rock. In the region of 3500 minerals have so far been discovered, with about 100 being commonly found in the crust of the Earth. The rocks around us contain clues to the history of the Earth. A geologist is able to study the layers of rock laid down over many years and build up a picture of what the environment was like at the time.

Depending on their composition, rocks are used for a variety of purposes such as building and landscaping. Many rocks used in the construction of buildings are extremely hard wearing; indeed we can see historic buildings that are many hundreds of years old which were often built using locally quarried rock.

STARTER
Begin by letting the children look at and handle a range of rock types, some may be in their 'natural' condition, others may have been shaped. Encourage

Differentiation
The children can record their findings in different and appropriate ways, a simple checklist could be prepared for some children, others can record in words, pictures or tables. When drawing concept maps some children could do so using ready-made word, cards or pictures to simplify the process. Others may develop more complex links between words and phrases.

the children to share their ideas about the rocks and their characteristics. There is no need at this stage to expect the children to identify the rock type although some may be able to do so.

MAIN ACTIVITY
Ask the children to think about some of the ways in which rock is used, for example, as a construction material on buildings, walls and roads. The children may also be able to identify other uses for rocks such as for decorative purposes and in garden features. You may want to explain how some rocks are modified, worked or changed before they have been used. Concrete, for example, is a mixture of sand, cement and gravel and whilst not a rock, is clearly made using rocks. This is a good, discussion starting point.

GROUP ACTIVITIES
1 In small groups discuss and draw a concept map. Encourage the children to share all they know about rocks and soils with each other, together with the uses of rocks. They should write down some of the key words and phrases they use. As you work with the children avoid correcting misconceptions at this stage, since it is important that the children feel free to air all their ideas. Try to ensure that the children make links between some of the words and phrases to establish concepts and ideas. This could also be done using one of the many concept-mapping software packages that are available.
2 Make an annotated drawing of some uses of rocks. Some children may be able to find out more about different types of rock and how they are used.

ICT LINK
Children could use concept mapping software or the interactive whiteboard as a means of creating, storing and returning to a group concept map.

ASSESSMENT
Through discussion and questioning, together with scrutiny and discussion of the concept maps, assess the children's ability to recognise and record the ways in which rocks are used.

PLENARY
Share and discuss the concept maps, encouraging children to ask questions and make suggestions. Begin to group the ways in which rocks are used and discuss criteria for these categories. You could also create a shared concept map using the interactive whiteboard that can be returned to later in the unit.

OUTCOME
● Can identify the ways in which humans use rocks.

LINKS
This lesson is further developed in Lesson 5, Rock trail.

Lesson 2 ▶ Types of rock

Objective
● To be able to recognise and describe a range of different rocks.

RESOURCES
Main activity: A selection of rock samples with their names written on cards. Rock kits containing samples of sandstone, limestone, marble, granite, chalk and slate are available from Hardy Aggregates, Torr Works, East Cranmore, Shepton Mallet, Somerset BA4 4SQ; tel: 01749 880735; e-mail: info@hardy-aggregates.co.uk; website: www.hardy-aggregates.co.uk

Vocabulary
chalk, granite, igneous, limestone, marble, metamorphic, sandstone, sedimentary, slate

Group activities: 1 Hand lenses and magnifiers; paper; pens; pencils; secondary sources of information. **2** Paper; pens; pencils; secondary sources of information; large sheets of coloured paper; papier-mâché 'rocks'.

BACKGROUND

The surface of the Earth – the Earth's crust – is made up of rock, though some of this rock is covered by soil or water.

Rocks are widely used for a variety of building purposes and a walk around any town will give plenty of examples. Towns are often characterised by the colour of the local stone which has been used for their buildings: pink or grey mottled granite, red-brown sandstone, white or yellow limestone. There are many different types of rock that can be identified by looking at factors such as colour, texture and hardness.

Rock is classified according to the way in which it was formed, many millions of years ago. Three types of rock make up the Earth's crust. Igneous rocks such as granite were formed from molten or partially molten material, during volcanic eruptions and make up nearly 95% of the Earth's crust. Sedimentary rocks such as sandstone and limestone make up about 5% of the Earth's crust and were formed when sediment settled and then became compressed. Metamorphic rocks are made from existing igneous and sedimentary rocks that have undergone extreme changes, due to heating or pressure. Slate, for example, is formed from shale, and marble is formed from limestone or dolorite.

STARTER

Relate this lesson to the ideas developed in Unit 3c, Lesson 6 'Natural and man-made materials' by asking the children to recall the two groups into which we can classify materials: natural and man-made (or manufactured). Remind the children that part of one of their tasks was to find out which materials come from under the ground. Ask the children to recall some of these and ask if they can tell you where rocks come from. Discuss whether rocks are man-made or natural, and consider some ways in which they are used.

MAIN ACTIVITY

Have available in the classroom a selection of rock samples for the children to look at and touch. Ask the children to describe the rock samples using characteristics such as: size of particles (different visible pieces in the rock's structure) – none, tiny, small, large; shape of particles – angular or smooth and round; colour – black, white, grey, pink, green or yellow, for example, and shiny or dull; texture – rough or smooth.

Create a class table of the observations. Now put the name labels with the correct rock samples, and associate the characteristics from the children's descriptions with the rock types.

GROUP ACTIVITIES

1 Using the labelled rocks to reinforce the variety of distinguishing characteristics, ask the children to identify similar small rock samples. Ask them to group the rocks by considering their characteristics. The children can record their work by drawing carefully coloured observational sketches of the rock samples, naming them and, depending on their ability, writing a brief description of one or more of the rock samples.

2 Ask the children to use secondary sources to find out more about the three rock types: igneous; sedimentary; metamorphic. The children can present their findings as a 'Rock factfile' or mounted on to coloured rocks that are either painted stones or papier-mâché rocks to form a mountain as a display.

Differentiation
Some children may need to research some basic facts about one or two rock types. Other children will be able to research in more detail and find examples of each rock type.

ICT LINK
Visit this useful website: www.virtualquarry.co.uk.

ASSESSMENT
Assess the children's work for evidence of their ability to recognise the samples of the rocks. Most should be able to recognise the majority of the samples having studied the bigger pieces; the most able should recognise them all.

PLENARY
Use the descriptions produced to see if the children can identify the samples from each other's work. Discuss their findings about the three main rock types. Show the children a piece of concrete/aggregate – 'manufactured rock' – and talk about its similarities to natural stone.

OUTCOMES
● Can recognise and describe a range of different rocks.
● Can put rocks into groups.

LINKS
Geography: investigating our local area.

Lesson 3 ▪ Rock rubbing test

Objective
● To know that rocks can be tested for their wear.

RESOURCES
A selection of different rock samples; hand lenses; sandpaper; paper; pens; pencils.

MAIN ACTIVITY
Compare rock samples by testing to see how easily they wear. Use hand lenses to observe and sketch the surface of each rock sample. Carry out a 'rubbing test' to compare how easily the samples are ground down: rub each sample ten times with a piece of sandpaper. Try to rub the same place each time and with the same force. Use the hand lenses to carry out a second observation and again record as an observational drawing.

ASSESSMENT
Through scrutiny of the children's work, observation, discussion and during the Plenary, look for evidence that the children know that rocks can be tested in this way.

PLENARY
Ask the children to present their findings and to say which rock sample was the hardest-wearing and which the easiest to wear away. Begin to think about the uses these rocks could be put to.

Differentiation
Differentiate by outcome.

OUTCOME
● Can compare and rank rocks according to their ease of wearing.

Lesson 4 ▪ Rock permeability

Objective
● To know that rocks can be tested for their permeability.

RESOURCES
A selection of different rock samples; water; pipettes; paper; pens; pencils; secondary sources of information.

Differentiation
Differentiate by outcome.

MAIN ACTIVITY

Use a variety of rock samples to test for permeability by dropping small amounts of water onto the samples and observing how quickly the water is absorbed, if at all. Drop five drops of water on to the same place on each sample. Observe and record the results in a table which gives the opportunity for the children to identify the rock samples using secondary sources.

After this lesson and Lesson 10, take the children outside. Look around at the local environment for evidence of wear on rocks and stones, for example, on carvings on buildings. Speculate on the causes of the wear.

ASSESSMENT

Look for evidence that the children have been able to carry out the investigation in a fair way.

PLENARY

Bring the children together and ask them to share their work with each other. Discuss what the disadvantages of building using very permeable rock would be, for example, it may not be weatherproof. To illustrate this you may wish to discuss and demonstrate the effects of water freezing and thawing (the rock surface is broken up).

OUTCOME

● Can compare and rank rocks according to their permeability.

Lesson 5 ▪ Rock trail

Objective
● To know that rocks are chosen for particular purposes because of their characteristics.

RESOURCES

Clipboards, a pre-determined route for a 'Rock trail'; digital cameras; appropriate numbers of adult helpers.

BACKGROUND

Rocks are used for a variety of different purposes, largely in the construction of buildings and roads. Many have distinctive characteristics that make them appropriate for use in very specific ways. For example, rock such as granite is often used in stairs because it is particularly hard wearing. Other examples might include sandstone and flint in buildings and walls, marble for statues, monuments and fireplaces, and slate for roofing. However, there are a number of other building materials that are manufactured from different kinds of rock. Brick, concrete and plaster are all derived from rocks, as are glass and ceramics such as tiles and bathroom fittings.

STARTER

Begin the lesson by reminding the children about previous lessons. Ask the children to recall the three different ways in which rock is formed. They may also be able to identify and name some of the most common types of rock. Use the rock samples from previous lessons to reinforce their ability to identify these. Ask the children if they can think of any of the ways in which we use rocks and compile a list. Talk further and ask the children if all rock types can be used in these different ways. Establish that this is not so and that we often select specific rocks for particular uses. Explain to the children that they are going to take part in a rock-use survey and that they are going to go on a 'Rock trail' to see if they can find out how rock is used and the way in which rocks are used as a result of their characteristics.

Differentiation

Group activity

Children who need support could be asked to find just one example of rock use in buildings, roads and pavements and decorative items, and suggest reasons for its use. Other children could be asked to find three or four examples of each and also be asked to try to identify the rock type.

MAIN ACTIVITY

With appropriate and adequate support and preparation, take the children on a 'Rock trail'. Walk around the school or the local area to identify the ways in which rocks are used and the characteristics that these rocks have which determine their use. For example, particular types of rock are used in building walls and for pathways or are crushed to be used on paths and roads. Others are used for decorative purposes. Some of the uses are quite obvious since the rock has only been shaped, others are less so, as materials may have been manufactured from rock. This may be an idea that you wish to develop with some children. In general, however, talk with the children initially about uses of rock that are clearly seen. Ask the children to write down examples of uses of rock in buildings, roads and pavements and decorative uses and reasons for these uses. If you have access to digital cameras ask some children to additionally record their observations by taking a series of photographs.

GROUP ACTIVITY

On return to the classroom ask the children to work in small groups to prepare to share their findings. Suggest some of the different methods that the children could use, for example: pictures on a map, drawings of a street scene, an ICT presentation using digital images taken, a 'Rock trail' guide or leaflet, or a 'Uses of rocks' factfile.

Whichever reporting method is used, ensure that the children are considering why each of the rock types are used as they are. Why, for example, granite is used for steps and slate is used for roofing.

ASSESSMENT

Through scrutiny of work and questioning and discussion, assess the children's ability to understand that rocks are used for specific purposes as a result of their characteristics. Ask questions such as: *Can you tell me which rock is used for building walls? Why is that rock used in that way? Why not other rocks?*

PLENARY

Discuss the visit you have made to observe rock uses, ask the children to select one use and to explain the reason it was used and if appropriate its name and characteristics. Give each group the opportunity to share their observations in their particular way.

OUTCOME
● Know that rocks are used for particular purposes because of their characteristics.

Lesson 6 ▪ Under our feet

Objective
● To understand that rock is below all surfaces.

RESOURCES
Illustrations of rocky outcrops; cliffs and quarries, displayed on an interactive whiteboard if available; modelling materials.

MAIN ACTIVITY
Remind the children of the range of rocks that there are and that these can be grouped by origin as igneous, sedimentary and metamorphic. Ask the children to think about what might be below the surface of the Earth. Show the children a number of pictures that show rocky outcrops, cliff faces and quarries. Ask the children to consider why they can see the rocks in these places. Use plaster bandage or other modelling materials to create a model landscape showing rocky outcrops and layering of rocks.

LIBRARY LIVERPOOL L17 6B
231 5218/5299

Differentiation
Some children could identify the different layers of rocks and write annotations for a guide to the landscape model.

ASSESSMENT
Through discussion and questioning, assess the children's understanding that rock exists below all surfaces and that, in places, this is visible on the Earth's surface.

PLENARY
Discuss with the children why some rocks are more exposed than others, identify reasons why soil may have been eroded from the rock surface.

OUTCOME
● Can explain some rock is exposed due to erosion and the structure of the Earth's crust.

Lesson 7 ▪ Types of soil

Objectives
● To know there are different kinds of soil.
● To know that there is rock beneath soil.

Vocabulary
bedrock, humus, soil, subsoil, topsoil

RESOURCES
Main activity: A piece of rock; some crushed rock; a container of soil; a container of water and a dead plant (a weed); paper; pens; pencils.
Group activities: 1 Soil samples; hand lenses; dishes or shallow trays.
2 Secondary sources of information.

BACKGROUND
Soil is a mixture of tiny pieces of rock that have become mixed with decaying plants. This decaying vegetation becomes a substance called 'humus'. The humus sticks all the particles together and absorbs water. This mixture slowly changes and becomes a habitat for plants and minibeasts. Just as there are different rock types, there are also different soil types. The different types of soil are produced depending on the rock types that are underlying the area. As you dig down into the ground, you go through different layers of soil, each slightly different in composition. In Britain, you are likely to find three layers: topsoil, which is the decomposed remains of living things mixed with tiny rock particles; subsoil, which is larger pieces of rock with less decaying plant life; and bedrock, which is the rock from which the soil is made. Each different layer then has different amounts of rock and water in it thus making them different colours and textures.

STARTER
Take into the classroom a piece of rock, some crushed rock, a container of soil, a container of water and a dead plant (a weed). Ask the children if they can think how these things are all linked. Talk about the possible links that the children suggest.

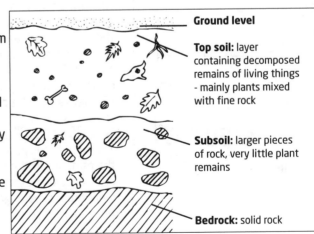

Ground level

Top soil: layer containing decomposed remains of living things - mainly plants mixed with fine rock

Subsoil: larger pieces of rock, very little plant remains

Bedrock: solid rock

MAIN ACTIVITY
Introduce the idea of how the soil was created. Ask the children to help you to put the items in order to show how soil is made. This should be: rocks become the crushed rocks, to which the decaying plant material and water is added, resulting in the soil. Ask the children to draw a series of illustrations to explain how soil is formed. Remind them of the importance of washing their hands after handling any soil samples.

Differentiation
Because of the nature of the activities in this lesson differentiation is largely by outcome.

GROUP ACTIVITIES

1 Ask the children to collect soil samples carefully from the school grounds. Perhaps the children could bring samples from their own gardens. (In an urban area you may need to provide trays of local soils for the children to use.) Ask the children to describe each type of soil and how they differ from those found in the school grounds.

2 Ask the children to use secondary sources to investigate the recognised soil types. Can they find sufficient information to draw an illustration showing the different layers of soil to be found under the ground? This could become a group collage picture.

ASSESSMENT

Through scrutiny of the children's work, assess their level of understanding. All of the children should be able to describe how soil lies on top of rock and most should recognise that there are different types of soil.

PLENARY

Use illustrations to show and talk about how soil can be made up of several different layers of different colours.

OUTCOMES

- Can describe how soil lies on top of rock.
- Can recognise that there are different kinds of soil.

LINKS

Geography: investigating our local area.

Lesson 8 ◗ Soil observation

Objective
To know that different soils have different-sized particles and different colours.

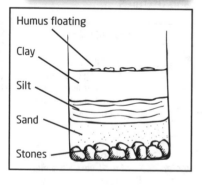

Humus floating
Clay
Silt
Sand
Stones

RESOURCES

Soil samples from Lesson 7; plastic beakers; water; paper; pens; pencils.

MAIN ACTIVITY

Use the different soil samples collected from different locations. Put approximately 5cm of one sample in a clear plastic beaker. Fill the beaker with water, stir, and leave the solution to settle (this may take a couple of days). Different groups of children can look at the different soil samples. As the water clears and the materials settle you should begin to see different layers of particles, with the heavier ones generally settled at the very bottom. Ask the children to record the results for each soil sample by drawing what they see. You may want to provide photocopies of an outline of a beaker for the children to record their observations on.

ASSESSMENT

Through discussion and observation, assess the children's ability to compare the particles in the soil. Most should be able to explain the observable differences. They should be able to describe how darker soils usually contain more humus; pale, gritty soils may be very sandy, while reddish soils with fine particles tend to be clay-based.

PLENARY

Discuss the different layers with the children and compare the contents from the different soil samples.

Differentiation
Differentiate by outcome.

OUTCOME

- Can compare soils in terms of particles and colour.

Lesson 9 ▪ Separating soil particles

● To understand that particles of differing sizes can be separated by the use of sieves.

RESOURCES
Wholemeal seeded flour; a range of sieves with different-sized holes. (These may range from a garden sieve to a cook's sieve.) Sieves can also be made using plastic pots or containers with holes punctured into the base using different sized tools or nails.

BACKGROUND
Rock and stone excavated from a quarry is brought out in a huge range of shapes and sizes. For this to be useful it needs to be sorted and graded to ensure consistency of size. This often requires the rocks to be broken, crushed or ground to an appropriate size. The sorting and grading takes place in a series of grids, grills, sieves or filters, which allows stone of a particular size to be separated out. This is important to the way in which these rocks are used. For example, if you are using gravel as a pathway the aggregate needs to be of a generally uniform size, likewise it would be difficult to use sand if there were large pieces of sandstone in it.

STARTER
Talk to the children about a problem you have been presented with. Somehow the local DIY store had a mix up in its deliveries and has unfortunately now got lots of different sizes of sand, gravel and stone mixed together. They have asked if the class can suggest some method of sorting out the mixture. Ask the children to share their ideas about how the large and small particles could be separated. You may like to demonstrate the time-consuming task of separating these by hand as an encouragement to the children to consider using sieves.

MAIN ACTIVITY
Talk about different types of sieves and how the sieving and grading process works, by demonstrating sieving something like wholemeal, seeded flour using sieves with different sized holes. The sieved flour products can then be clearly presented, sorted into groups of different sizes.

GROUP ACTIVITIES
1 Give the children the prepared sand and gravel mixture and have available a selection of sieves with different-sized holes. The children should then sieve and classify by size the materials they have.
2 Ask the children to prepare a poster in a collage style to illustrate and record the activity. The poster should indicate the initial problem and explain in simple illustrated steps how the process was carried out.

ASSESSMENT
Through discussion and observation, assess the level of understanding of how particles of differing sizes can be separated. Assess understanding of the methodology and equipment used and how this skill and process can be used in other ways. Most children should understand this process quite well.

Differentiation
Differentiation can be by the level of support given to the children both during the practical and recording stages. Alternatively, children could be given a simpler or more complex mixture of materials that require fewer or more sieves.

PLENARY
Ask the children to share their outcomes and to explain the process of sieving. Discuss ways in which this process can be applied in other areas such as in the garden and in the kitchen. This could also be extended to the ways in which foods, are graded, particularly fruit and vegetables.

OUTCOME
● Can understand that particles of differing sizes can be separated by the use of sieves.

Lesson 10 ▪ Growing seeds in different soils

Objectives
● To use simple apparatus to measure volumes of liquids and to measure time.
● To recognise when a test is unfair.

RESOURCES

Main teaching activity: Pictures of rainy days and flooding; soil samples from Lesson 7 plus extra samples; clay and sand; water; beakers; a plastic tray, a timer.
Group activity: Pots; soil samples; cress seeds; copies of photocopiable page 116 (also 'Growing seeds in different soils' (red), available on the CD-ROM); paper; pens; pencils.

BACKGROUND

Different soils and subsoils have different properties: some are fine, some are gritty and open and some are more solid with finer particles that stick together. These different soil types allow the water that falls on them to drain away at different rates. When it rains, you will notice how the water lies for longer in some areas than in others. This is often related to the soil type and its permeability (its ability to allow water through). Clay soils, for example, are not very permeable, whereas sand drains quickly.

STARTER

Talk to the children about rainy days and flooding and show them some pictures. Ask: *Why do you think the water stays on some surfaces longer than others?* Talk about the effects of such flooding and ask them to think about some of the times when they may have experienced playing on the beach or in sand and ask them to describe what happens to water on sand.

MAIN ACTIVITY

Demonstrate how we can show that different soils have different qualities of permeability, by pouring water simultaneously through two different soil samples . Use the clay and sand for the demonstration. Use different amounts of water for each and also do not give equal time to allow the water to drain through. Ask the children if they think that the test was a fair test. Encourage them to identify that you should use equal amounts of water and allow equal time for the water to drain through. Talk about how this can be tested in real life when growing plants.

GROUP ACTIVITIES

Distribute photocopiable page 116 and ask the children to follow the instructions carefully. They should plant cress seeds in two different types of soil and care for them both equally well. A record of their work can be kept on a simple storyboard.

ASSESSMENT

Scrutiny of the children's work and your questioning will help you to assess the children's ability to identify an investigation that is not a fair test and one that is a fair test. Ask questions such as: *Did you use the same amount of water for each plant? Why? Did you use the same amount of soil? Why? How was this fair or unfair?*

Differentiation
This task could be used as a means of assessing the children's ability to identify when a test is unfair and to carry out a fair test. Differentiate by outcome.

PLENARY

Give children the time to look at each other's work and to share their findings. Reinforce the concept of permeability and ask the children how they could improve areas where water does not drain away very quickly. Explain how plants need the right amount of water - neither too much (waterlogged soil is cold and airless) nor too little.

OUTCOMES
● Can use simple apparatus to measure volumes of liquids and to measure time.
● Can recognise when a test is unfair.

Lesson 11 ◗ Testing soil permeability

Objectives
● To plan a fair test.
● To make and record measurements of time and volume of water.
● To use results to make comparisons, and draw and explain conclusions.

Vocabulary
permeability, permeable, drainage, waterlogged

RESOURCES ◉
Main activity: Soil samples from Lesson 7 plus extra samples; clay and sand; water; beakers; a plastic tray; a timer.
Group activity: Soil samples from Lesson 7 plus extra samples; clay and sand; water; beakers; funnels; filter paper or paper towels; a plastic tray; a timer; paper; copies of photocopiable pages 96 and 97 from Unit 3c, (also 'Investigation - 2' (red) and 'Investigation - 3' (red)), available on the CD-ROM), pens; pencils.

BACKGROUND
This investigation is a fair test into the permeability of different types of soils and follows on from Lesson 10. Permeability is a term that is used to describe materials that have holes or pores that let water in. In geological terms it is the ability of rock to transmit fluids such as water. However, whilst all rocks can be said to be permeable, some are more so than others. This is dependent on the size of the grains that make up the rock. When the grains are large, such as in sandstone and limestone, the rock is highly permeable. When the grains are small and tightly packed there is less room for water to get through, making the rock much less permeable. The same principle applies to soils. Highly permeable soils such as sandy, loamy soils are those that have a coarse texture and therefore many holes and pores that water can flow through. Less permeable soils, such as those containing clay, tend to have fewer holes and therefore do not allow water to flow through as easily.

STARTER
This is a good opportunity to bring together aspects of previous lessons on the way in which the characteristics of rocks determine their use and the permeability investigation. Links could be made in terms of the ways in which some rocks are less permeable and are therefore more suitable to be used, for example, in roofing and building. Discuss with the children how we can test for permeability and recap the lesson on investigations that are clearly unfair in the nature of the test.

MAIN ACTIVITY
Talk with the children about fair testing. Ensure that they are aware of how to make sure that their investigation is a fair test and that only one thing at a time should be changed and that everything else should remain the same. The children could share their ideas about how to carry out this investigation before planning and carrying it out in groups. You may want to agree to all use the same method and for each group to test just one of the soil samples. Alternatively, you could let each group use their own method to test several soil samples. Ensure that the children understand how they are going to measure the amount of water poured over the soil samples, the amount collected and the time taken for this to happen.

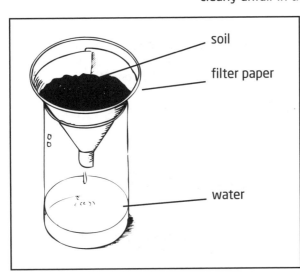

soil

filter paper

water

Differentiation
Some children will continue to need support particularly in the planning of the investigation while others should be moving towards a greater degree of independence. You might also want to differentiate the way in which the children report their findings. Some children may be able to report their findings without the support of the photocopiable sheet.

GROUP ACTIVITY

The children should devise together, with support, a fair test to investigate permeability of soil types. Ensure the children consider what factors will make the investigation a fair test. The test should involve pouring equal amounts of water over equal quantities of soil and timing how long it takes for the water to drain through, or how much water drains through in a given time. On this or a future occasion, the children should carry out their tests on the soil samples. The children could record their findings in a table format using photocopiable pages 96 and 97 as a basis for their report.

ASSESSMENT

Scrutiny of the children's work and your questioning will help you to assess the children's ability to plan and carry out a fair test. Ask questions such as: *Did you use the same amount of water each time? Why? Did you use the same amount of soil? Why? Can you explain what you were trying to find out?*

PLENARY

Bring the groups together to share, compare and discuss their results. Display the results in a class table and encourage the children to consider the data and begin to draw conclusions. You may need to support and encourage the children in this. It is important also to ask them to explain the conclusions they come to, drawing on the evidence shown in the data collected.

OUTCOMES
● Can plan a fair test.
● Can make and record measurements of time and volume of water.
● Can use results to make comparisons, and draw and explain conclusions.

Lesson 12 ◗ Assessment

Objectives
To assess the children's knowledge and understanding of rocks and soils.

RESOURCES ◉
Starter: Objects brought from home (less familiar than the usual classroom items).
Assessment activities: 1 Copies of photocopiable page 117 (also 'Assessment – 1' (red), available on the CD-ROM); pens; pencils. **2** Copies of photocopiable page 118 (also 'Assessment – 2' (red); available on the CD-ROM); pens; pencils.
ICT link: 'Rocks and soils' interactive, on the CD-ROM.

STARTER

Ask the children to bring in one simple object from home (a letter home may ensure they do not bring valuables to school). Ask them to help you to sort the objects according to the materials they are made from. Discuss alternative groupings. Encourage the children to begin to identify the natural raw materials that are used in some of the objects.

ASSESSMENT ACTIVITY 1

Distribute copies of photocopiable page 117 and ask the children to complete the sheet unaided. The tasks are designed to give the children the opportunity to identify the different types of rocks and how soil is formed.

ICT LINK ◉

Display 'Rocks and Soils -1' on an interactive whiteboard and complete as a whole-class activity using the drawing tools on the CD-ROM.

ANSWERS

1.

I was formed from a volcanic eruption.	I am igneous rock.
I was formed from small particles of animals and plants.	I am sedimentary rock.
I was formed when rocks were squeezed together.	I am metamorphic rock.

2. Examples may include:
Igneous: granite, pumice and basalt;
Metamorphic: marble and slate;
Sedimentary: Chalk, limestone, sandstone and shale.

LOOKING FOR LEVELS

All the children should be able to identify the rock types from their descriptions and most should be able to give examples of rocks. Most should also be able to give an explanation of how soil is formed.

ASSESSMENT ACTIVITY 2

Distribute copies of photocopiable page 118 and ask the children to complete the sheet unaided.

ANSWERS

1. The brick, drinking glass and jewellery are made from (processed) rock.
2. Three pictures to show uses of rock could include: stone walls, dressed building stone, roads, bricks, glass, walls, monuments and so on.
3. Soil is formed when crushed rock is mixed with humus and the mixture is bound together with water.

ICT LINK 🔘

Children can use the 'Rocks and soils' interactive to sort materials into groups according to whether or not they are made from rock.

LOOKING FOR LEVELS

All the children should be able to identify which objects are made from rocks, and most should be able to identify another use of rock. Some will identify more than one other use and some will be able to explain how soil is formed.

PLENARY

Discuss the Assessment activities and address any further misunderstandings. Reinforce the link between rock and how soil is made.

PHOTOCOPIABLE

Growing seeds in different soils

■ You are going to grow some cress seeds in two different soils.

■ Put different types of soil into each of the two pots. Label them A and B.

■ Sprinkle the seeds onto the soil and gently press them in.

■ Water the seeds carefully before putting the pots on a window sill. Make sure you give each the same amount of water.

■ Draw a storyboard to show what you have done so far.

■ Keep an eye on the seeds, water them regularly and equally.

■ Predict in which soil the seeds will grow the best and why.

_____

_____

■ Draw a storyboard of the pots as the cress grows.

A	A	A
B	B	B

Assessment – 1

1. What type of rock am I? Match the sentences together.

| I was formed from a volcanic eruption. | I am a metamorphic rock. |

| I was formed from small particles of animals and plants. | I am igneous rock. |

| I was formed when rocks were squeezed together. | I am sedimentary rock. |

2. Give some examples of these rock types.

Igneous _____

_____

_____

Metamorphic _____

_____

_____

Sedimentary _____

_____

_____

3. Label this diagram to show the layers beneath the ground and how soil is formed.

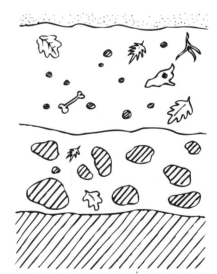

Illustration © Kirsty Wilson

Assessment – 2

1. Circle the objects that are made from rocks.

2. Can you think of some more ways that we use rocks?
Draw three pictures.

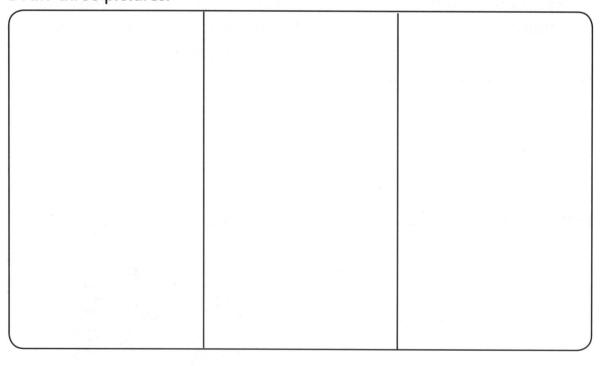

3. Explain how soil is formed. These words will help you.

humus	crushed rock	water

CHAPTER 6 Magnets and springs

Lesson	Objectives	Main activity	Group activities	Plenary	Outcomes
Lesson 1 Forces and motion	• To ascertain the children's current knowledge of forces and motion from their work in Key Stage 1/Primary 1–3.	Concept mapping.	Drawing concept cartoons. Looking at magnetic and non-magnetic materials.	Sharing ideas and asking questions.	• Teacher can assess the level of the children in the class. • Teacher can arrange children in appropriate class groups.
Lesson 2 Magnets	• To know that there are forces between magnets which push and pull. • To make observations.	Looking at the poles of magnets.	Completing a worksheet on magnets. Looking at magnets and their properties. Investigating repulsion and attraction in magnets.	Agreeing a general rule for the attraction and repulsion properties of magnets.	• Can demonstrate how a magnet is attracted and repelled by another magnet. • Can make observations.
Lesson 3 Magnetic materials	• To know that some materials are magnetic and others are not. • To be able to make observations and comparisons.	Testing materials for attraction by a magnet.	Testing different types of metal for magnetic attraction. Researching magnetic attraction in metals.	Comparing results and research.	• Can recognise magnetic and non-magnetic materials.
Lesson 4 Uses of magnets	• To know that magnets have uses.	Looking at the uses of magnets.	Using secondary sources to explore uses of magnets. Writing a 'Guide to…' the uses of magnets.	Drawing conclusions about the range of uses of magnets.	• Can describe a range of uses of magnets.
Lesson 5 Magnet strength test	• To know that magnets can be tested for strength. • To be able to plan and carry out a fair test.	Planning an investigation to test the strength of magnets.	Investigating the strength of magnets. Making magnets.	Discussing findings and feedback on ensuring a fair test was carried out.	• Can consider what makes a fair test. • Can use simple equipment safely. • Can describe their observations using scientific vocabulary.
Lesson 6 Do magnets work through materials?	• To investigate whether magnets will work through a range of materials.	Planning an investigation to test which materials magnets will work through.	Testing a range of materials to see if magnets will work through them. Writing a poem or rap to report findings.	Discussing the investigation and sharing poems.	• Can investigate whether magnets will work through a range of materials.
Lesson 7 Springs	• To know that springs and elastic bands exert forces.	Brainstorming knowledge of springs.	Experiencing and describing a selection of springs and elastic bands. Looking at the direction of the forces exerted by springs and elastic bands.	Demonstration of push and pull forces in springs.	• Can recognise the pushes and pulls made by springs. • Can recognise the forces exerted by a stretched elastic band.
Lesson 8 Jack-in-the-box	• To know that when a spring is compressed downwards and released a force is exerted upwards.	Handling and exploring jack-in-the-boxes and relating them to work on springs. Role-playing being a jack-in-the-box.	Making a simple jack-in-the-box.	Explaining how their Jack-in-the-boxes works.	• Knows that when a spring is compressed downwards and released a force is exerted upwards.
Lesson 9 Uses of springs	• To know that springs are used in a variety of ways.	Completing a survey of springs.		Sharing of survey findings.	• Can describe how springs are used in a variety of ways.
Lesson 10 Springs in action	• To investigate the forces exerted by springs and elastic bands.	Designing and making a simple ballista.		Demonstration by the children.	• Know that an elastic band can exert a force. • Can recognise that a force acts in a particular direction.
Lesson 11 Testing a rubber band	• To know that the force exerted by an elastic band depends on how much it is stretched. • To make observations, measure in standard units and to draw conclusions from results.	Using simple catapults to project a missile.	Investigation using a flat board catapult into the relationship between stretch and the force exerted by an elastic band. Making a simple paddle boat.	Children's explanation of their findings and the relationships.	• Can describe the relationship between the amount an elastic band stretches and the force that it exerts. • Can make observations, measure in standard units and draw conclusions from results.

Lesson	Objectives	Main activity	Group activities	Plenary	Outcomes
Lesson 1 Forces and motion	• To ascertain the children's current knowledge of forces and motion from their work in Key Stage 1/Primary 1–3.	Concept mapping.	Drawing concept cartoons. Looking at magnetic and non-magnetic materials.	Sharing ideas and asking questions.	• Teacher can assess the level of the children in the class. • Teacher can arrange children in appropriate class groups.
Lesson 2 Magnets	• To know that there are forces between magnets which push and pull. • To make observations.	Looking at the poles of magnets.	Completing a worksheet on magnets. Looking at magnets and their properties. Investigating repulsion and attraction in magnets.	Agreeing a general rule for the attraction and repulsion properties of magnets.	• Can demonstrate how a magnet is attracted and repelled by another magnet. • Can make observations.

Assessment	Objectives	Activity 1	Activity 2
Lesson 15	• To assess the children's knowledge of the properties of magnets, types of forces and the uses of springs.	Describing bar magnets and attraction and repulsion.	Identifying pushes and pulls and the uses of springs.

SC1 SCIENTIFIC ENQUIRY

Which cotton reel travels the furthest?

LEARNING OBJECTIVES AND OUTCOMES
● Decide how to find the answer to the question.
● Decide what equipment and materials to use.
● Make a fair test.
● Take action to control risk.
● Review work.

ACTIVITY
Use cotton reels and elastic bands to build elastic-band-powered vehicles. The children should test the vehicle to see how many turns are needed to make the vehicle move.

Record the number of winds and the distance the vehicles travel. The children can present their findings in an appropriate way - written, diagrammatically or verbally.

LESSON LINKS
This Sc1 activity forms an integral part of Lesson 12, Driving force.

Lesson 1 ▸ Forces and motion

Objectives
● To ascertain the children's current knowledge of forces and motion from their work in Key Stage1/Primary1-3.

RESOURCES
Main activity: Flipchart or board; pens.
Group activities: 1 and **2** Large sheets of paper; pens; pencils.

BACKGROUND
In Key Stage 1/Primary 1-3 the children will have had the opportunity to become familiar with some of the basic principles of magnets when investigating the properties of some materials. They will probably not have used or considered magnets in terms of a force which can make something move, stop or change direction or shape.

STARTER
Begin the lesson by talking to the children about work they will have covered in Key Stage 1/Primary 1-3. Explain that they will be building on what they learned then and discovering a little more about forces.

MAIN ACTIVITY
The children should work in small groups to develop a concept map of forces and, in particular, ways of making things move and stop. They should express all their ideas and knowledge about the subject and then attempt to join their ideas with lines and arrows to produce a map. A large class concept map can be drawn using the groups' ideas. Some of the key ideas, which are relevant to Key Stage 1/Primary 1-3 will include: forces make things move; forces can make things go faster, change direction or slow down; there are many types of force including friction, pushes, pulls, gravity and magnetism; and magnets attract some materials but not others.

GROUP ACTIVITIES
1 Ask the children to draw a concept cartoon to show that magnets: attract certain materials, do not attract some materials, can attract each other, and have uses.

TEL. 0151 231 5216/5299 ... LIVERPOOL L17 6BU

Differentiation
Some children will need prompting by an adult when compiling the concept map. Other children will be able to work independently to annotate their concept cartoon in detail.

2 Write two headings on the board or flipchart: 'Attracted by magnets' and 'Not attracted by magnets'. Ask the children to copy the headings and write the names of as many materials that they can think of in each column, giving very careful consideration to their choices.

ASSESSMENT

In using the Group activities look for evidence that the children have some understanding of forces, motion and magnetism. Most children will know that pushes and pulls make things move and most should be able to recognise that some materials are attracted by magnets while other materials are not. It is unlikely any will have connected the two and understood that magnets exert forces, although they may suggest that magnets can make things move.

PLENARY

Share ideas and encourage the children to begin to formulate their own questions about what they think they would like to find out about.

OUTCOMES

- Teacher can assess the level of the children in the class.
- Teacher can arrange children in appropriate class groups.

Lesson 2 ▪ Magnets

Objectives
- To know that there are forces between magnets which push and pull.
- To make observations.

Vocabulary
attract, magnet, magnetism, north, poles, repel, south

RESOURCES 💿

Introduction: A magnetic travel game.
Main activity: A selection of bar magnets of different strengths, preferably one or more per child.
Group activities: 1 The magnets from the Main teaching activity, photocopiable page 140 (also 'Magnets' (red), available on the CD-ROM).
2 Strong, thin thread, pieces of polystyrene (for example, from packing, cut into pieces big enough to sit a magnet on); trays of water.

PREPARATION

Check the magnets are sufficiently magnetic to repel and attract one another. School magnets often become demagnetised!

BACKGROUND

It is difficult to provide a definition of magnetism other than to say that magnetism is a force that attracts certain materials to it. Iron, cobalt, nickel and their alloys such as steel and alnico are all attracted to magnets, whereas all other materials do not have any magnetic attraction.

Magnetism, unlike most other forces except gravity, can work from a distance. A force is a push or a pull: it can make something slow down, speed up or change direction or shape. Magnetism can do just that. Since magnets come in different strengths their effects can be similarly different. A strong magnet can be effective over a much greater distance or through much thicker non-magnetic materials. Magnets of the same strength can, like all equal forces, counterbalance each other: if you placed a piece of iron between two magnets of equal strength the iron would remain stationary. If on the other hand one magnet was brought closer, its magnetic force would have a greater effect and the iron would move.

Every magnet, whatever its shape, has a north pole and a south pole. It is at these poles that the magnetic force is concentrated. When the poles of the two magnets are brought together, like poles (two north poles or two south poles) repel each other, and unlike poles (a north pole and a south pole) attract.

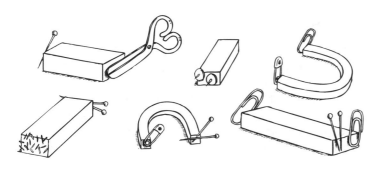

Magnets can be made by bringing iron into close contact with a magnet, by stroking it with another magnet or by inducing magnetism with a current of electricity. Heating, hammering and banging magnets can cause the domains to become jumbled again and so the material will lose its magnetism. It is important then that magnets are treated carefully, not dropped or damaged, and because magnetic properties are used in televisions, cassette tapes and computer floppy disks it is also important to keep these well away from the effects of magnets.

The Earth itself acts like a huge bar magnet. Perhaps confusingly, the Earth's geographic North Pole is magnetically a south pole. This is because the Earth's magnetic north pole attracts the north poles of magnets – because unlike poles attract, it must be that the Earth's magnetic north is really a south-seeking pole. It must also be remembered that the geographic North Pole and the magnetic north pole are not at the same point on the Earth.

STARTER

Begin the lesson using a children's magnetic travel game or magnetic letters and numbers as a visual aid to encourage the children to begin to think about magnets. Ask them why the letters appear to stick on the board and why the pieces on the travel game do not fall off. Most should be able to tell you that they are magnets or magnetic. Ask the children if they can think of the words we use when a magnet 'sticks'. Introduce the words 'attract' and 'repel' (although we shall see that repel in magnetic terms has a more active effect than simply 'not sticking').

MAIN ACTIVITY

Distribute magnets to the children and ask them to tell you about the magnets they have. Talk about and introduce the idea that there are two ends to a magnet called poles. These poles, indicated by N and S, are the north and south poles of the magnet. Ask the children to work in pairs to see what happens when these poles are brought together. Ask them to try like poles and unlike poles. Discuss the outcomes

GROUP ACTIVITIES

1 Distribute copies of photocopiable page 140 and ask the children to read through the sheet with you, and then complete it by experimenting with the magnets. If resources are short, let the children work in pairs or fours with two magnets.
2 Let the children investigate repulsion and attraction further. Different groups could try suspending a magnet so that it spins freely, then bringing another magnet towards it. Repeat at each end of the magnet. They could also try floating a magnet on a small piece of polystyrene in a tray of water. Again bring the poles together in different combinations.

In each case, the children should observe what happens and attempt to answer: *In which direction does the magnet point when allowed to move freely? Can you make up a general rule based on what you have found out about magnets repelling and attracting?*

ASSESSMENT

Mark the children's work for evidence of understanding. The diagrams should indicate that like poles repel and unlike poles attract.

Differentiation
Some children may prefer to record their findings diagrammatically. Other children can go on to record their findings in writing.

PLENARY

Bring the children together to discuss the activities during the lesson and for them to share with each other their ideas for a general rule about repulsion and attraction. Attempt to come to an agreed statement that can be used to reinforce the aims of the lesson, such as: 'When we brought two ends of magnets together that were the same, they repelled each other.' And 'When we brought two ends of magnets together that were different they were attracted to each other.' Use the work carried out during the Group activities to reinforce these statements.

OUTCOMES

● Can demonstrate how a magnet is attracted and repelled by another magnet.
● Can make observations.

Lesson 3 ▪ Magnetic materials

Objectives
● To know that some materials are magnetic and others are not.
● To be able to make observations and comparisons.

Vocabulary
attract, magnet, magnetised, magnetism, north, poles, repel, south

RESOURCES

Main activity: A collection of different magnetic and non-magnetic materials (in trays); magnets.
Group activities: 1 A collection of objects as for the Main teaching activity; magnets; large sheets of paper; pens; pencils. **2** Secondary sources of information.

PREPARATION

Gather the materials and magnets together and have these to hand.

BACKGROUND

Some materials cannot be made into magnets and similarly are neither attracted to nor repelled by them. Magnets attract metals, but not all metals. Be aware that in carrying out investigations into which materials are attracted by a magnet and which are not, it is important to remember that the only materials attracted are iron, steel, nickel and cobalt. Some objects may be made out of an alloy, which contains large amounts of iron. Some coins, for example, are magnetic because of this, while others have less or no iron and so are not magnetic. Similarly, things which you may think should not be attracted to magnets may have a coating under which is steel. So everything may not be as it seems.

The area around a magnet that experiences the effects of the magnetic force is called the 'magnetic field'. While the magnetic field cannot be seen, its effects can. By using iron filings or a plotting compass it is possible to see the extent of the magnetic field. This force exerted by a magnet is used widely (see Lesson 4) but, as we have already seen, its effects can only be felt by certain materials.

STARTER

Revise magnets repelling and attracting. Ask the children if they can tell you what sort of materials (or objects, such as the fridge) magnets are attracted to. Compile a list of suggestions on the board. Talk about the difference between 'repulsion' (a push away) and 'non-attraction' (no reaction). Tell the children that in this lesson they will be finding out about materials that are magnetic and those that are not.

MAIN ACTIVITY

Write the headings 'Attracted by magnets' and 'Not attracted by magnets' on the board or flipchart. Distribute large sheets of paper, the magnets and selections of various materials/objects. Ask the children to test each item to see if it is attracted to the magnet or not. This could be done in groups, or each child's results could be collated on to a large sheet of paper using the headings you have written. Provide each group of children with a tray containing the necessary resources (see above). These trays could be different and passed around after a given time. Each child in the group could have a responsibility, such as object selector, material identifier, predictor, tester, recorder. The children could change responsibilities so that each gets a 'turn'.

GROUP ACTIVITIES

1 Distribute further large sheets of paper. The children should investigate further items in the classroom and around school. This time, however, they should concentrate specifically on items that are metal or appear to be metal. Children record their thoughts about the objects that are and are not attracted by the magnet.

2 The children could use secondary sources to try to research which metals are attracted by magnets and which are not. Aluminium and tin cans are good examples.

ASSESSMENT

Looking at the children's work will give a good indication of whether the children have learned that some materials are attracted by magnets or not. Discussion during the Group activities will support this judgement.

PLENARY

Bring the children together and discuss the list they have made. Compare it with the lists written earlier. Those who have been researching metals could feed back their findings.

OUTCOME

- Can recognise magnetic and non-magnetic materials.

LINKS

Unit 3c: Characteristics of materials.

Lesson 4 ▪ Uses of magnets

Objective
- To know that magnets have uses.

Vocabulary
burglar alarms, compasses, door latches, metal detectors, telephones, vending machines

RESOURCES

Main activity: Flipchart or board; pens; examples of objects that use magnetism to work (preferably that can be taken apart to expose the magnet, such as electric bells, motors, loudspeakers); an old cassette recorder and/or computer disc drive (try car boot sales).
Group activities: 1 and **2** Paper; pens; pencils; secondary sources of information such as books; videos; CD-ROMs or the internet.

PREPARATION

Ensure that the secondary resources are available and contain appropriate information. Search for suitable websites.

BACKGROUND

Magnets and the characteristics and properties of magnetism are used in a wide variety of ways all around us, though the children are unlikely to recognise many of them. The children need only to know that these items use magnets, not all the science of how - keep it simple.

Bells, motors and loudspeakers use electricity to make magnetism. In an electric bell, a magnet attracts the bell clapper. Another major use of magnetism is in the recording of data. Magnetic tape is used in tape

Differentiation
Some children may need support in making their list. Others should be able to undertake some independent research which could be presented with annotated diagrams.

recorders where patterns are applied to the tape by the tape head. On replay, this magnetic patterned tape causes an electrical signal in the head that then reproduces the sound. Data on computer hard disks is recorded in the same way. (CD-ROMs are different, however, and are recorded and reproduced using a tiny laser beam.) Other uses of magnets include: burglar alarms, telephones, door latches, vending machines, metal detectors, moving large quantities of iron and steel, separating materials, compasses.

STARTER
Reinforce the concepts covered so far. Ask the children if they can think of any uses for magnets. If they have difficulty, show them again your magnetic travel game, or magnetic letters.

MAIN ACTIVITY
Show the children any resources you have collected together: an electric bell, a (classroom) motor, or an old loudspeaker. Show the children that these all have magnets in them to make them work. Talk about cassette tape and how they use magnets to record data. Highlight the dangers of putting magnets near such items. (You will lose the data stored on the tape.) Begin to compile a list of uses for magnets.

GROUP ACTIVITIES
1 Ask the children to write down all the uses of magnets you have discussed and then to add more from any available secondary sources of information.
2 Tell the children to go on to use the secondary sources to investigate one or two uses of magnets in more detail according to their abilities. They could present their findings as an information sheet or poster as a 'Guide to...' the uses of magnets.

ASSESSMENT
The children's posters will indicate their level of understanding. All the children should be able to find some uses for magnets.

PLENARY
Come back together and discuss the uses that the children have found. Draw a conclusion about the use of magnets in terms of being widespread - if hidden - and very important in a range of everyday objects.

OUTCOME
● Can describe a range of uses for magnets.

Lesson 5 ▪ Magnet strength test

Objectives
● To know that magnets can be tested for strength.
● To be able to plan and carry out a fair test.

Vocabulary
horseshoe magnet, bar magnet

RESOURCES
Main activity: Paper; pens; pencils.
Group activities: 1 Bar magnets; horseshoe magnets; paper clips; paper; card; cloth; writing and drawing materials. **2** Bar magnets; steel pins or nails; paper clips.

BACKGROUND
Magnets come in different strengths depending on what they are made from, how they are magnetised and how they are kept. Not all magnets are the same: iron is usually easier to magnetise, but loses its magnetism much more quickly and is used to form temporary magnets. Steel, however, retains its magnetism much better and is used to make permanent magnets. More expensive magnets are likely to last longer than cheaper ones, but if

Differentiation
In this lesson the children could support each other in mixed-ability groups.

magnets are not treated with care they will lose their magnetism. The incorrect storage, heating and hitting of magnets will all cause damage.

Strong magnets can attract other magnetic materials over larger distances, through non-magnetic materials and through a vacuum. The strongest area of the magnetic field is at the poles; the area down the length of, a bar magnet is generally much weaker.

STARTER
Remind the children that last lesson they were looking at how magnets have a wide variety of uses. Ask the children if they think, therefore, that all magnets are the same. Talk about magnets being of varying sizes and strengths. Ask the children if they can think of a fair way to test a magnet to find out how strong it is. Collect suggestions.

MAIN ACTIVITY
Together, plan an investigation to test the strength of the magnets you have. The children could look at: the number of paper clips which can be attracted in a line; whether the size of the magnet affects its strength; which are stronger – horseshoe or bar magnets; how close something needs to be to a magnet before it is attracted; the thickness of materials through which a magnet can attract, for example, layers of paper, card or cloth.

The class could work in groups to plan their investigations into one of these different factors. Write on the board or flipchart a writing frame to help the children with the format and to direct their thinking under the following headings: 'My question'; 'What I will do to find the answer'; 'What I will need'; 'What I think will happen'. Highlight the importance of making this a fair test. They should then record appropriate details below the headings.

GROUP ACTIVITIES
1 In groups, the children should carry out their investigation, recording their work as they go along under headings such as: 'This is what I did', where they record how they carried out their test; 'This is what I found out' where they should draw up a table for results something like the one shown below; and 'This is what I now know' where they should write down what they have learned from this investigation. Write these headings on the board or flipchart for children to copy if need be.
2 Ask the children to use a bar magnet and a steel nail or needle to create a new magnet. (Make at least twenty strokes in the same direction with a magnet to magnetise the nail.) The group can test the new magnet's strength.

ASSESSMENT
Review the children's reports of their investigation, looking for their ability to plan and carry out the investigation and for their understanding that magnets can be tested for strength. Do they understand what they have done that makes this a fair test?

PLENARY
Discuss with the children the investigation they have carried out. Ask the children to explain what they have done, what they have found out and how they ensured a fair test.

Type of magnet	Number of paper clips

OUTCOMES
- Can consider what makes a fair test.
- Can use simple equipment safely.
- Can describe their observations using scientific vocabulary.

Lesson 6 ▪ Do magnets work through materials?

Objectives
● To investigate whether magnets will work through a range of materials.

RESOURCES

Magnets; paper clips; a variety of materials such as card, paper, fabrics, aluminium foil, thin wood, water, iron, sufficient for group work. You will also need a selection of magnetic games such as face disguises, table football, magnetic draughts or chess

BACKGROUND

As we have seen in earlier lessons magnets come in all shapes and sizes and have a variety of uses. This lesson looks at using magnets through other materials and encourages the children to consider which materials these may be. Materials are either attracted by magnets or not; however, even those materials that are not attracted by magnets may allow the force of magnet to be effective through it. For example, a piece of paper is not attracted by a magnet yet the magnetic field can still be observed and used through the paper. Clearly one of the factors that will be important in this is the thickness of the material and the nature of the material itself. Additionally, the strength of the magnet is important. These are factors that the children can become aware of and discuss during the investigation.

STARTER

Begin the lesson by recapping on previous learning in which the children will have had opportunity to learn about the way in which some materials can be attracted by magnets and others not. Ask the children to share their thoughts and ideas about which materials this may apply to and to make a list of 'Materials that are attracted by magnets'. They may also have had some opportunity to learn about some of the uses of magnets. Introduce the idea of using them in games. Share with the children a selection of games that make use of magnets and encourage them to consider how the magnets are used and the materials that the game is made from. Elicit from the children some understanding that for these games to work some of the materials do need to be attracted and others not. Talk about these materials and make a second list of 'Materials that magnets do not attract'.

MAIN ACTIVITY

Present the children with a challenge. Say that the manufacturers of these games would like them to test a range of materials that could be used in their games. Their task is to see if magnets will work through them. Show the children the selection of materials that you have gathered together. Encourage them to share their ideas about how they could carry out the test and which materials they think would pass the test and which would not. Reassure the children that when they are making these predictions there is not really a right or wrong answer, at this stage what is important is what they think. Having talked about a number of ways in which this investigation could be carried out, tell the children that they are going to work in groups and decide for themselves how to test each of the materials. However, they must ensure that they carry out this in a fair way.

GROUP ACTIVITY

Give each group samples of the materials, together with a magnet and a few paper clips. Tell the children that they have to make a prediction about and then test each of the materials. They should devise a simple table to enable them to do this. As a fun way of reporting their findings, ask the children to work together on writing a simple poem or rap. This does not need to rhyme but should enable the children to report on the materials.

ASSESSMENT
Through discussion and questioning, together with scrutiny of work, assess if the children were able to identify which materials allowed magnets to be used through them and which did not.

PLENARY
Bring the children together to discuss their investigations, how they completed the test and the outcomes. Draw some conclusions about the materials that they have tested and what feedback they should give to the magnetic games manufacturers.

They could also share their poems in groups, or individual pupils could present their poems to the class.

OUTCOME
- Can investigate whether magnets will work through a range of materials.

Differentiation
Some children may need support to compile a result table; you may want to give these children a prepared table to complete. They may also need some assistance writing the poem. You may want to give some starter phrases, lines to complete or a model to follow. Other children will be able to test a wider range of materials and should be able to work independently on devising the table and writing their poem.

Lesson 7 ⬤ Springs

Objective
- To know that springs and elastic bands exert forces.

Vocabulary
elastic band, exert, force, pull, push, spring

RESOURCES 💿
Main activity: Flipchart; paper; pens.
Group activities: 1 A collection of springs and elastic bands (for example, from the inside of ballpoint pens, from an old clock, from machinery, from an old push-chair or pram). **2** Springs; elastic bands; copies of photocopiable page 141 (also 'Springs' (red), available on the CD-ROM).

BACKGROUND
Forces exist all around us. A force acting on an object or body can make the object move, speed up, slow down, change direction, and can change the shape of the object.

There are several different types of forces, the two we are concerned with here are stretching and compression. The children will have already looked at forces in terms of push and pull, so these can now be introduced in terms of a stretching force being the same as a pull, and a compression force being the same as a push.

Springs of varying sizes have an equally varying range of uses, from the tiny spring in a ballpoint pen to the suspension springs on large vehicles, but all work in the same way. When a mass is hung from a spring, the force of gravity pulling on the mass pulls the spring and causes it to stretch. The spring itself can support this weight because it in turn exerts a pull force on the mass. This pull in the spring is called tension.

The opposite of stretching, in this sense, is compression. When a spring is compressed, a force is exerted by the spring on whatever is causing the compression and at the same time the mass compressing the spring is also exerting a force on it. For example, if you were to sit on a sprung chair your mass, together with gravity, would exert a downward force on the springs causing them to compress. At the same time, the springs would be exerting an upward force on you. When the two forces are equal you stop sinking into the chair and remain still: the upward force from the springs is effectively supporting you.

Springs, then, can exert two forces: a stretching force and a compression force. Elastic bands are slightly different. Springs stretch and compress because of the way the material has been shaped - the material the spring is made from only stretches to a limited extent. However, some materials do stretch rather more and still return to their original size when the force on them is removed. These materials are said to be elastic. While the spring may be said to have elastic properties, its material does not stretch as much as, rubber, for example. A rubber band is very elastic and will stretch when a

Differentiation

Group activity 2

For children who need support in Group activity 1, use 'Springs' (green) from the CD-ROM, which uses the terms 'push' and 'pull' rather than 'force'.

To extend children, use 'Springs' (blue), which includes an additional question about why it is difficult to repeat the push test with elastic bands.

force is exerted upon it. When the force is removed it will return to its original shape. This is not compression since the material is merely returning to its original shape. If you tried to exert a compression force upon a rubber band you would not succeed, since there is no useful or significant opposite force.

STARTER

Begin the lesson by looking at a simple retractable ballpoint pen. Ask the children if they know how the pen refill clicks in and out. Take it apart to investigate. Show the children the spring, ask them what it is and what they think it does.

MAIN ACTIVITY

Elicit from the children what they already know about forces. They should know in simple terms that a force is a push or a pull (or a twist or a squash, maybe), can make an object move, and then change speed and/or direction, and can change the shape of an object.

Talk about how springs can be used with a push or pull and that when we push or pull a spring we are exerting a force on it. Discuss also that the spring itself is exerting a force: this is easily felt pushing back when a spring is squashed. Ideas can be collated onto a simple class concept map on a large sheet of paper or the board.

GROUP ACTIVITIES

1 Distribute a selection of springs to the children for them to look at and handle. Ask them to pull and push the springs and to describe the direction of the force on their hands. The children should record their work with comments such as: 'When I stretch the spring, I feel a pull on my hand' or 'When I push the spring, it pushes on me'. Remind the children to take care when using springs - overstretched springs may break and could injure.

2 Distribute copies of photocopiable page 141 and read through it together. Explain the tasks to the children. Say that for every force, not just in springs, there is a force the opposite way. The sheet asks them to mark on the diagrams the direction of the forces exerted by themselves and by the spring.

ASSESSMENT

Discuss with the children their experiences of pushing and pulling the springs and elastic bands; try to encourage them to describe what they felt and to explain what is happening. Listen for use of appropriate vocabulary that shows understanding and knowledge of the exertion of a force. Looking at the children's work will also give an indication of understanding if the children have been able to mark the direction of the forces correctly on the worksheet.

PLENARY

Bring the children together at the end of the lesson and recap on the Group activities. Ask the children to demonstrate both types of force - pushes and pulls - and to begin to discuss how these forces are used.

OUTCOMES

- Can recognise the pushes and pulls made by springs.
- Can recognise the forces exerted by a stretched elastic band.

Lesson 8 ▪ Jack-in-the-box

Objectives

● To know that when a spring is compressed downwards and released a force is exerted upwards.

RESOURCES 💿

A selection of jack-in-the-boxes; a pogo stick; copies of photocopiable page 142 (also 'jack-in-the-box' (red), available on the CD-ROM) copied on to card.

BACKGROUND

Springs can come in one of two forms, they can either be a spiral coil of material or a concertina fold of material. They have essentially one of three functions: they can return something to a previous position, as in a jack-in-the-box; measure the force needed to stretch the spring, as in a spring balance; or store energy, as in a clockwork mechanism. This lesson focuses on the first. When a force is applied to a spring, be it a compression or stretching force, the make up of the material and the way in which it has been coiled or folded means that when that force is released there is a force that operates in the opposite direction. For example, if you squeeze a spring exerting a force downwards there is an opposite force that acts upwards when the spring is released. This happens vice versa - if you compressed a spring upwards, when released the force would be downwards. The jack-in-the-boxes and pogo sticks featured in this lesson work in this way.

STARTER

Begin the lesson by recapping on previous learning. Ask the children to recall the uses for springs. Have available a collection of springs for the children to handle. Talk about the way in which springs exert forces, remind them that springs can exert forces in two directions depending on whether they are compressed or stretched. If available, look at the way in which the spring in a pogo stick is compressed and then when released exerts a force in an upwards direction. You may want the children to experience this first hand. Talk about the forces exerted and illustrate this with small springs that the children can handle. Take care that they don't allow them to spring up into their faces.

MAIN ACTIVITY

Continue the lesson by showing and sharing with the children a jack-in-the-box. If you have access to several, give the children the opportunity to handle and explore these simple toys. Encourage them think about how the toy's mechanism operates and to relate this to the springs they have handled and the pogo stick experienced. To help them understand the principles behind springing upwards and exerting a force you could ask the children to role-play being a jack-in-the- Box. Encourage them to explain what it felt like and to share their understanding of the direction in which the force is being exerted. Compile a list of words that the children used to describe these activities.

GROUP ACTIVITY

Using photocopiable page 142 the children can make a jack-in-the-box of their own. They should use the long squared strip, folded in a concertina fashion, to make a spring. Encourage the children to try different sizes before determining which size of spring they would like to use. The net can be decorated in an appropriate way before being cut out and assembled, though take care that this does not become the main focus for this lesson. Ask the children to make up their box, ensuring that the lid is not glued down, then to assemble their jack-in-the-box. Encourage the children to evaluate their own designs and in a positive way those of others in their group.

ASSESSMENT

Through discussion and scrutiny of work, assess the children's understanding. Are they able to explain that there is a relationship between a downwards compression and the resultant upwards force?

PLENARY

Bring the children together to share their finished jack-in-the boxes. The children could explain how they work and the way in which the 'jack' is sprung out of the box. Ask the children to look for further examples of how the released force works in the opposite direction to the compression force at home and around school.

OUTCOME

● Knows that when a spring is compressed downwards and released a force is exerted upwards.

Lesson 9 ◗ Uses of springs

Objective
● To know that springs are used in a variety of ways.

RESOURCES

A collection of objects with springs; access to other parts of the school, secondary sources of information.

MAIN ACTIVITY

Carry out a survey of your classroom or school to find as many uses for springs as you possibly can. You might find springs in doors, pens, spring balances, clocks and watches. Choose one of the uses for springs and examine it in more detail. Find out and record in words and pictures how the spring works, what it does and what would happen if it was not there. *Does this spring use a push or a pull to perform its function?*

ASSESSMENT

Assess the children's understanding through discussion with them during the survey. Can they identify a number of different uses of springs?

Differentiation
Some children will need to concentrate on identifying uses for springs. Others will move more quickly on to what function the spring performs.

PLENARY

Bring the class together to share findings and discuss how many uses they have found. Ask: *Can anyone explain the function of the spring?* (For example, in a ballpoint pen it causes the refill to retract.)

OUTCOME

● Can describe how springs are used in a variety of ways.

Lesson 10 ◗ Springs in action

Objective
● To investigate the forces exerted by springs and elastic bands.

RESOURCES

A variety of pieces of wood, elastic bands, simple hand tools, glue, safe missiles.

MAIN ACTIVITY

Design and make a simple ballista that will project a missile in a particular direction. In projecting the missile, the children should understand that the force required to move the missile is being exerted in a particular direction. The ballistas could be tested and a challenge arranged to see which group's device can project a missile the furthest, most accurately, or the highest.

Apart from the concept of the direction of the force there is also the

Differentiation
Some children could make a simple catapult device. Others could investigate the trajectory of the missile.

possibility of investigating variables that affect the performance of the device: weight of missile, pull back on the sling, angle of release of the missile.

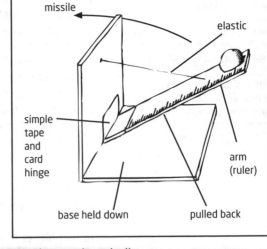

ASSESSMENT
During construction and testing ask the children to explain what they are doing and look for the use of appropriate language and an ability to explain how the forces are acting on the missile.

PLENARY
Bring the class together and test the ballistas under a challenge situation. Discuss the notion of the force being exerted and it acting in a particular direction, such as sending the missile towards its target.

OUTCOMES
- Know that an elastic band can exert a force.
- Can recognise that a force acts in a particular direction.

Lesson 11 ▫ Testing a rubber band

Objectives
- To know that the force exerted by an elastic band depends on how much it is stretched.
- To make observations, measure in standard units and to draw conclusions from results.

Vocabulary
exert, force, measurement, prediction

RESOURCES ◉
Main activity: Simple toy catapults; projectiles.
Group activities: 1 Flat board catapults (one per group – see Preparation), toy cars; rulers; photocopiable page 143 (also 'Testing a rubber band' (red), available on the CD-ROM). **2** Thin balsa wood; simple hand tools; nails; card; elastic bands; a water trough (guttering).

PREPARATION
Make flat board catapults to project your toy cars similar to the one shown below.

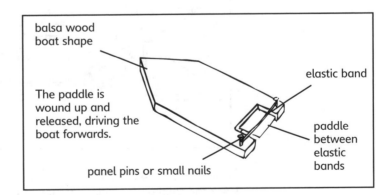

BACKGROUND
Most materials will stretch to some extent when a force is applied to them. The 'elasticity' of a material is the extent to which it will return to its original size and shape following the application of a force to it. English

Differentiation 💿
Group activity 1
To support children, give them 'Testing a rubber band' (green), on the CD-ROM, which provides multiple choice answers to some of the questions. Some children may also require support to measure how far back the band is pulled and the distance the car travels.

inventor and scientist Robert Hooke (1635-1702) is best remembered for his work on elasticity. Hooke found that the stretch (in an elastic band, for example) is directly proportional to the added load, up to a certain point. Clearly if you were to continue adding masses, there will come a point where the elastic band will no longer return to its original size and shape when the mass is removed. At this point the material is said to have reached its extent of elasticity and will remain in a deformed state. This principle clearly has it uses, mainly in weighing equipment.

Materials like steel, iron, copper and concrete have very little elasticity, while a material like rubber (or more usually plastic these days), is very elastic.

STARTER

Begin the lesson by recapping the learning from previous lessons, asking the children to tell you all they can about forces. Ask the children to recall the work they have done using elastic bands and how they exert a force upon objects to make them speed up, slow down or move in a particular direction. Ask the children to think of ways that this idea is used - give hints along the lines of Robin Hood's bow and the use of medieval ballistas to lead the discussion into catapults. Ask the children if they know how a bow and arrow works and how someone like Robin Hood was able to get his arrows to travel over great distances. Tell the children that they are going to use simple catapults to see who can send something over the greatest distance. Remind the children of the dangers of catapults and stress that they must not fire at anyone.

MAIN ACTIVITY

Sit the children in a horseshoe shape, behind the catapults, and fire the toys away from the group. Using a number of simple catapults, the sort available cheaply from many toy shops, carry out a challenge to see who can catapult an object the furthest distance. During this time talk to the children about the fairness of this as a scientific investigation. Would this be a good way to accurately measure the effect of pulling the elastic back further in order to send the projectile further?

Ask the children to consider all the factors that determine the distance that the projectile will travel. Variables may include: the angle of projection; the strength of the person; the mass of the projectile. These are all factors that will affect the trajectory of the projectile. Ask the children to think of a way of limiting these variables and of testing to see if the force exerted by an elastic band has an effect on the distance a projectile will travel. A flat board catapult will go some way to addressing some of these variables.

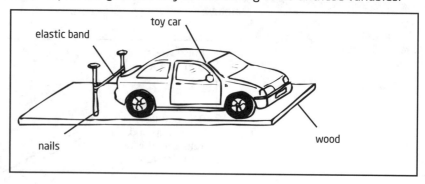

GROUP ACTIVITIES

1 Ask the children to work in groups of four to use the flat board catapult to investigate the relationship between the amount an elastic band stretches and the force that it exerts by catapulting a toy car along a surface. They should predict what they think will happen before using the flat board catapult to help them determine the distance the elastic is stretched and the distance the car travels.

This equipment and the careful measuring of the retraction should mean that a fair test can be carried out without uncontrollable variables. During the investigation the children should record their results on a copy of photocopiable page 143 and then complete the questions.

2 Make a simple paddle boat using balsa wood (see diagram on page 133). Investigate the relationship between the number of turns of the paddle and the distance travelled. Test them in a long trough of water – a section of guttering is ideal.

ASSESSMENT
Scrutinise the children's work for evidence of understanding. Are they able to explain what happens when the elastic band is pulled back further? (The force exerted is greater.)

PLENARY
Discuss the investigation with the children and the conclusions they have come to. Ask some of them to explain their understanding of the relationship between the amount the elastic band stretches and the force that it exerts. They can demonstrate its effect with their flat board catapult: 'The further I pull the band back, the further the car travels, so the bigger the force that I am making must be.'

OUTCOMES
● Can describe the relationship between the amount an elastic band stretches and the force that it exerts.
● Can make observations, measure in standard units and draw conclusions from results.

Lesson 12 ▪ Driving force

Objective
● To know that elastic bands exert forces that can be used to drive things along.

RESOURCES
Cotton reels; elastic bands; spent matches; a candle.

MAIN ACTIVITY
Use cotton reels and elastic bands to make an elastic-band-powered vehicle. Thread an elastic band through the cotton reel, anchoring it at one end with a piece of match. At the other end, wax the cotton reel or thread a bead onto the elastic. Next, insert a match through the elastic band and wind it up until secure. Continue to wind before allowing the elastic band to unwind and drive the vehicle forward.

Test the vehicle to see how many turns are needed to make the vehicle move. Remind the children not to under- or over-wind the elastic band.

Differentiation
Differentiate by outcome.

ASSESSMENT
Through looking at the children's findings, observations and by discussion, establish if the children have understood that it is the elastic band exerting a force that drives the vehicle. Ask questions such as: *What made the toy car move? Why did it stop?*

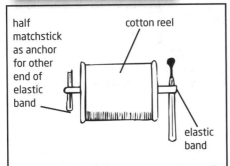

half matchstick as anchor for other end of elastic band

cotton reel

elastic band

PLENARY
Ask the children to demonstrate their investigation and to explain the forces that started and stopped their cotton reel vehicles. Hold a 'Cotton reel Grand Prix'.

OUTCOME
● Can recognise that elastic bands exert forces that can be used to drive things along.

ENRICHMENT
Lesson 13 ▪ Energy

RESOURCES 💿
Main activity: Springs and elastic bands.
Group activities: 1 Photocopiable page 144 (also 'Energy' (red); available on the CD-ROM); pens; pencils **2** Model-making materials; tools; glue; LEGO® or similar construction sets.
ICT link: 'Energy' interactive activity, from the CD-ROM.

BACKGROUND
In everyday terms the meaning attached to the word 'energy' is often different from that used in the science. 'Energy' does not make things move – forces do. We cannot see or feel energy itself; we can only observe its effects. Energy is needed to make objects move, speed up, change direction, heat up and so on, but these are all manifestations of energy being transferred from one thing to another. For example, when you play on a pogo stick, energy is moved from you into the spring of the stick. Energy, therefore, cannot be created or destroyed; it can only be moved from place to place and can come in a number of forms: thermal (heat) energy, sound energy, solar (sun) energy, nuclear energy, kinetic (movement) energy, light energy, electrical energy, chemical energy; stored (potential) energy. These and others can be reduced to two forms: stored (potential) energy, for example, a stretched spring or elastic band has stored energy and when the energy is released it can make objects move; and movement (kinetic) energy, for example, a spring or elastic band moves as it is released.

STARTER
Begin with a mind-mapping session about energy: *What is it? Where does it come from? What forms does it come in?* Collect the children's ideas together and come to some agreement. Talk to the children about energy being needed in order to make things move, change speed or direction and to heat things up: *Can you name any different types of energy?* They may need prompting. Try to come up with a list of different forms of energy that includes: thermal energy (heat energy), sound energy, solar energy (sun energy), light energy, electrical energy, nuclear energy (the children may have heard about this through TV, but without much actual understanding) and chemical energy (the children may suggest 'food energy').

MAIN ACTIVITY
Ask the children if they know where all this energy comes from. Introduce the idea that we cannot create or destroy these energy forms; we can only change them from one to another. Give some examples: electrical energy can be changed to heat energy in an electric fire or to light in an electric lamp; movement energy can be changed to sound energy by banging a drum; wind and water movement energy can be changed to electrical energy.

Ask the children to think of further examples. Talk in simple terms about the ideas of stored and movement energy. Use a spring or elastic band to demonstrate by saying that if you stretch a spring and hold it still or pull back a catapult there is some energy in that spring or elastic band, and because it is just there and not causing movement we call it stored. When we release the spring or elastic band the energy causes movement so we call that movement energy.

GROUP ACTIVITIES
1 Distribute copies of page 144 for the children to complete. The children have to identify the energy changes taking place. The answers to the

examples on the sheet are: 1. electrical to sound; 2. electrical to heat; 3. light (from sun) to light (from electricity); 4. stored energy to sound and movement; 5. wind (movement) to light.

2 Ask the children to design (and make, if you have sufficient and suitable resources) a simple model vehicle that demonstrates the change in energy from stored or electrical energy into movement energy. The vehicle could be battery-powered so the change would be from electrical energy to movement energy, or powered by an elastic band which would be stored energy changed to movement energy.

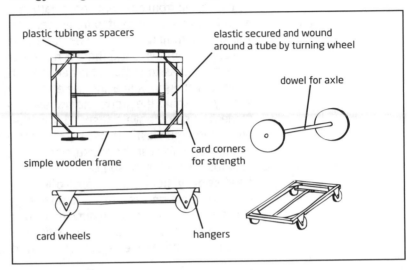

plastic tubing as spacers

elastic secured and wound around a tube by turning wheel

dowel for axle

simple wooden frame

card corners for strength

card wheels

hangers

ICT LINK ☉
The children could use the 'Energy' interactive, from the CD-ROM, to identify different types of energy.

ASSESSMENT
Observe whether the children can identify various types of energy. Through observation and discussion, assess if they can recognise that stored or electrical energy can be changed into movement energy. Ask, for example: *What sort of energy is in the battery? What type of energy is making the vehicle move?*

PLENARY
Bring the children together to demonstrate models and reinforce the concept of energy change.

OUTCOMES
● Can recognise that energy can change forms.
● Can recognise that stored and electrical energy can be changed into movement energy.

ENRICHMENT
Lesson 14 ▫ Where do we get our heat from?

RESOURCES ☉
Main activity: Flipchart or board and felt-tipped pens.
Group activities: 1 Copies of photocopiable page 145 (also 'Where do we get our heat from?' (red), available on the CD-ROM); pencils and pens.
2 Paper; pens; pencils.

Vocabulary
energy, transfer, heat energy, fuel sources

BACKGROUND

Energy sources: nearly all the energy used on Earth can be traced back to the Sun. All the fossil fuels that we use – coal, oil and gas – were formed many millions of years ago from plants, trees and animals that grew using energy from the Sun. Heat energy is released and transferred when fuels are burned. This energy can be transferred and put to a number of uses, including cooking, generating electricity, keeping warm and driving vehicles.

Energy transfer: energy cannot be created nor can it be destroyed but it can, however, be transferred when we perform an activity. The energy can be converted from one form into another. If we consider what happens when a stone is fired from a catapult, we can see an example of how energy is transferred from its kinetic to its potential form and back to kinetic again. As the elastic is drawn back, there is movement (or kinetic) energy used in stretching it. As the catapult is held, the energy is stored in the elastic (potential energy). Releasing the elastic allows movement again (kinetic energy), pushing the stone and transferring this kinetic energy into the stone. The stone travels at speed from the catapult, still using kinetic energy and the elastic comes to rest because it has transferred all its energy to the stone. You can, of course, trace these energy transfers back further towards their ultimate source.

Heat energy: heat is also a form of energy and it too can be transferred. It can also be created as a result of an energy transfer, when coal, oil, gas or wood are burned and when movement takes place, such as friction. The more energy that is required and which we use in carrying out a task (such as running), the more energy is transferred into heat energy.

STARTER

Remind the children about the work they have done on stored and movement energy; recall what they have learnt about types of energy.

MAIN ACTIVITY

Talk in simple terms to the children about heat being a form of energy. Ask the children to talk about the many different ways in which we use heat energy. Use a flipchart or board to record 'Uses of heat'. Discuss with the children the fuels that produce our heat energy. Again brainstorm ideas about heat energy sources.

GROUP ACTIVITIES

1 Distribute photocopiable page 145 for the children to complete. They are asked to identify the means we have of using heat energy and the sources of fuel used to produce that energy.

2 Ask the children to think of a number of different activities that require them to use energy, such as walking on the level, walking up and down stairs, running slowly, running quickly and so on. They should try out some of these simple movements to see how warm they feel after each exercise. They could record their results in a table using simple terms that describe how they feel, such as: 'I did not feel any different', 'I felt quite warm', 'I felt very warm', 'I felt hot'.

Differentiation 💿
Group activity 1
To support children, give them 'Where do we get our heat from?' (green) from the CD-ROM, which omits the extension question included on the core sheet.

ASSESSMENT

Assess the children's worksheets for understanding and by devising a quiz about heat sources and talk with the children, during the group activities to assess their understanding of energy transfer to heat.

PLENARY

Share ideas about the sources of heat energy and how different forms of exercise requiring us to use more energy produce more heat in us.

OUTCOMES
● Can recognise that heat is a form of energy.
● Can recognise different sources of heat.
● Can recognise different applications of heat in everyday life.

Lesson 15 ▪ Assessment

Objective
● To assess the children's knowledge of the properties of magnets, types of forces and the uses of springs.

RESOURCES 💿
Assessment activities: **1** Copies of photocopiable page 146 (also 'Assessment – 1' (red), available on the CD-ROM); pens; pencils. **2** Copies of photocopiable page 147 (also 'Assessment – 2' (red), available on the CD-ROM); pens; pencils.

STARTER
Begin the Assessment activities by briefly recapping on previous activities.

ASSESSMENT ACTIVITY 1
Distribute copies of photocopiable page 146 for the children to complete individually.

ANSWERS
1. The children's picture of the bar magnet should include the poles marked with N and S for north and south.
2. When the poles are the same the magnets will repel each other, and when the poles are different they will attract each other.
3. Six uses of magnets could include: bells, burglar alarms, telephones, door latches, vending machines, metal detectors, moving large quantities of iron and steel, separating materials and compasses.

LOOKING FOR LEVELS
For Assessment activity 1, all of the children should be able to draw a bar magnet with most of them being able to label the poles. Most should be able to explain that 'like' poles repel and 'unlike' poles attract and they should be aware of some uses of magnets. Some children will be able to identify a greater number of less obvious uses such as magnetic tape and hard disks.

ASSESSMENT ACTIVITY 2
Distribute copies of photocopiable page 147, for the children to complete individually. For children who need support, you may wish to add a word list to the photocopiable page from which the children can choose the missing words before completing the page.

ANSWERS
For the first section of photocopiable page 147 accept any sensible object which uses springs and is either pushed or pulled. The words to complete the sentences are: 1. force, 2. spring, 3. elastic band, 4. push, 5. pull, 6. exert, 7. speed up; slow down, 8. pushing.

LOOKING FOR LEVELS
For Assessment activity 2, all of the children should be able to identify uses of springs and most should be able to say whether those uses involve pushes or pulls. Most children should be able to complete sentences 1 to 3, with some able to complete them all.

PLENARY
Discuss the Assessment activities, perhaps allowing an element of self-marking before discussing any misconceptions the children may still have.

PHOTOCOPIABLE

Magnets

- ◧ Draw and colour a diagram of a bar magnet.
- ◧ Colour one end red and the other end blue.
- ◧ Mark N at the red end and S at the blue end.

◧ Complete these sentences

N stands for _____. S stands for _____.

The ends of the magnet are called the _____.

◧ Bring the ends of two bar magnets close together.

Bring N to N.   What do you notice? _____

Bring S to S.   What do you notice? _____

Bring N to S.   What do you notice? _____

◧ Draw a diagram to show what happens each time.

Magnets	Diagram	What happened?
N to N		
S to S		
N to S		

◧ SCHOLASTIC

Springs

◗ Use springs to test for their push or pull.

◗ Push the spring together from both ends.

◗ Draw red arrows to show the direction of your force. Draw blue arrows to show the direction of the force of the spring.

Push

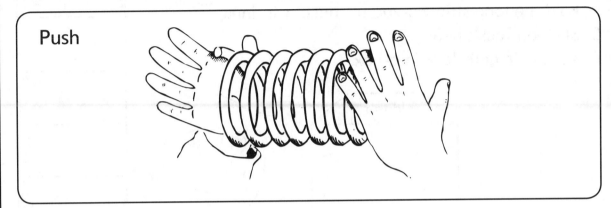

◗ Pull the spring gently from both ends.

◗ Draw red arrows to show the direction of your force. Draw blue arrows to show the direction of the force of the spring.

Pull

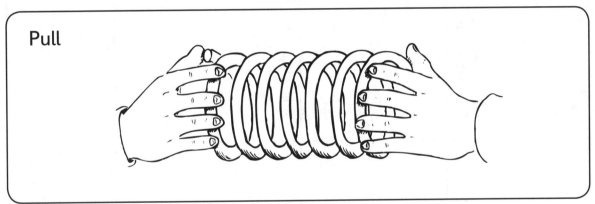

◗ Now try the pull test with a rubber band. Draw what you see below.

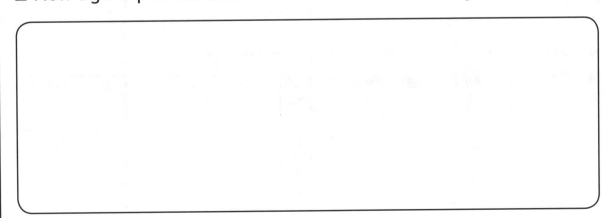

Illustration © Kirsty Wilson

PHOTOCOPIABLE

Jack-in-the-box

To make a Jack in the Box

1. Carefully cut out the net of the box
2. Fold the box where shown.
3. Assemble the box by sticking the tabs.
4. Fold the long strip zig-zag to make a spring.
5. Stick on Jack's head.
6. Assemble your Jack-in-a-box.

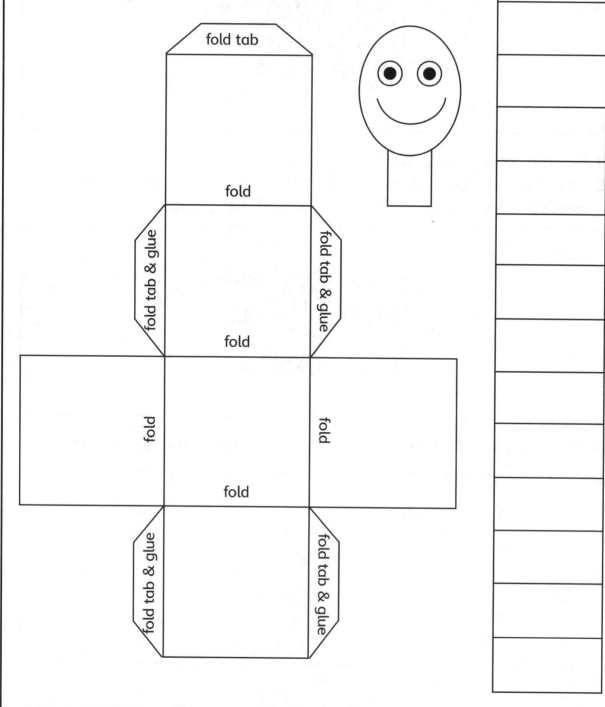

SCHOLASTIC

Testing a rubber band

◧ You will need a flat board catapult, a toy car, a ruler, a tape measure and a flat, clear surface.

◧ Catapult the toy car along the flat surface.

◧ Draw a diagram here.

◧ What do you think will happen if you pull the rubber band back further?

_____

_____

◧ Test your prediction by measuring the distance you pull the rubber band back and the distance the car travels.

Pull back on rubber band (cm)	Distance car travelled (cm)

◧ What happens as you pull the rubber band back further?

_____

_____

◧ Is this what you predicted would happen?

_____

_____

◧ Explain why this happens.

Energy

■ Energy can change forms from one type of energy to another. Can you identify the types of energy in these pictures?

1.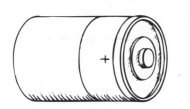

_____   _____

2.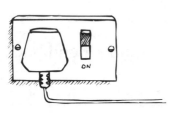

_____   _____

3.

_____   _____

4.

_____   _____

5.

_____   _____

◗ SCHOLASTIC

Illustration © Kirsty Wilson

Where do we get our heat from?

■ Think about all the times we need heat.
■ Complete this table to show the ways in which heat is supplied and its sources.

In the classroom		Around school	
How it comes to us	Source fuel	How it comes to us	Source fuel

At home		Outside	
How it comes to us	Source fuel	How it comes to us	Source fuel

■ Think about all these sources of heat energy. Where does the energy come from in the first place?

PHOTOCOPIABLE

Assessment – 1

1. Draw a picture of a bar magnet. Show what is usually written at the ends.

What happens when two magnets are brought together?
Draw sketches to help explain your answers.

2. a)   When the poles are the same:

_____

_____

_____

_____

   b)   When the poles are different:

_____

_____

_____

_____

3. Write down six uses of magnets.

_____

_____

📖 S C H O L A S T I C

Assessment – 2

■ Write down or draw all the things you can think of that use springs.
■ Say whether the spring is being pulled or pushed.

Object	Pull or push?

pushing	exert	spring	slow down	elastic band
push	force	speed up	pull	

■ Complete these sentences.

1. A push or a pull is called a _____.

2. A coil of metal used to make things move is called a _____.

3. A loop of rubber or elastic used to make things turn round is an

_____ _____.

4. A compression force is a _____.

5. A stretching force is a _____.

6. Springs _____ forces.

7. Forces can make things _____ _____ or _____ _____.

8. A catapult uses _____ forces to project a missile through the air.

CHAPTER 7 Light and shadows

Lesson	Objectives	Main activity	Group activities	Plenary	Outcomes
Lesson 1 Light	• To ascertain the children's levels of understanding of light and how shadows are formed.	Concept mapping.	Looking at uses of light. Letting light through.	Formulating questions.	• Teacher can assess the children's level of understanding of light and shadows. • Teacher can arrange children in appropriate class groups.
Lesson 2 Shadow walk	• To encourage children to question their own ideas about light.	Observing shadows in the playground.	Annotated drawings to explain what a shadow is.	Discuss the range of ideas held.	• The teacher has a greater awareness of children's existing understanding. • The children are more aware of their own ideas and are ready to question them.
Lesson 3 How does light travel?	• To begin to recognise that light travels from a source in straight lines. • To explore and make notes about relevant observations.	Discuss how a mirror can be used to see behind you.	Activities using mirrors, torches and ray boxes to explore how light travels in straight lines.	Introducing the idea that light travels in straight lines.	• Can begin to recognise that light travels in straight lines. • Can recognise that the sharp edge to a shadow is due to light travelling in straight lines.
Lesson 4 Me and my shadow	• To know that when light from the Sun is blocked by an object a shadow forms.	Looking at how shadows are formed.	Casting shadows, observation and recording. Completing a worksheet looking at shadow formation.	Discussion and reinforcement of how shadows are formed.	• Can recognise that a shadow forms when sunlight is blocked.
Lesson 5 Matching shadows	• To know that shadows are in the shape of the object blocking the light.	Explanation of how shadows are formed.	Worksheet on shadows. Looking at shadow formation.	Reinforcing ideas about shadows.	• Can describe how shadows are formed when objects block light from the sun.
Lesson 6 Light sources	• To know that when light from sources other than the Sun is blocked, shadows are also produced.	Using a variety of light sources to cast shadows.	Completing a worksheet on how shadows are formed. Survey of light sources.	Reinforcing shadow formation and size.	• Can recognise that light from a range of sources produces shadows. • Can describe how the shape and size of the shadow varies with the position of the light source.
Lesson 7 Shadow puppets	• To apply knowledge that when light is blocked, shadows are produced.	Making shadow puppets using different materials.		Making a puppet show and reinforcing the concept of shadow creation.	• Can recognise that light from a range of sources produces shadows. • Can describe how the shape and size of the shadow varies with position of the light source. • Can use knowledge of shadows.
Lesson 8 Changing shadows	• To know that shadows of objects in sunlight change during the course of the day.	Observing and drawing shadows.		Looking at observations and drawing conclusions about how shadows change.	• Can observe, record and understand how the shadows of objects change during the course of a day.
Lesson 9 Shadow graphs	• To know that the shape and position of a shadow change at different times of day. • To know that the shape and position of a shadow can be measured at different times of day.. • To be able to measure in standard units and present results in tables and bar charts.	Measuring the length of shadows cast by a rounders post at intervals throughout the day.		Sharing findings and addressing misconceptions.	• Can measure in standard units and present results in tables and bar charts.

Lesson	Objectives	Main activity	Group activities	Plenary	Outcomes
Lesson 10 The Sun in the sky	• To know that the Sun appears to follow a curved path across the sky every day.	Observing and recording the path of the Sun.	Making a sunshine recorder to plot the path of the Sun on paper. Researching the Sun.	Looking at an outline drawing of the path of the Sun and describing it.	• Can describe the shape of the path of the Sun across the sky.
Lesson 11 The Sun's path	• To know that the Sun appears to follow a curved path across the sky every day.	Relating results from previous investigations to see the relationship between the Sun's position and shadow length.		Discussing findings.	• Can describe the shape of the path of the Sun across the sky.
Enrichment Lesson 12 Shadows	• To understand that the position of a shadow is dependent on the direction of the light source. • To make and test predictions.	Predicting the position of a shadow cast by a torch shining on a Plasticine figure.	Predicting and testing the position of shadows when the position of the torch is changed.	Relating the position of the shadows to how light travels in straight lines.	• Can make and test a prediction. • Can understand how the position of the light source affects the position of the shadow.
Lesson 13 The Sun and the Earth	• To know that the path of the Sun is due to the movement of the Earth, not the movement of the Sun. • To understand that the Sun is at the centre of the solar system and that the Earth orbits it.	How the Earth and other planets orbit the Sun.	Completing a worksheet looking at the relationship between the Sun and the Earth. Researching the solar system using secondary sources.	Demonstration of modelling. 'Guess the planet' quiz.	• Can explain why the Sun appears to move across the sky even though it stays in the same position in space relative to the Earth. • Can understand that the Sun is at the centre of the solar system and that the Earth orbits around it.
Lesson 14 Telling the time with shadows	• To know that shadows can be used to tell the approximate time of day.	Looking at sundials and how they are used.	Making and using a simple sundial. Completing a worksheet looking at how shadows can be used to tell the time on sundials.	Discussing the effectiveness of sundials.	• Can make a sundial. • Can use a sundial to tell the approximate time of day.
Enrichment Lesson 15 Sunlight	• To know that day and night are caused by the movement of the Earth. • To know that day lengths are different in summer and winter.	Concept mapping.	Completing a daylight worksheet.investigating light sources.	Sharing ideas and formulating questions.	• Teacher can assess the level of the children in the class. • Teacher can arrange children in appropriate class groups.
Lesson 16 Letting light through	• To know that materials can be grouped as opaque, translucent or transparent according to how light behaves when it is shone on to them. • To carry out a test. • To use light meters. • To interpret results and draw conclusions.	Demonstrating how to compare the amount of light that can pass through different materials.	Carrying out tests on how much light passes through a range of materials.	Grouping materials as transparent, translucent and opaque.	• Can distinguish between opaque, translucent and transparent materials. • Can use a light meter/ data-logger. • Can interpret own data to draw conclusions.
Lesson 17 Shadow or no shadow?	• To know that translucent and opaque materials form shadows and transparent ones do not. • To make predictions and suggest explanations based on previous knowledge.	Investigating the shadows cast by transparent, translucent and opaque materials.		Suggesting reasons for results of investigations.	• Can recognise that opaque and translucent materials form shadows and that transparent materials do not.
Enrichment Lesson 18 Colour	• To know that there is a wide range of colours that can be seen. • To know the colours of the rainbow.	Looking at the colours of the spectrum and colour collections.	Completing a worksheet on colour, and pictures and collage work of the spectrum.	Reinforcement of the colours of the spectrum.	• Can recognise the colours in the spectrum.

Lesson	Objectives	Main activity	Group activities	Plenary	Outcomes
Enrichment Lesson 19 Colour in nature	• To know that colours are used for decoration and to give messages in the natural world.	Using secondary sources to investigate how animals use colour.		Sharing research with each other.	• Can describe how plants and animals use colours.
Enrichment Lesson 20 Colour on the roads	• To know that colours are used for decoration and to give messages in the man-made world. • To know that colour and light are important in road safety.	Looking at the messages different colours give us, including traffic light sequences.	Looking at the many uses of colour in road safety and giving descriptive illustrations.	Looking at colour families.	• Is aware that humans use colour to send out messages. • Can describe the use of colour in road safety. • Can describe the use of light in the local environment, for example, for road safety.
Enrichment Lesson 21 Light energy	• To know that light is a form of energy.	Discuss different forms of energy, including solar energy.	Investigate the effect of light on a solar cell. Leave trays of water in Sun and shade to find out what happens. Find out some uses of solar energy.	Report findings.	• Know that light is a form of energy.

Assessment	Objectives	Activity 1	Activity 2
Lesson 22	• To assess the children's level of understanding of the sources of light. • To assess the level of understanding of the path the sun takes across the sky and the relationship between the Earth and the Sun. • To assess the understanding of the use of shadows in telling the time.	Completing a worksheet on the position of the Sun in the sky.	Completing a worksheet on sundials

SC1 SCIENTIFIC ENQUIRY

How do shadows change during the day?

LEARNING OBJECTIVES AND OUTCOMES
- Decide what equipment and materials to use. Make simple observations.
- Use ICT to present findings.
- Use data to draw conclusions.

ACTIVITY
The children should use vertical posts to cast shadows on the playground. These should be in the same place all day so that the children can make regular observations.

The children should measure and record the length of their post's shadow and tabulate the results in a simple chart. They should then use their results to draw a bar graph that will show how the shadow length shortens towards midday. The graphing tool (from the CD-ROM) could be used to present this data.

LESSON LINKS
This Sc1 activity forms an integral part of the Lesson 9, Changing shadows.

Lesson 1 ▪ Light

Objective
- To ascertain the children's levels of understanding of light and how shadows are formed.

RESOURCES 💿
Main activity: Flipchart or board; large sheets of paper; pens; pencils.
Group activities: 1 Paper; pencils; pens; coloured pencils; large sheets of coloured paper; scissors. **2** A copy of photocopiable page 179 (also 'Light' (red), available on the CD-ROM) for each child; pens; pencils.

BACKGROUND
From their work in Key Stage 1/Primary 1–3 the children should be able to recognise that light is needed to see and that 'dark' is the absence of light. They should know that the Sun is our main source of light, but that there are other light sources. They should recognise that different materials let varying amounts of light pass through, and should also be able to explain that shadows are formed when light is blocked. They may also know that light is a form of energy (but this is not a curriculum requirement throughout the UK).

STARTER
Begin the lesson by talking to the children about the work they have covered in Key Stage 1/Primary 1–3 on light. Ask the children to begin to think about what they can recall about light. Ask questions such as: *Where does light come from and how do we use it?* Explain that they will be building on what they already know and discovering a little more about light.

MAIN ACTIVITY
The children should work in small groups on developing a concept map of light. They should express all their ideas and knowledge about the subject and then attempt to join their ideas with lines and arrows to produce a map. A large class concept map can be drawn on a flipchart or board using the groups' ideas.

Differentiation 💿
Group activity 2
To support children, use 'Light' (green) from the CD-ROM , which provides multiple choice answers for the first part of the sheet.

To extend children, use 'Light' (blue), which asks them to think of their own items that fit into the table rather than selecting items from a list.

GROUP ACTIVITIES

1 Ask the children to discuss the uses of light, such as to illuminate buildings, torches, warning lights or to show an appliance is working. Share out the ideas among the groups and ask each child to draw a picture and write a paragraph highlighting one use of light. The children should then present their work in an imaginative way. They could stick all the 'uses' on to a giant cut-out of a lamp, stick them on smaller individual lamps to make a string of lamps or make a catalogue.

2 Distribute copies of photocopiable page 179 and ask the children to complete it unaided. The tasks are designed to assess the children's understanding of how light can pass through some materials and not others, thus creating shadows. The answers are that if you shine a torch at a clear drinking glass, the light would pass through the glass; and if you shine a torch at a book, the light would not pass through and a shadow would be formed.

ASSESSMENT

Through observation, discussion, and scrutiny of work, assess the children's understanding of the uses of light, how shadows are cast and how light passes through some materials and not others. All the children should be able to name some uses of light; most should also be able to say that only some materials allow light through. Some children will be able to describe how shadows are formed.

PLENARY

Share ideas and encourage the children to begin to formulate their own questions about what they think they would like to find out about.

OUTCOMES

● Teacher can assess the children's level of understanding of light and how shadows are formed.
● Teacher can arrange children in appropriate class groups.

Lesson 2 ▪ Shadow walk

Objectives
● To encourage children to question their own ideas about light.

Vocabulary
light, shadow

RESOURCES

Main activity: 'Shadow' from *Star Poems* by Michael Rosen (ASE Publications, 2000).
Group activity: Writing materials.

PREPARATION

Take advantage of a sunny ten minutes to do the 'shadow walk', in case the sun isn't shining on the day of the lesson.

BACKGROUND

This activity will enable you to help the children question their ideas about light and shadows from Lesson 1. It is quite common for children to confuse shadows and reflections, and their drawings may show this. Other children may not have yet realized that a shadow is an absence of light; that light has been blocked. Light travels in straight lines and this can be used to explain why shadows have sharp edges.

When working outside, it is important that the children are told not to look directly at the sun as this could damage their eyes.

STARTER

Read the poem 'Shadow' by Michael Rosen to the children and discuss it using the suggested questions below. If you do not have a copy of the poem to stimulate interest in shadows, then engage children in thinking about shadows by asking them: *Have you ever noticed your shadow? Can you describe it to me? When do you notice that you have got a shadow?* (On a sunny day.) *What else can you tell me about shadows? Is your shadow always the same?* This will help to focus the children's observations during the 'shadow walk'.

MAIN ACTIVITY

Go for a ten-minute 'shadow walk'. Ask the children to look out for any shadows and to think about how they are made. This could be replaced by five minutes of observation within the classroom if there are shadows cast by lights and windows.

Back in the classroom, ask the children to briefly describe what they saw and explain that you are interested in finding out their ideas about light and shadows.

GROUP ACTIVITY

Ask the children to work individually and do an annotated drawing of themselves with a shadow on a sunny day. Explain that you want the picture and writing to show as much as possible about what they understand about light and how a shadow is made.

Circulate, asking questions to assess understanding, for example: *Do you ever get a coloured shadow? Why have you shown the shadow there – could it be on the other side?*

ASSESSMENT

Analyse the annotated drawings – are shadows represented by solid blocks or are they like reflections? Are the shadows drawn starting at their feet? Are they in the correct place with respect to the light source? Is there evidence of understanding that the light has been blocked?

PLENARY

Choose several children who have represented their shadows differently to show their work to the class. Point out that there are some different ideas here and that the class needs to do some investigations to check out their thoughts. Explain that scientists are always trying to understand things better and this means they change their ideas when they find new evidence.

OUTCOMES

● The teacher has a greater awareness of children's existing understanding.
● The children are more aware of their own ideas and are ready to question them.

Lesson 3 ▸ How does light travel?

RESOURCES

Main activity: A flat mirror.
Group activities: 1 A flat mirror. **2** Torches; cards with holes in the centre; a wall or other surface to shine the torch on to. **3** Ray boxes (home-made ones can be made using a simple bulb and battery circuit in a container such as a short crisp tube that has a slit cut into the bottom edge).
Plenary: A torch and object.

PREPARATION

Have the resources for the Main teaching activity to hand. Set up the Group

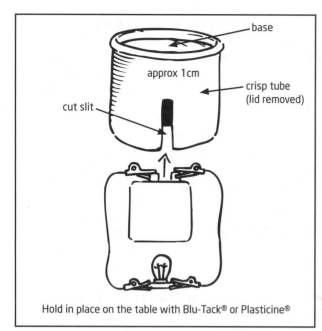

base

approx 1cm

crisp tube
(lid removed)

cut slit

Hold in place on the table with Blu-Tack® or Plasticine®

mirror

activities on the tables. Have the children sitting on the carpet in front of you.

BACKGROUND
The three Group activities will help children to get a 'feel' for light travelling in straight lines, but the Plenary is important to pull these experiences together and articulate a clear idea: light always travels in straight lines. Be sure to leave plenty of time for discussion. This is a start point for the development of this concept. It can be more helpful to think of it in terms of what light does not do - go around things.

STARTER
Ask two children to come out to the front and stand one in front of the other. Give the child in front a mirror. Tell the child behind to pull a silly face and ask the child in front to see if they can copy the face by using the mirror. Ask the children: *How can Josh see what Alice is doing?*

MAIN ACTIVITY
On a board or flipchart, model an annotated drawing that expresses the children's explanations of how Josh can see Alice.

GROUP ACTIVITIES
Explain that in the Group activities the children will need to record their ideas by drawing and writing. Explain that there are three different activities and they will all get a chance to do each one in turn.
1 As in the starter, ask the children to stand or sit in pairs and take turns to use a mirror to copy the silly faces pulled by the child behind. Children record their ideas as an annotated drawing.
2 Working in pairs, shine a torch on to a card with a hole in it and look at the spot of light it makes on a wall. Take another card with a hole in it and place it so that there is still a spot of light. *Can you do it with three cards?* Children record their ideas as an annotated drawing.
3 Look at the light coming out of a ray box. Explore putting different pieces of card with slits in front of the light and observe what happens. Cut your own design of slit in card and see what happens. (These are often provided with commercially produced ray boxes.)

ASSESSMENT
Is light indicated by straight lines in the children's drawings? Do the children realise that light cannot go around corners unless a mirror is 'helping'?

PLENARY
Ask the children to feed back any interesting observations they have made, and any things they tried out in their exploration. Ask: *Can light go around things?* (No.) *How do you know that?* (There are examples from Group activities 2 and 3.)
Introduce the idea that light always travels in straight lines. Use a torch to cast a shadow on an object. Explain that because light travels in straight lines, when it is blocked it cannot get around the corner to fill up the gap, so there is a sharp edge to the shadow.

Differentiation
Scribe or provide a key wordbank for children with weaker literacy skills. Extend the exploration by encouraging children to add extra mirrors or extra children in Group activity 1; using extra cards or different sizes of hole for Group activity 2, or moving and combining the card slits for Group activity 3.

OUTCOMES
● Can begin to recognise that light travels in straight lines.
● Can recognise that the sharp edge to a shadow is due to light travelling in straight lines.

Lesson 4 ◗ Me and my shadow

Objective
● To know that when light from a source such as the Sun is blocked by an object, a shadow forms.

Vocabulary
block, light source, shadows, Sun

RESOURCES ◉
Main activity: An OHP; various opaque objects.
Group activities: 1 A sunny day; paper; pencils. **2** Copies of photocopiable page 180 (also 'Me and my shadow' (red), available on the CD-ROM); pens; pencils.

BACKGROUND
The Sun is the 'source' that gives us most of our light and our heat. Light is a form of energy. It is transmitted by electromagnetic waves that, like other forms of energy, we cannot see. What we can see are the objects on which light falls.

Light travels in straight lines and at a tremendous speed - 3,000,000km per second. In fact, nothing travels faster. Despite its speed, it can travel only through certain materials. When it meets the surface of a material, light can either be transmitted (allowed to travel through, such as with glass), absorbed (as in a black surface) or reflected (as with a mirror, but also by all the objects we can see). It is reflected light that travels to our eyes that produces an image on our retina, thus allowing us to see objects.

Because some light is usually reflected from an object, and because light cannot travel around corners, the area behind an object comes into shadow. A shadow therefore is simply an area from which light is blocked. Clearly there is some light reaching that area otherwise behind, say, a building there would be complete darkness. Usually, this is light reflected from other objects. Shadows are strictly areas of less light rather than no light at all.

Begin by giving the children a number of statements that will lead to the identification of a mystery thing - a shadow. When they think they know the answer, the children should write it down secretly. The statements could be: *This thing can change shape. It can appear and disappear instantly. It can be anywhere, at any time. Its shape can change before your eyes. It does not have any colour. One of these can follow you around. Sometimes they can be scary. Sometimes they can be useful. They can move, but they are not alive. Without light, they simply do not exist.*

MAIN ACTIVITY
When the children have the answer, ask them if they know how shadows are made. Use the light from an OHP to demonstrate how shadows are formed. Use an object and explain that the light is being blocked when it reaches the object, hence the darker area behind it. Ask the children to think about where most of our light comes from and therefore gives most of our shadows. Discuss the Sun as being a major light source and, if appropriate, that light is actually another form of energy.

GROUP ACTIVITIES
1 In the playground, and working in groups, the children should make shadows while other members of the group observe and record their observations as sketches. Ask the groups to observe and record their shadows at different times during the school day (perhaps each break time may be possible). What, if anything, do the children think will be different?
2 Distribute photocopiable page 180 to the children and explain the task. This sheet asks questions about the way in which shadows are formed, so it

Differentiation 💿
Group activity 2
For children who need support, use 'Me and my shadow' (green), which includes fewer and less complex questions than the core sheet.

To extend children, use 'Me and my shadow' (blue), which also asks them to write a description of their shadow.

may be useful to have your demonstration from the Main teaching activity available for them to refer to. The final section asks the children to draw a picture of the Sun and a shadow that it may cast. At this point it is worth reinforcing the importance of never looking directly at the Sun.

ASSESSMENT
Mark the children's work for evidence of an understanding of how shadows are formed. The questions and diagrams should reflect the knowledge that a shadow is formed when light from the Sun or other light source is blocked.

PLENARY
Discuss with the children how shadows are formed, asking them to explain shadow formation in their own words. Look at the pictures of the Sun and shadows that the children have drawn. Reinforce understanding of the concept that when an object blocks the Sun's light a shadow is cast. If the children draw a Sun with rays coming from it, use that to illustrate the concept that the object blocks the Sun's rays, even though we cannot see the rays as such.

OUTCOME
● Can recognise that a shadow forms when sunlight is blocked.

LINKS
Unit 3e, Lessons 13 and 14: forms of energy and energy transfers, including heat and light.

Lesson 5 ▪ Matching shadows

Objective
● To know that shadows are in the shape of the object blocking the light.

Vocabulary
Sun, shadows, cast, sunlight, long, short

RESOURCES 💿
Main activity: An OHP or torch, various objects with which to make shadows.
Group activities: 1 Copies of photocopiable page 181 (also 'Matching shadows' (red), available on the CD-ROM) for each child; pens; pencils.
2 Paper; pens; pencils; drawing materials.
ICT link: 'Matching shadows' interactive activity, from the CD-ROM.

BACKGROUND
When light from the Sun reaches an object on Earth, it is not always able to pass through the object. Materials that let most of the light through are said to be transparent; those that let a little of the light through are translucent, and those that let none at all through are opaque. It is this last group which tend to form the best shadows. A shadow from the Sun is never still, unlike those made by many other light sources. Since the Earth is constantly moving in relation to the Sun, shadows cast by objects lit by the Sun change shape continually from sunrise to sunset. Of course, the Sun does not actually move at all.

Shadows first thing in the morning and late in the evening are longer because of the angle of the Sun's light to the Earth: the Sun appears much lower in the sky at these times. As the day progresses towards midday, the shadows become shorter as the Sun apparently 'climbs' higher in the sky to its peak. The same situation occurs on a seasonal basis, too: shadows at midday in summer are much shorter than those at midday in winter, again due to the apparent path of the Sun across the sky.

STARTER
Begin the lesson by asking the children to think about walking down the street on a dark night where the main source of light is the street lighting.

What is the one thing that always follows them along that street, that some people are frightened of, but is harmless? Discuss (scary) shadows and the children's experiences of shadows.

MAIN ACTIVITY

Remind the children about the previous lesson when they talked about how shadows are formed. Encourage the children to think about the Sun and the shadows cast when the light from the Sun is blocked by objects. Using a light source, for example an OHP or torch, demonstrate shadow-making with a variety of different-shaped objects (see Lessons 6 and 7 of this unit for ideas).

Ask the children if they have ever noticed what happens to shadows during the day. Many will already have noticed that shadows 'move' position as the Sun appears to move across the sky, and that the shadows change their size and shape. Using the light source show how, as an object moves across in front of a light source, not only is a shadow cast, but that the shadow moves as the object moves.

GROUP ACTIVITIES

1 Distribute copies of photocopiable page 181 which asks the children to match shadows with the objects that cast them.
2 Ask the children to explain in writing and diagrams how shadows are formed. Their work should go on to explain how the Sun's shadows change during the day.

ICT LINK 💿

Children can use the 'Matching shadows' interactive to match shadows to pictures of the objects that cast them.

ASSESSMENT

Mark the written work and worksheet for evidence that the children have developed their understanding of how and why shadows change during the day. Can they explain what happens to the shadows? (They change size and position.)

PLENARY

Bring the children together to look at their findings from the Group activities and to reinforce the concept of changing shadows.

OUTCOME

● Can describe how shadows are formed when objects block light from the Sun.

Lesson 6 ◦ Light sources

Objective
● To know that when light from sources other than the Sun is blocked, shadows are also produced.

Vocabulary
light source, Sun

RESOURCES 💿
Main activity: Candles; torches; a computer screen.
Group activities: 1 Copies of photocopiable page 182 (also 'Light sources' (red), available on the CD-ROM); pens; pencils. **2** Clipboards; paper; pens; pencils.

BACKGROUND
It is a common misconception that seeing involves something being emitted from our eyes as though we are some superheroes! Another is that the Moon and planets, for example, are light sources. They are not. They can be seen because they reflect light from the Sun. We can see objects because light is reflected from them, which comes from a light source such as:

the Sun - the light from the Sun supplies us with our daylight and also heat energy; the light energy from the Sun is also used by plants to make their food (photosynthesis)
an electric light - electricity passes through the filament in the light bulb which heats up so much that light is emitted
a candle - chemical energy is released by the burning of the candle wax which causes heating, and when the fuel becomes white hot the candle produces a light.

All light sources can produce shadows, but their intensity will vary depending on the strength and intensity of the light source. The intensity of a shadow can be varied by moving the object casting the shadow nearer or further away from its light source. The shadow also loses its definition, but gains in size as the object is moved nearer to the light source - this happens because more reflected light is able to fall in the shadow. Similarly the intensity and sharpness of shadows is affected by the intensity of the light source. On a bright sunny day, shadows are very sharp and distinct, whereas on an overcast day when the light is diffused by clouds the shadows are far less distinct.

STARTER
Ask the children if they can think of or remember any other sources of light apart from the Sun. Compile a list of these on the board. Discuss briefly the concept of needing light to be able to see anything, whether it is the light from the Sun or elsewhere, and that we see because light bounces off (is reflected from) objects and enters our eyes.

MAIN ACTIVITY
Use a variety of light sources so the children can see that shadows will be cast by any light source. A candle, torch and computer screen can all be used and will produce shadows of varying quality and intensity. Ask the children to think about what will happen as the light source is moved nearer and further away from an object. Demonstrate with the help of the children.

GROUP ACTIVITIES
1 Distribute copies of photocopiable page 182 and ask the children to complete the sheet based on the things they have just seen and talked about.
2 Carry out a survey around school of the many and varied different light sources to be seen. The children can present their findings as a 'We spy' booklet of light sources, such as desk lamps, an OHP or a computer monitor.

ASSESSMENT
Check that the children have been able to identify a number of other light sources and that their diagrams show that when a light source comes nearer

Differentiation
Group activity 1
To support children, use 'Light sources' (green), from the CD-ROM, which asks them just to draw rather than write about their findings. To extend children, use 'Light sources' (blue), which omits the prompt words included in the drawing space.

to an object the shadow becomes larger. Aim only for a general understanding here – the children will explore this more systematically in future years.

PLENARY
Use an OHP as a light source for the children to demonstrate their understanding of light sources and shadow sizes by making shadow puppets with their hands. Encourage them to use their knowledge from this lesson to add feeling to their shadows by varying their sizes.

OUTCOMES
- Can recognise that light from a range of sources produces shadows.
- Can describe how the shape and size of the shadow varies with the position of the light source.

Lesson 7 ▸ Shadow puppets

Objective
- To apply knowledge that when light is blocked shadows are produced.

RESOURCES
Craft materials with varying light-blocking qualities; small garden canes or dowel; glue or tape; a light source such as an OHP; a screen (for example, a wooden frame covered with tracing paper).

MAIN ACTIVITY
Talk about traditional shadow puppetry, for example, in Asian culture, where shadow puppets are sometimes used to tell the traditional legends of the gods at festival time. Demonstrate how the shadows are made. Show the children how to make their own shadow puppets. The puppets can then be manipulated by the children to tell an existing story, or they could devise one of their own.

ASSESSMENT
During the Main activity, talk to the children about their shadow puppets and the materials they are using. Ask them which materials cast better shadows than others and why. See if they know what they need to make effective shadow puppets.

PLENARY
Bring the children together and allow them time to present their shadow puppet stories.

OUTCOME
- Can recognise that light from a range of sources produces shadows.
- Can describe how the shape and size of the shadow varies with the position of the light source.
- Can use knowledge of shadows.

Differentiation
Differentiate by outcome.

screen   shadow puppet   light source

Lesson 8 ⬛ Changing shadows

Objective
● To know that shadows of objects in sunlight change during the course of the day.

RESOURCES
A sunny day; paper; pencils.

MAIN ACTIVITY
Remind the children of what they already know about shadows: that shadows are made by objects blocking the light and that the shadow formed is in the shape of this object. Ask the children if they have ever noticed that sometimes their shadow makes them appear very tall and sometimes it makes them appear very short.

During the day the shadows of various objects, cast by the Sun, change. Ask the children to work with a partner. At regular intervals throughout the day, they should stand in the same place in the playground; one child should cast a shadow while the other partner observes and draws the shadow cast. Ensure that the children observe each other.

ASSESSMENT
Through discussion with the children and scrutiny of their sketches, ensure that the children understand that the shadows change in two ways: position and size.

PLENARY
Look at each other's records and try to draw conclusions about how the shadows have changed – not just their position, but the length of the shadows cast as the day progresses. Ask questions, such as: *At what time of day were your shadows longest? At what time of day were your shadows shortest? What happened to your shadows when the Sun was high in the sky?*

Differentiation
Differentiate by outcome.

OUTCOME
● Can observe, record and understand how the shadows of objects change during the course of a day.

Lesson 9 ▪ Shadow graphs

Objectives
● To know that the shape and position of a shadow change at different times of day.
● To know that the shape and position of a shadow can be measured at different times.
● To be able to measure in standard units and present results in tables and bar charts.

RESOURCES 💿
Wooden posts (such as rounders posts and stands); metre rulers or measuring tapes; paper; graph paper; graphing tool from CD-ROM.

MAIN ACTIVITY
Use pieces of wood fixed vertically (rounders posts in stands would be ideal), to cast shadows on the playground. Leave them in the same place all day where they will not be disturbed. At regular intervals throughout the day (hourly on the hour, or some other convenient regular time), observe the shadows of the posts. The children should measure and record the length of their post's shadow and tabulate the results in a simple chart.

They should then use this information to draw a bar graph that will show how the shadow length shortens towards midday.

ICT LINK 💿
Children could use the interactive graphing tool on the CD-ROM to convert their table of results into a graph.

ASSESSMENT
Assess the children's work for evidence of their ability to collect the relevant data and present information as a clear graph.

Differentiation 💿
Some children may prefer to use the graphing tool (from the CD-ROM) to draw a simple bar chart, or make a cut out of the shadow each hour and stick these on the wall to make a 'living' graph by the hour. Other children could use the graphing tool to produce a variety of graphs.

PLENARY
Share findings, look at each other's graphs and draw conclusions. Try to correct any misconceptions still held about how and why shadows change during the day.

OUTCOME
● Can measure in standard units and present results in tables and bar charts.

Lesson 10 ▪ The Sun in the sky

Objective
● To know that the Sun appears to follow a curved path across the sky every day.

Vocabulary
arc, curved, Earth, rotation, sky, Sun, sunrise, sunset

RESOURCES
Main activity: Clipboards; paper; pencils.
Group activities: 1 Sheets of paper; pencils; dowel; pots of sand, Plasticine®. **2** Paper; pencils; secondary sources of information.

PREPARATION
Gather the resources together, and make a demonstration model.

BACKGROUND
The Sun is at the centre of our solar system. The planets, of which Earth is just one, travel around the Sun, each in a different orbit. The Earth's orbit takes 365.25 days, which we call one year. Because of the effective loss of one quarter day every year we add an extra day into our calendar every four years, in a leap year.

At the same time as the Earth is orbiting the Sun, it is rotating about its own axis. The time taken for this to occur is 24 hours or one day. At any time, only half of the Earth is being lit by the Sun - the other half is turned away and is, therefore, in darkness. As the Earth rotates, the half of the Earth in darkness changes. This is the change from night to day. Daytime begins as the Sun appears to rise. Of course, it does not actually rise; it is simply our perspective of it as we rotate. The Sun then begins its apparent

Differentiation
Differentiate by outcome.

journey across the sky. The path this apparent journey takes varies depending on where you are on Earth and on the time of year. In Britain, the Sun appears to rise in the eastern sky and set in the western sky, passing on its journey through the southern sky. The path it takes is always the same general symmetrical curve or arc. The Sun is at its highest in our southern sky around midday (but this varies depending on GMT or BST). There are a number of differences in the seasonal paths that the Sun takes. In summer, the Sun appears to rise north of east and set north of west, thus if you were in the Arctic you would experience a period when the Sun did not appear to set at all, it would simply travel around the sky. In winter, the converse applies as the Sun appears to rise south of east and set south of west. There are in fact only two days when the Sun appears to rise over Britain due east and appears to set due west: 21 March and 21 September. Both are mid-way between the longest and shortest days, when the Sun rises and sets at its earliest and latest respectively.

While we still talk about the Sun rising and setting and about it travelling through the sky, it is worth reminding the children that the Sun is not moving, but that the Earth is rotating.

STARTER

Remind the children of the work they have done previously and their observations of how shadows change. Look at the shape of their charts.

MAIN ACTIVITY

Early in the day, take the children outside and ask them to draw the general outline of the scene from where they are standing in the playground. Without looking directly at the Sun, they should also mark on the position of the Sun relative to the objects in their outline drawing. As they mark on the position of the Sun, they should also record alongside it the time of the observation.

Back inside, tell the children that throughout the day they are going to carry out observations of the position of the Sun in the sky. Ask them to predict where they think the Sun will be in one hour. After one hour, return to exactly the same spot and observe the position of the Sun now. Were the children's predictions correct? Continue this pattern of observation and prediction hourly throughout the day, recording each time on their outline drawing.

Safety: continue to stress the importance of not looking directly at the Sun, but simply observing its general location relative to their drawings.

GROUP ACTIVITIES

1 Each group should fix a small length of dowel into a pot of sand to make a small 'sunshine recorder'. Stand the pots on sheets of paper and position them on a sunny window sill. At regular intervals throughout the day, one of the children should record the position of the end of the shadow. When seen together this will indicate the path taken by the Sun across the sky. The

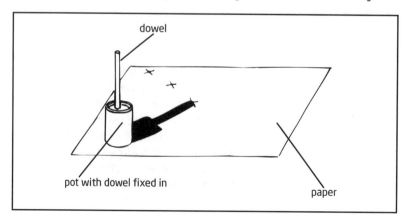

dowel

pot with dowel fixed in

paper

points could be joined in a curve to give a more accurate representation of the path. Similarly, more frequent observations and points of reference will make the task easier.

2 The children should use secondary sources to carry out some research to strengthen their background knowledge of the Sun. Their findings could be presented on a large Sun cut from coloured paper.

ASSESSMENT
Through observation and discussion with the children throughout the day, assess their understanding of the path the Sun takes across the sky. Ask the children to explain what they are doing and to describe the shape of the path that they have plotted.

PLENARY
Use the children's outline drawings to look at the path of the Sun. Reinforce the concept that this path is only apparent and that in reality it is the Earth that is moving.

OUTCOME
● Can describe the shape of the path of the Sun across the sky.

Lesson 11 ▪ The Sun's path

Objective
● To know that the Sun appears to follow a curved path across the sky every day.

RESOURCES
Information from previous lessons.

MAIN ACTIVITY
Relate the results from the activities in Lessons 9 and 10 to come to some conclusions about the relationship between the position of the Sun in the sky and the length of shadows cast. Encourage the children to see that when the Sun appears to be lower in the sky, the shadows are longer and that when it is high in the sky, the shadows are shorter.

ASSESSMENT
Look for evidence of the ability to describe the path of the Sun.

PLENARY
Discuss the findings of the children and their conclusions. Reinforce the children's knowledge and ability to describe the path of the Sun across the sky and how the path is related to the position and length of shadows.

Differentiation
Differentiate by outcome.

OUTCOME
● Can describe the shape of the path of the Sun across the sky.

ENRICHMENT
Lesson 12 ▪ Shadows

Objectives
● To understand that the position of a shadow is dependent on the direction of the light source.
● To make and test predictions.

RESOURCES 💿
Main activity: A Plasticine® figure or toy play person; a torch; a large sheet of white paper; two different-coloured felt-tipped pens; rulers.
Group activities: 1 Plasticine®; a torch; white paper and felt-tipped pens for each group. **2** Copies of photocopiable page 183 (also 'Shadows' (red), available on the CD-ROM); rough paper; writing equipment.

Vocabulary
beam, light, ray, shadow

PREPARATION

Put the Group activities resources on the tables. Sit the children in a circle with the white paper and Plasticine® figure in the centre.

BACKGROUND

This lesson aims to develop the children's ability to make and test predictions, and to understand how their predictions relate to their practical experience. It will further develop the children's understanding that light travels in straight lines and how shadows are formed when light is blocked.

STARTER

Remind the children of the drawings they did of their shadows. Ask them what they have learned about light from Lesson 3. (Light travels in straight lines/cannot go around corners.)

MAIN ACTIVITY

Put the Plasticine® figure or toy person on a sheet of white paper in the centre of the circle. Point a torch at the figure, but don't switch it on. Ask: *Where do you think the shadow is going to be?* Ask several children to point to where they predict the shadow will fall. Make sure that they understand the word 'predict'. Show how their predictions can be drawn onto the paper. Switch on the torch and ask a child to draw around the shadow in a different coloured pen. Explain that they are going to do a similar activity in their groups – making predictions and testing them.

GROUP ACTIVITIES

1 Each group carries out ten predictions and tests, with the children taking turns to hold the torch and draw the predictions and outcomes.
2 If resources limit the number of groups give some groups photocopiable page 183 and ask them to devise an acrostic for the word 'shadow'.

ASSESSMENT

Are the children able to make and test predictions? Do their predictions show an understanding of how the position of the shadow is related to the position of the torch? Can they use the idea that light travels in straight lines to explain this?

PLENARY

Repeat pointing the torch and ask a child to predict where the shadow will fall. *Can you explain why you think the shadow will be there?* Help the class to visualise the light ray by using a ruler to show its straight-line path.

OUTCOMES
● Can make and test a prediction.
● Can understand how the position of the light source affects the position of the shadow.

Differentiation
Have mixed-attainment groups to allow cross-fertilisation of ideas. Extend individuals by asking them to explain the reasons for their predictions in terms of light travelling in straight lines.

Lesson 13 ▪ The Sun and the Earth

Objectives
● To know that the path of the Sun is due to the movement of the Earth, not the movement of the Sun.
● To understand that the Sun is at the centre of the solar system and the Earth orbits it.

RESOURCES ◉

Main activity: OHP or torch; globe; name cards for the nine planets and the Sun; paper; pens; pencils.
Group activities: 1 Photocopiable page 184 (also 'The Sun and the Earth' (red), available on the CD-ROM). **2** Secondary sources of information about the solar system – books; CD-ROMs; videos; access to the internet (see Preparation opposite).

Vocabulary
rotation, orbit, solar system, universe

PREPARATION

You will need to find, in advance, web addresses with content suitable for the age and ability of your class if you wish the children to research further on 'space' topics on the internet. There is a vast amount of 'space' information on the Internet, and much is far beyond the access of 7–8 year olds. The NASA website www.nasa.gov contains much useful information.

BACKGROUND

The Earth has a diameter of 12,756km at the equator and is the third planet from the Sun in our solar system. The Sun is at the centre of our solar system and in all there are nine planets that orbit the Sun.

The Earth rotates around the Sun, a journey that takes 365.25 days. At the same time as it is orbiting the Sun, the Earth is rotating on its own axis in an anti-clockwise direction. For the Earth to rotate once on its own axis takes 24 hours – an Earth day. At any one time only half of the Earth is lit by the Sun and is in daylight; the other half is in darkness – night-time. Because of the rotation of the Earth these halves are continually changing. Throughout this, the Sun remains static so that any apparent movement of the Sun across the sky is in fact due to the rotation of the Earth.

A similar effect is experienced when you are sitting on one of two trains standing side by side in a railway station. If you watch the other train as yours departs you experience an illusion that the other train may be moving when in fact it is still in the station. Because you have no fixed points of reference you assume that the other train is moving. Similarly with the Earth and Sun, it is the Earth's rotational movement that causes us to experience the illusion that the Sun is travelling across the sky.

It is important also to realize that this effect is due to the Earth's rotation on its own axis and not its orbiting around the Sun. A simple orbit with axial rotation would not produce the same effect.

STARTER

Begin the lesson by recapping on the work from previous lessons looking at the path the Sun takes across the sky. Ask the children to once again explain this to you. Ask the children if they know which is moving, the Earth or the Sun.

MAIN ACTIVITY

Talk to the children about the solar system, how the Sun is at its centre and that the planets orbit the Sun. Demonstrate this by using the children, in groups, to model the solar system. You will need one child to be at the centre and represent the Sun. Other children, carrying name cards for the planets, should orbit the Sun. As they are orbiting the Sun, ask the children to rotate on their own axis and to look straight ahead at all times. This will mean that they see the Sun for only part of the time (each planet's daylight hours).

Working with one large group at a time, and using a light source such as an OHP or torch and a globe, model the relationship between the Sun and the Earth to recreate the effect of the Earth rotating on its axis as it orbits around the Sun. The children should record their observations in words and diagrams.

GROUP ACTIVITIES

1 Distribute copies of photocopiable page 184 for the children to complete. There are six mixed-up sentences to rewrite correctly. These sentences reinforce the key concepts being taught in the lesson and when correctly written should read:
The Sun is the centre of our solar system.
All the planets orbit the Sun.
As the Earth spins, half of it turns to face the Sun.

During the day, the Sun appears to move across the sky.
The Sun does not really move from east to west in the sky.
Really, the Earth moves around the Sun.

The children are then asked to draw a diagram to show the Earth and Sun and to explain why the Sun appears to move across the sky during the day to reinforce their prior learning.

2 The children could use secondary sources to find out more about the solar system and the orbits of the nine planets to create a series of 'factfiles' with key information about each planet.

ASSESSMENT

Mark the children's work for evidence of understanding of why the Sun appears to move across the sky even though it stays in the same position in space relative to the Earth. All of the children should be able to match up the sentences correctly and most should be able to give some explanation of how the Earth orbits the Sun. Check that this is clearly stated and that the children do not still hold the misconception of the Sun moving across the sky.

PLENARY

Ask some of the children to demonstrate the modelling of the Earth rotating around the Sun and the Sun remaining stationary. Reinforce this concept.

Ask some other children to share their research into the Solar System with the class. Play a game of 'Guess the planet' by asking some of the children to give some simple 'planet facts' for the others to guess the identity of the planet.

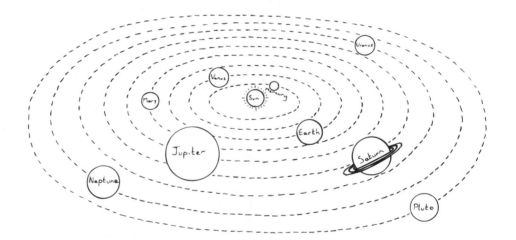

OUTCOMES

● Can explain why the Sun appears to move across the sky even though it stays in the same position in space relative to the Earth.
● Can understand that the Sun is at the centre of the solar system and that the Earth orbits it.

ICT LINKS

Use the internet and CD-ROMS as secondary sources of information. Visit the 'NASA for Kids' website at: http://www.nasa.gov/audience/forkids/home/index.html

Lesson 14 ▪ Telling the time with shadows

Objective
● To know that shadows can be used to tell the approximate time of day.

Vocabulary
approximate, calibrate, cast, estimate, measure, shadows, sundial

RESOURCES ⊙
Main activity: A sundial (or a picture of one).
Group activities: 1 Flat wooden boards with a central hole drilled to fit pieces of dowel (one per group, but can be shared, if necessary); paper templates (one per group); art materials; glue to fasten the dowel in place; reference materials; such as guidebooks for stately homes showing old sundials (optional). **2** Copies of photocopiable page 185 (also 'Telling the time with shadows' (red), available on the CD-ROM).

PREPARATION
Prepare materials for making sundials.

BACKGROUND
Shadows are formed because light travels in straight lines and is unable to bend to go around objects that will not allow light through. On a bright sunny day, the Sun casts shadows that are very sharp at the edges. On overcast days the shadows are more indistinct and fuzzy.

Shadows have been used for many centuries to help us mark time. We know that the Earth rotates around the Sun giving the illusion that the Sun is travelling across our sky. This has been used to mark out the passage of time during the day. The first sundials were used, it is thought, over 4000 years ago by the Chinese. Today they are generally only used for decorative purposes due to the unreliability of certain climates. A sundial works by casting a shadow from a simple pole on to the dial below. After calibration, they can be used alongside our time-keeping and measuring system.

STARTER
Begin by asking: *What time is it? How do you know?* Most children will be able to tell you about clocks and watches and many will have a sound understanding of time. Ask the children if they know how people used to tell the time before watches and clocks were invented. They may identify ways to measure the passage of time, such as using sand timers or tickers.

MAIN ACTIVITY
Lead the discussion by suggesting that one method of telling the time is connected with something that is always present even though we may not be able to see it. Give clues that will lead the children to think about the Sun as a means of telling the time. Introduce the idea of a sundial and show the children an actual sundial (or a picture of one). Set the sundial up and see if the children can use it to tell the time.

GROUP ACTIVITIES
1 Use flat boards with a vertical piece of dowel to make a simple sundial. A face can be made from a circle of paper with a central hole that can be slotted on to the sundial. (See diagram on page 167). The children could research historic designs of sundials, reproducing them or using them as inspiration for their own designs. Guidebooks from stately homes and historic houses or gardens often contain pictures. The children may observe that real sundials do not usually cover the full 24-hour period; ask them why this is. (There is no sunlight at night.)

The sundial will need to be set up and calibrated by marking the position of the shadow at specific times, preferably on the hour. This will need to be repeated every hour, so that a calibrated dial can be set up. After this, the children can use the sundial to estimate the time. Set them a series of challenges to estimate the time using the sundial and then checking the time on a clock. With experience, can they improve the accuracy with which they use the sundial to estimate the time (although there will be an accuracy range of several minutes)? The children can record their estimates in a table:

2 Distribute copies of photocopiable page 185 for the children to complete. This involves the children looking at sundials and estimating the time shown on them.

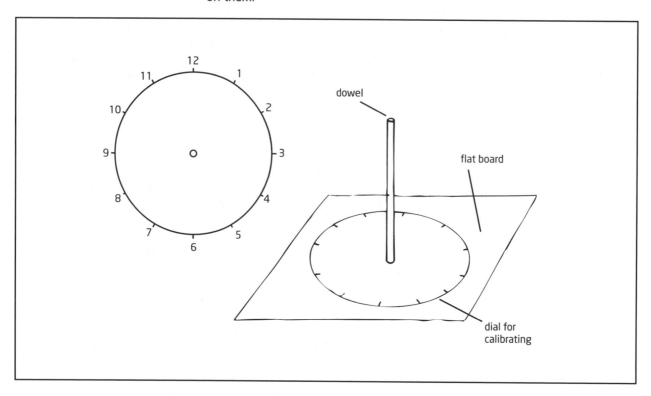

ICT LINK
Children could use a digital camera to record observations during this investigation.

ASSESSMENT
Using photocopiable page 185 and through observation and questioning, assess the children for their ability to tell the approximate time using a sundial. The answer to question 1 is shown on the right. For question 2, most of the children should be able to tell the approximate time. (The time would be 12 noon.) More confident learners will be able to be more specific and precise in telling the time. For question 3, sundials are not used very often today for several reasons: they are inaccurate, they are unreliable and we have alternative methods of telling the time.

PLENARY
Ask the children to demonstrate their sundials and their skill in telling the (approximate) time using them. Ask the children to think about why sundials are not a very efficient, reliable or accurate way of telling the time.

OUTCOMES
● Can make a sundial.
● Can use a sundial to tell the approximate time of day.

Differentiation 💿
Group activity 2
To support children, give them 'Telling the time with shadows' (green), from the CD-ROM, which omits the extension question included on the core sheet. Some children will need adult support to help them complete the sheet.
  To extend children, use 'Telling the time with shadows' (blue), which asks them to tell the time from the illustrated sundial with the sun in various positions around it.

ENRICHMENT
Lesson 15 ◗ Sunlight

RESOURCES ◉
Main activity: Large sheets of paper on a flipchart or board.
Group activities: 1 A copy of photocopiable page 186 (also 'Sunlight' (red), available on the CD-ROM), for each child. **2** Paper; pencils; pens; drawing materials; pictures of the Sun or sunny scenes cut from magazines; large sheets of paper; glue; scissors.

BACKGROUND
Like all stars, the Sun is an extremely hot place. All of the energy on the Earth comes from the Sun and without it, life here on Earth would not exist. The sun is some 149,600,000km (93,000,000 miles) away and the light from it takes eight minutes to reach the Earth. The Sun is a sphere of atoms that generates its energy from a nuclear reaction at its core. The temperature at the core is thought to be 14–16,000,000°C (water boils on Earth at 100°C), while the surface is a rather cool 6000°C!

From work previously carried out, you can expect most children to know something about the Sun's relationship with day and night. Through work related to light and shadows the children should have learned that the Sun is just one of many sources of light and that darkness is the absence of light. They may also have learned something about the relationship between the Sun and the seasons.

STARTER
Begin the lesson by talking to the children about work they will have covered in Key Stage 1/Primary 1–3. Explain that they will be building on what they learned then and discovering a little more about the Earth.

MAIN ACTIVITY
Ask the children to give you words that are in some way connected with the Sun. Make a list of suggestions on the board, a flipchart or an OHP, recording key words and phrases. Look for contributions from as many children as possible. In discussion with the children, try to link some of the words together to form a concept map that will indicate their level of understanding.

GROUP ACTIVITIES
1 Distribute copies of photocopiable page 186 and ask the children to complete it without working together; highlight that you want to find out what they each know individually.
2 Ask the children to think of as many light sources as they can. Tell them to make a list of light sources and use pictures to make a group collage.

ASSESSMENT
Most children should have a good grasp of the concepts covered in Key Stage 1/Primary 1–3; however, some will not, and may continue to hold misconceptions such as that the Sun literally rises and sets or goes behind a cloud, that at night the Sun has gone to Australia, or that the Moon emits light. This activity will help to identify these misconceptions.

PLENARY
Share ideas and encourage the children to begin to formulate their own questions about what they would like to find out about next.

OUTCOMES
● Teacher can assess the level of the children in the class.
● Teacher can arrange children in appropriate class groups.

Lesson 16 ◗ Letting light through

Objectives
● To know that materials can be grouped as opaque, translucent or transparent according to how light behaves when it is shone on to them.
● To carry out a test.
● To use light meters.
● To interpret results and draw conclusions.

Vocabulary
light meter, opaque, translucent, transparent

RESOURCES 💿
Main activity: A selection of materials from the collection below.
Group activities: 1 A collection for each group of materials that are opaque such as card, aluminium foil and wallpaper; are transparent such as sticky tape and clingfilm and that are translucent such as tracing paper; light meters (or data-logging equipment if available); torches. **2** Copies of photocopiable page 187 (also 'Letting light through' (red), available on the CD-ROM).

PREPARATION
Put one collection of materials on each group's table. Keep the torches out of sight in case the children request them. Have data-logging equipment or light meters set up ready at the side.

BACKGROUND
Opaque materials do not let any light through and so they make dense shadows. Transparent materials let light through and so they do not form shadows. Translucent materials such as bathroom windows let some light through, but scatter it, so the shadows are not as dark. The terminology is not as important as the ideas, but the children may enjoy using the scientific vocabulary. Avoid using the word 'see-through' as this encourages the idea that rays are coming out of the eyes, rather than the correct idea that light is going into them.

Light meters and data-logging equipment can be used by children to measure how much light is coming through. However, if these are not available, the children can develop their own index instead with 0 meaning 'no light comes through' and 5 meaning 'all the light comes through', with the numbers in between representing degrees of translucence.

STARTER
Give each group a collection of materials to sort in as many different ways as they can.

MAIN ACTIVITY
Explain that some materials let more light come through than others. Ask the children to pick out items from their collection that they think let no light through, and lots of light through. Ask: *How could we test how much light each material lets through?* Suggestions will probably include holding them up and shining a torch on them. Ask: *How will we know how much light is coming through?* Explain that there are devices that can measure how much light there is, and demonstrate how to use the light meters or data-loggers. It is important to point out that the normal daylight will be measured too, so they are looking for a change in the reading on the meter.

As part of the demonstration, exaggerate putting the light meter very close to the torch, then much further away and ask the children: *Is that fair?* (No.) *Why not?* (Because when it is nearer it might get more light.) *How can I make it fair?* (Keep it the same distance away.)

GROUP ACTIVITIES
1 Ask each group to plan and carry out a test to find out how much light comes through some of the materials in their collection. The groups are to decide how many materials to test. Ask each group to record their results in a table, as shown on the left and encourage the children to explain their test design. Ask each child to write down two or three sentences about what they found out.

Opaque	Transparent	Translucent
Card Foil	Clingfilm	Tracing paper

2 Give each child a copy of photocopiable page 187 and ask them to look at the graph and interpret it by answering the questions.

ASSESSMENT

Can the children use the light meter effectively? Have they carried out a test? Can they give examples of materials in their collection that let a lot/a little/no light through?

PLENARY

Bring the class to sit in a circle on the carpet. Ask each group to give you a piece of the material that let all the light through. Put these in a group with the label 'transparent'. Ask each group for a material that lets no light through. Put these materials together and label them 'opaque'. Ask: *Were there any materials that let a bit of light through, but you can't see things clearly?* Put these in a group labelled 'translucent'.

Bring out some new samples of materials and ask the children which group they think they would belong to and why. Put them with the relevant group.

OUTCOMES

- Can distinguish between opaque, translucent and transparent materials.
- Can use a light meter/data-logger.
- Can interpret own data to draw conclusions.

LINKS

Maths: measurement, interpretation of measurement.
Unit 3c Characteristics of materials: properties of materials.

Differentiation

Have the children working in mixed-attainment groups to support each other. Target questions about the test according to the child, for example: *Why did you choose those materials? Which one do you think will let most/least light through? Why? Are you doing anything to make the test fair? Can you tell me what you have found out so far?* Scaffold the data interpretation by providing phrases such as: 'We found that (x) let the most light through and (Y) did not let any light through. This is a list of objects in order of how much light went through.'

Lesson 17 ▪ Shadow or no shadow?

Objective

- To know that translucent and opaque materials form shadows and transparent ones do not.
- To make predictions and suggest explanations based on previous knowledge.

RESOURCES

A collection of materials as for Lesson 16; an OHP; a screen or wall area for projection.

MAIN ACTIVITY

Explain that you want the children to use what they learned in the previous lesson to help them with a new investigation. Hold up an opaque material. Ask: *Do you think this would make a shadow if I put it in the way of the light? Why?*

Ask the children to work in pairs to choose five materials and discuss what they think the shadow would be like. Ask them to record their predictions in a table (see below). The children carry out the test and record their findings. Remind them to think back to the previous lesson to help explain why they got the results.

Material	What I predict will happen	What did happen	Why I think this happened

ASSESSMENT

Can the children make predictions? Are they drawing on the previous lesson in their suggested explanations? Can they explain why shadows are formed by some materials and not others?

PLENARY

Ask the children for some of their explanations, then clarify them. Hold up a new material, ask the children to make a prediction about what the shadow will be like and to explain their reasoning.

OUTCOME

● Can recognise that opaque and translucent materials form shadows and that transparent materials do not.

ENRICHMENT

Lesson 18 ▪ Colour

Objective
● To know that there is a wide range of colours that can be seen.
● To know the colours of the rainbow.

Vocabulary
red, orange, yellow, green, blue, indigo, violet, spectrum

RESOURCES 💿

Main activity: Soundtrack recording of Andrew Lloyd Webber's musical *Joseph and the Amazing Technicolor Dreamcoat*; children's story Bible (optional).
Group activities: 1 A small collection of objects that are one particular colour, copies of photocopiable page 188 (also 'Colour' (red), available on the CD-ROM), pens, pencils. **2** Paper, painting equipment, collage materials, glue, scissors.

PREPARATION

Set up a 'colour display' of objects that are one particular colour – perhaps you have a school colour that you could use as a basis for this.

BACKGROUND

We are able to see things around us when light from a light source reaches an object, hits it, is reflected and enters our eyes. But what about seeing colour? The light that is all around us is 'white', but it is accepted that it is made up from seven colours. Together, these colours are called the 'spectrum'. They are: red, orange, yellow, green, blue, indigo and violet. We can see these colours split apart in a rainbow, where red is on the outside and the rest follow in this order, in bands, to the violet on the inner edge.
   In this spectrum of light, there are three 'primary' colours: red, green and blue. It is important to remember that the primary colours of light and the primary colours of paint are different (red, blue and yellow). Different rules apply to mixing light compared to mixing paint.
   When white light hits, for example, a blue object, the red and green elements of the white light are absorbed by the object. The blue light is reflected into our eyes by the pigments in the object, and we see a blue object. The same applies to the other primary colours. If the object is a mixture of colours, then the colour pigments in the object reflect some of the constituent colours and absorb the rest.

STARTER

How many colours can you see in the classroom? What is your favourite colour? Carry out a quick and simple survey of favourite colours.
   Alternatively, play 'When I went to market', where each item has to be a different colour. For example: *When I went to market, I bought a green apple; When I went to market I bought a green apple and a pink bag* and so on.

MAIN ACTIVITY

Talk about how we may wear clothes in our favourite colours. Introduce and play the song 'Joseph's coat' from *Joseph and the Amazing Technicolor Dreamcoat*. Tell the children that Joseph's story is in the Bible as is Noah's, and something else that is multicoloured appears in that story – the rainbow. You may like to read the end of the Noah story to the children. Ask them to name the colours of the rainbow. Teach them to remember the colours in order using a mnemonic such as: Richard Of York Gave Battle In Vain.

You may wish to explain, very simply, how we see colour.

GROUP ACTIVITIES

1 Give out copies of photocopiable page 188 for the children to complete. Encourage different groups to make different colour collections on their own of items from around the classroom.
2 Paint a picture or make a collage of a rainbow. The children could also make up new versions of the 'ROYGBIV' mnemonic as the centrepiece for a display of work from the unit.

ASSESSMENT

Look for evidence in the children's completed photocopiable pages that they are able to name the colours of the spectrum and correctly complete the cloze procedure.

PLENARY

Ask some of the children to share their work with the class. Reinforce the concept of a range of colours and knowledge of the colours of the spectrum. Listen to new versions of the 'ROYGBIV' mnemonic. You may like to read more of the stories of Noah or Joseph to round off this lesson.

OUTCOME

● Can recognise the colours in the spectrum.

LINKS

RE: biblical stories of Noah and Joseph.
Art: colour recognition and colour mixing.

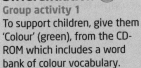

Differentiation
Group activity 1
To support children, give them 'Colour' (green), from the CD-ROM which includes a word bank of colour vocabulary.

To extend children, give them 'Colour' (blue), which includes an extension question about how rainbows are formed.

ENRICHMENT
Lesson 19 ▸ Colour in nature

Objective
● To know that colours are used for decoration and to give messages in the natural world.

Differentiation
Some children might benefit from researching one specific item, perhaps camouflage or warnings. Other children could try more complex research that investigates a range of animals, plants and uses of colour, and uses a range of media to present findings, such as images from the Internet.

RESOURCES

Secondary sources of information, such as books; CD-ROMs and so on; art materials.

MAIN ACTIVITY

Use secondary sources to investigate colours in nature, how animals and plants use colour as a warning, as camouflage or as a means of attracting another of the same species. The children could work in small groups and present their findings with artwork to add to a class display. Provide a background of green art paper leaves, where green bugs can hide. Let the children make 'blot' butterflies, but discuss what colours they should use to give warnings (red = 'I'm not nice to eat'; yellow and black = 'I sting'), or to attract a mate (the peacock's greens and blues, for example). Emphasise the symmetry of the patterns, too.

ASSESSMENT

Look for evidence of an understanding of how plants and animals use colour for camouflage, attraction or warning.

PLENARY
Ask the children to share their findings and allow an opportunity for the children to read and look at each others' work.

OUTCOME
● Can describe how plants and animals use colours.

ENRICHMENT
Lesson 20 ▪ Colour on the roads

Objective
● To know that colours are used for decoration and to give messages in the man-made world.
● To know that colour and light are important in road safety.

Vocabulary
amber, danger, green, red, reflective, safe, traffic

RESOURCES 💿
Main activity: Flipchart or board; road safety posters; pictures of emergency vehicles; copies of photocopiable page 189 (also 'Colour on the roads' (red), available on the CD-ROM); pens; pencils.
Group activities: 1 Paper, pencils, colours. **2** Large sheets of paper; decorating paint charts, painting equipment.
ICT link: 'Colour on the roads' interactive activity, from the CD-ROM.

PREPARATION
Display the posters and pictures where the children can see them easily.

BACKGROUND
As in nature, humans often use colour to send messages. We paint our homes in certain colours to create particular atmospheres: green is said to be calming, whereas blue is generally considered cold. The colour of the clothes we wear sends messages: they may indicate what sort of person we may be or even which football team we support. But certain colours have particular associations: red we associate with danger, fire engines and a warning to stop; green we associate with nature, the environment and traffic lights telling us it is safe to go; colours are 'adopted' by certain organisations and sections of our society.

On the roads, we make great use of colour and light. Not only do we use lamps to light the streets, but also to control the traffic (see the DfT Highway Code for more information), and for vehicles to signal when they are manoeuvring or stopping. Pedestrians too may wear appropriate clothing to warn of their presence. Many children who walk to and from school wear coats with reflective patches or armbands, and people working on the roads wear bright reflective jackets in orange, bright green or yellow.

STARTER
Begin by asking the children how they travelled to school this morning. Introduce some elements of road safety. Ask the children how they keep themselves safe on the roads, particularly when it is dark. Encourage them to consider street lighting, crossing at pelican crossings (the green man), and wearing reflective clothing or armbands.

Differentiation 💿
Main activity
To support children, use 'Colour on the roads' which includes a simplified version of the traffic lights activity and asks them to make a list of uses of light, but not colour.

As extension, give children 'Colour on the road' (blue), which omits the word bank included on the core sheet.

MAIN ACTIVITY
Discuss with the children how colour and light are very important in road safety. Red is often used as a warning colour to tell people that there is danger ahead; green is used generally as a sign that things are safe. Amber is used as a warning that danger may lie ahead. Make a list of examples on the flipchart, one of these should be traffic lights. Ask the children if they know the colours that are used in traffic lights. Tell them the sequence of traffic light changes, and what each one means. Distribute photocopiable page 189 and allow the children time to complete it. The children will have to recall the sequence of traffic lights, which should be: red; red and amber together; green; amber; red.

GROUP ACTIVITIES

1 Ask the children to think about colour use outside in the local environment. Ask them to draw a picture of a street scene and to mark on as many uses of colour and light as possible. In particular, they should indicate how light and colour are used in road safety, including: traffic lights, street lighting, emergency vehicles, reflective clothing, road signs, cat's eyes, roadside barriers and markers. Alternatively, this could be a collaborative display, with the children drawing and cutting out their individual contributions to stick on to a group or class scene.

2 Ask the children to think about colour use inside the home. Give out some decorating paint charts and ask the children to look at variations in colour among the colour groups. Ask the children to choose one colour family and to create their own paint chart. Each chart should have about six blocks of colour and the children should give each an appropriate name. Encourage systematic mixing, with the children adding white or black to a starting hue.

ICT LINK ⊙

Children can use the 'Colour on the roads' interactive on the CD-ROM. This is a drag-and-drop activity where the children have to arrange five traffic lights into the correct order.

ASSESSMENT

Have the children been able to indicate appropriate uses for colour and light in road safety, and/or other human situations?

PLENARY

Reinforce the importance of colour and how certain colours send out certain messages: In Britain, red is for danger and green for safety. Have a quiz where one child gives a traffic light colour or colours and another has to give the sequence that either follows or comes before it.

OUTCOMES

- Is aware that humans use colour to send out messages.
- Can describe the use of colour in road safety.
- Can describe the use of light in the local environment, for example, for road safety.

ENRICHMENT
Lesson 21 ◗ Light energy

Objective
- To know that light is a form of energy.

Vocabulary
heat, light, movement, change, energy, electrical energy, solar power

RESOURCES

Main activity: A torch; a battery-powered calculator; a solar-powered calculator.

Group activities: 1 A solar-powered calculator for each group (make sure the calculator is not dual-powered or it will continue to work on batteries even in the dark); small pieces of tissue paper to cover the solar cells on the calculators; writing materials. **2** For each group: two shallow trays (of the same size and colour); water; two thermometers; a sunny day; writing materials; reference materials about the use of solar power. The Centre for Alternative Technology in Machynlleth, Powys, Wales (tel: 01654 705950; www.cat.org.uk) provides information on all kinds of alternative and sustainable energy sources.

BACKGROUND

Energy is needed to make things, including our bodies, work. We get our energy from the food we eat: that is our fuel. A car gets its energy from petrol or diesel, and many devices use electrical energy. A torch uses electrical energy from a battery, while a ceiling light or table lamp uses electrical energy from the mains supply.

Energy comes in many forms and can be changed or transferred from one form to another, most of which are too complicated or abstract for children of this age. They should, however, be able to understand that energy is needed to make things work and that we can get energy in different ways. Energy can be stored in the form of fuels (energy in the form of light and heat is released from the wax in a candle as it burns; we get light and heat from burning wood or coal). Sometimes this energy is used to create movement (in a steam engine or in a power station to drive turbines and produce electricity). Light is a form of energy that we can get directly from the Sun. It can be used as light, heat or can be changed into electrical energy.

STARTER

Ask the children what they think the word 'energy' means. Where have they heard it used? They may have heard parents or teachers saying: *You have got a lot of energy today. You must have had an extra egg for breakfast!* or something similar. While this is not strictly a definition of energy, it may help the children to understand that energy is needed for something to work. If we have no energy, we do not feel like doing anything.

MAIN ACTIVITY

Electricity is one form of energy and most children can understand that electrical devices need electrical energy to make them work. Ask the children if they can name some things that need electricity. (Lights, food mixer, kettle, fan, heater, torch, radio.) Tell them that electricity is a form of energy and that energy is needed to make things work. All the devices that they have named require energy in the form of electricity.

Show them a torch and switch it on to show that it works. Then take the batteries out and switch it on again. *Why doesn't it work?* (It has no energy supply.) Replace the batteries and ask the children if they think it will work now. (It should do!) Show them a calculator that uses a battery and talk about it needing the electrical energy from the battery to make it work. Now show them a solar-powered calculator. Does anyone know how this works? It doesn't have any batteries so how does it get its energy? (From sunlight or artificial light falling on special light-sensitive cells.) Explain that light is another form of energy and some things can use light to make them work. Remind them how plants need light to make their food so that they can grow. Plants use the light to provide the energy they need to do this.

GROUP ACTIVITIES

1 Divide the children into groups of three or four and give each group a solar-powered calculator. Ask them to look carefully to find the solar cells. Explain that these are special things that can change light energy into electrical energy to make the calculator work. Ask them to investigate placing layers of tissue paper over the solar cells to see what effect this has. They should then write about what they find out.
2 Ask the children, working in groups of three or four, to put one small, shallow tray of water in a shady spot and a similar one in full Sun (or use a spotlight). Use a thermometer to measure the temperature of the water every hour or so to find out what happens.

Encourage the children to use the reference materials to find out other uses for solar energy. In some countries banks of mirrors are used to focus the Sun's rays to heat water. Some houses, even in this country, have solar panels on their roofs to help heat the water for the house. There are groups of people experimenting with solar-powered cars. Remind the children that they are going to report back to the rest of the class so they may need to make some notes.

ASSESSMENT
Listen to the children as they report back their findings from the Group activities and note those who make sensible contributions.

PLENARY
Ask the children from each group to report back on what they have discovered. Ask children from Group activity 1 to explain why the calculator does not work when the light-sensitive cells are covered. Then ask children from Group activity 2 to explain what happened to the trays of water. Can you explain why one got hotter than the other? Have you discovered any other uses for light energy?

OUTCOME
Know that light is a form of energy.

LINKS
Literacy: taking notes, using reference materials and a dictionary.

Lesson 22 ◖ Assessment

Objectives
● To assess the children's level of understanding of the sources of light.
● To assess the level of understanding of the path the sun takes across the sky and the relationship between the Earth and the Sun.
● To assess the understanding of the use of shadows in telling the time.

RESOURCES 💿
Assessment activities: 1 Copies of photocopiable page 190 (also Assessment -1', available on the CD-ROM); pens and pencils. **2** Copies of photocopiable page 191 (also 'The Assessment -2', available on the CD-ROM); pens and pencils.

STARTER
Begin the Assessment activities by giving the children a vocabulary test – this could be oral or written. Remember the activity is an assessment of scientific knowledge and understanding, not of writing skill. Either give a word and ask for a definition or a definition and ask for a word. You could also ask the children to recall the colours of the spectrum, they could devise a mnemonic to help others recall the seven colours, using 'Richard of York gave battle in vain' for inspiration.

ASSESSMENT ACTIVITY 1
Distribute copies of photocopiable page 190 to the children and allow them time to complete it individually. You may wish to tell the children that you want to find out what they have understood and that it is important to complete the sheet individually. You will need to collect these sheets in order to mark them effectively.

ANSWERS
1. The path drawn by the children should be arc-shaped from east to west.
2. The Sun appears to rise in the east.
The Sun appears to set in the west.
At midday the Sun is in the southern sky.
3. The illustration should show the Earth orbiting the Sun and not vice versa.

LOOKING FOR LEVELS
Assess the children's work in Assessment activity 1 for evidence of understanding. Most children should be able to answer questions 1 and 2. Many should be able to give an explanation of how the Earth orbits the Sun for question 3.

ASSESSMENT ACTIVITY 2

Distribute copies of photocopiable page 191 to the children and allow them time to complete it individually. You may wish to tell the children that you want to find out what they have understood and that it is important to complete the sheet individually.

ANSWERS

1. Children should write 'Sundials need the sun to be useful'; 'Sundials can be used to give approximate times'; and 'Sundials use shadows to show the time' in the 'True' column. The other five statements are false.
2. The illustration and explanation should give some indication of how sundials work and are used.

LOOKING FOR LEVELS

Although requiring a good level of literacy skill, most should be able to complete this task. You may like to read the sentences in question 1 for some children as this is not a test of reading but scientific understanding.

ICT LINK

Display the 'Assessment – 1' (red) and 'Assessment – 2' (red) from the CD-ROM on an interactive whiteboard. Complete the worksheets as a whole-class activity, or as part of the plenary, using the drawing tools provided on the CD-ROM.

PLENARY

Discuss the Assessment activities and address any misconceptions still held by the children.

Light

■ Some materials allow light through, some do not allow any through, and some allow only a little light through. Complete these sentences.

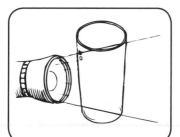

If you shone a torch at a clear drinking glass the light would

_____

_____.

If you shone a torch at a book the light would

_____

_____.

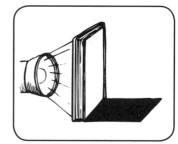

■ Can you sort these things into the correct column?

clear glass   frosted glass   newspaper   card   wood
metal   water   oil   cloth   curtains

Allows light through	Allows some light through	Allows no light through

■ Add some more of your own to each column.

Me and my shadow

What is a shadow?

_____

_____

How are shadows formed?

_____

_____

What do you need to make a shadow?

_____

_____

Draw a picture to help you with your answers.

Draw a picture of the Sun, the Earth's main light source, and a shadow of yourself.

Matching shadows

◗ Here are some shadows. Can you match them to the object that cast them?

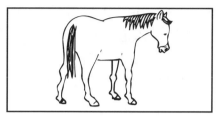

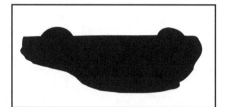

◗ Now see if you can draw some pairs of your own.

◗ Look at the objects and their shadows. Describe what you notice about the shape of each.

PHOTOCOPIABLE

Light sources

◀ A torch is a light source. All light sources can be used to produce shadows.

◀ Describe what happens when you use a torch to investigate shadows.

◀ What happens when you move the torch nearer to the object? Make a drawing in the space below.

Torch   Object   Shadow

_____

◀ What happens when you move the torch further away from the object? Make a drawing in the space below.

Torch   Object   Shadow

_____

■SCHOLASTIC

Shadows

▪ This is an acrostic poem for the word 'light':

L ifts the darkness
I n the morning
G iving rainbows
H ope ahead
T ravelling fast

▪ Write an acrostic poem for the word 'shadow'. Try out your ideas on rough paper first.

S

H

A

D

O

W

Illustration © Kirsty Wilson

PHOTOCOPIABLE

The Sun and the Earth

◼ Look carefully at all these phrases. They fit together to make six statements about how we see the Sun in the sky. Match up the parts and then write the statements correctly.

The Sun is	orbit the Sun.
All the planets	appears to move across the sky.
As the Earth spins,	around the Sun.
During the day, the Sun	from east to west in the sky.
The Sun does not really move	the centre of our Solar System.
Really, the Earth moves	half of it turns to face the Sun.

◼ Now write the six statements.

1. _____

2. _____

3. _____

4. _____

5. _____

6. _____

◼ Draw a diagram to show the Earth and the Sun. Explain why the Sun appears to move across the sky during the day.

Telling the time with shadows

- The first box shows a stick's shadow at 9.00am.
- Put a tick against the correct shadows for 12 noon and 3.00pm.

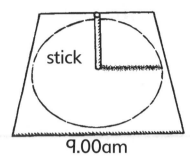

9.00am

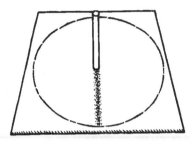

- A sundial can be used to tell the time.

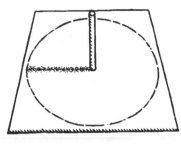

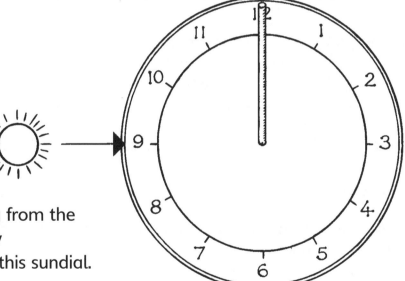

- If the Sun is shining from the direction of the arrow draw the shadow on this sundial.

The time would be _____ .

Why are sundials not used very often today?

_____

_____

_____

Illustration © Ray & Corinne Burrows

Sunlight

◼ Look at the diagram. Shade one side of the Earth to show the side that is dark. Write 'day' and 'night' on the correct sides of the Earth picture.

Sun  **Earth**

◼ Explain how day and night are caused.

Day _____

Night _____

◼ Complete these sentences. Choose from these words:

earlier	later	shorter	longer

In summer the days are _____ because the Sun sets _____.

In winter the days are _____ because the Sun sets _____.

Draw a picture of the Sun in the sky in summer and a picture of the Sun in the sky in winter.

Summer	**Winter**

Why is it dangerous to look at the Sun? _____

_____

◼ SCHOLASTIC

Illustration © Kirsty Wilson

Letting light through

■ Some children did an investigation to find out how much light can get through different materials. They presented their results in a bar chart.

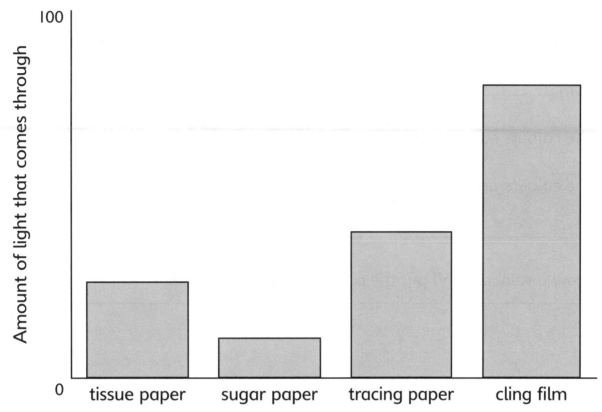

1. How many different materials did they try? _____

2. Which material let the most light through? _____

3. Which material let the least light through? _____

4. Tracing paper lets more light through than tissue paper. TRUE/FALSE

5. Cling film blocks more light than sugar paper. TRUE/FALSE

6. Write the materials in order on this line.

←———————————————————————————→

lets least light
through

lets most light
through

Colour

■ Complete these sentences.

We are able to see things because of _____.

We can see the _____ of things because light is made up

from _____ colours.

The colours can be seen in a _____.

The colours are _____, _____, _____,

_____, _____, _____, _____.

Draw a rainbow and put the colours in the right order.

■ SCHOLASTIC

Colour on the roads

◼ Colours are often used to give us a message or an instruction.

◼ Complete these sentences. Choose the correct words from the word bank.

a warning	dangerous	safe

Red is often used to indicate that something is _____.

Green is often used to indicate that something is _____.

Amber is often used to indicate _____.

◼ Now think about how traffic lights work. Can you remember the sequence in which the lights shine? Colour these traffic lights.

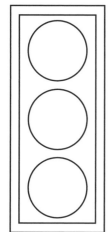 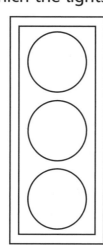 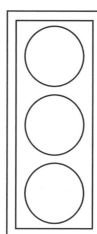 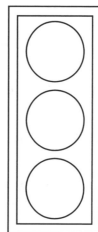 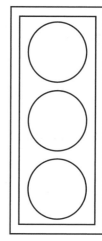

◼ Make a list of other uses of light and colour in road safety.

Light	Colour

PHOTOCOPIABLE

Assessment – 1

1. Draw the path of the Sun as it moves across the sky during the day.

east   west

2. Complete these sentences.

The Sun appears to rise in the _____.

The Sun appears to set in the _____.

At midday the Sun appears to be in the _____ of the sky.

3. Draw a picture to show how the Earth orbits the Sun.

Use this space to explain more about your drawing.

_____

_____

■ SCHOLASTIC

Illustration © Kirsty Wilson

Assessment – 2

1. Put these statements about sundials into the correct column:

A. Sundials are accurate.
B. Sundials can be used on cloudy, overcast days.
C. Sundials are easy to carry about.
D. Sundials can be used inside.
E. Sundials need the Sun to be useful.
F. Sundials can be used to give approximate times.
G. Sundials are a modern invention.
H. Sundials use shadows to show the time.

True	False

2. Draw a picture of a sundial and explain how to use it to tell the approximate time.

In this series:

ISBN 978-0439-94502-8

ISBN 978-0439-94503-5

ISBN 978-0439-94504-2

ISBN 978-0439-94505-9

ISBN 978-0439-94506-6

ISBN 978-0439-94507-3

ISBN 978-0439-94508-0

To find out more, call: 0845 603 9091
or visit our website www.scholastic.co.uk